Terry Johnson

Plays: 3

The London Cuckolds
Cleo, Camping, Emmanuelle and Dick
The Graduate

The London Cuckolds: 'fascinating and frequently very funny' *Daily Mail.*

Cleo, Camping, Emmanuelle and Dick: 'Again and again *Cleo, Camping* makes us laugh and again and again it wipes the laughter off our faces' *Financial Times*

The Graduate: 'better drama than the movie' *Financial Times*

Terry Johnson's work has been performed all over Great Britain, and in the USA, Europe and Australia. He is the recipient of nine major British theatre awards and has had seven productions, *Hitchcock Blonde, Entertaining Mr Sloane, The Graduate, Dead Funny, Hysteria, Elton John's Glasses* and *The Memory of Water* running in London's West End. He has written television drama that has been broadcast worldwide, most recently 'Cor Blimey' (an adaptation of *Cleo, Camping*) for ITV. He directed his most recent play *Hitchcock*, and is also director of a feature film about Peter Cook and Dudley Moore, *Not Only But Always.*

TERRY JOHNSON

Plays: 3

The London Cuckolds
Cleo, Camping, Emmanuelle and Dick
The Graduate

with an introduction by Stephen Jeffreys

Methuen Drama

Published by Methuen Drama 2004

1 3 5 7 9 10 8 6 4 2

First published in 2004 by
Methuen Publishing Limited

Methuern Drama
A&C Black Publishers Limited
36 Soho Square
London W1D 3QY

www.methuendrama.com

A CIP catalogue record is available from the British Library

ISBN 0 413 77372 8

Typeset by SX Composing DTP, Rayleigh, Essex

Contents

Terry Johnson:
A Chronology

1979 *Amabel* Bush Theatre

1981 *Days Here So Dark* Paine's Plough

1982 *Insignificance* Royal Court Theatre, SWET
nominations for Best Play and Best Newcomer.
Plays and Players Award, Evening Standard Award
(Most Promising Playwright). Performed US,
Germany, France, Australia, Israel, New Zealand,
Japan

1983 *Bellevue* Welfare State International

1984 *Cries from the Mammal House* Royal Court/Leicester
Haymarket
Unsuitable for Adults Bush Theatre. Performed in US,
New Zealand, Australia, Canada

1985 *Tuesday's Child* BBC TV. Co-written with Kate Lock
Time Trouble BBC TV
Insignificance Screenplay for Recorded Picture Co.

1986 *Tuesday's Child* Theatre Royal, Stratford East. Co-
written with Kate Lock

1991 *Imagine Drowning* Hampstead Theatre. Winner of the
John Whiting Award, 1991

1993 *Hysteria* Royal Court Theatre. Winner of the Olivier
Award for Best Comedy 1993, and Writers' Guild
Award for Best West End Play
99 to 1 Carlton TV

1994 *Dead Funny* Hampstead, Vaudeville and Savoy
Theatres. Winner of Critics' Circle Award for Best
New Play, Writers' Guild Award for Best West End
Play, 1994
Time Out Drama Award
The Bite, three-part television series for Warner
Sister/Carlton Television

1995 *Blood and Water* and *The Chemistry Lesson* for the BBC's Ghosts series.

1997 *The London Cuckolds* (adaptation of the play by Edward Ravenscroft) for the Royal National Theatre

1998 *Cleo, Camping, Emmanuelle and Dick* National Theatre. Winner of the Olivier Award for Best Comedy 1998

2000 *The Graduate* Gielgud Theatre

2003 *Hitchcock Blonde* Royal Court Theatre

Introduction

Terry Johnson was sitting in the stalls of Chicago's
Steppenwolf Theatre during a technical rehearsal of my
play *The Libertine* with a life-sized puppet of a monkey on his
arm. Terry was directing and the scene under discussion
depicted the protagonist, the Earl of Rochester, having his
portrait painted in the company of his favourite pet. The
monkey had been built to Terry's specifications and was
now being put through its paces. Terry was clearly a natural
puppeteer. He held the animal a couple of feet away from
his face and made it caper, snicker, mock and scrape. I
laughed; stage management laughed; even a few of the
actors laughed. But Terry's expression drifted in tiny
increments from blankness to profound depression. At last
he spoke: 'It's not good enough.' The monkey was axed and
one of the laughing actors was instructed to assume the role.

This vignette of a man employing considerable skill in a
desperate attempt to make himself laugh and failing
encapsulates the three characteristics which define, in my
eyes, Terry's work: he is, in more or less equal measure, a
superb technician, a great entertainer and a born
melancholic.

There is much of the technician in this volume: *The
London Cuckolds* sees him restructuring the narrative,
changing physical settings and providing pastiche
seventeenth-century dialogue to replace the occasional
obscurities of Ravencroft's original. The result is a
tremendous sharpening of focus: at every moment of the
play it's clear what the characters want, what stops them
from getting it and what desperate step they must now
entertain if they are to achieve their goals. In the theatre the
piece chimed effortlessly because the clockwork had been so
meticulously arranged.

But clever though *The London Cuckolds* is, it's not so sharp
as *The Graduate*. Though many plays have been transformed
into movies, few films have made the reverse journey and
the reason is clear: most screenplays feature between 150
and 250 scenes, while most plays manage with fewer than

twenty. Even Shakespeare, an epic writer par excellence, only exceeds thirty scenes in *Antony and Cleopatra*. So compressing a screenplay into fourteen scenes in the theatre requires some neat footwork. Terry is very astute at harnessing the audience's (likely) familiarity with the film to his advantage. The famous final scene on the bus, for instance, would be awkward to stage in the theatre, but by throwing in references to bus rides throughout the play, the writer activates that memory cell and makes us feel we've seen it. Then, when he has to conjure up a final scene, he comes up with an idea (the Cheerios scene) which provides the same dialectic between tentative optimism and what-the-hell-did-we-just-do panic that characterises the end of the movie.

The great technical trick of *Cleo, Camping, Emmanuelle and Dick* is so upfront it's easy to miss: it's the inspired notion of using the caravan as the sole setting. This coup simultaneously provides an atmospheric milieu, a playground for farce, a visual tension between interior and exterior and a metaphor for decay. Of the huge number of plays which are submitted to theatres but never reach the stage, a significant number are doomed because the writer hasn't come up with the simple idea that makes the play work. With this author, the nuts and bolts are always meticulously tightened.

As for Terry Johnson the entertainer, little need be said except that of all our current practising playwrights he is the unchallenged maestro at the art of selling a ticket on the basis of an idea. Some dramatists write big parts that will attract stars, some dramatise their consciences, some simply hope that the quality of their writing will shine through and draw a crowd. But when the blurb reads 'Marilyn Monroe explains relativity to Einstein' or 'Freud meets Dali' or 'Sid James, Kenneth Williams and Barbara Windsor bitch backstage' the box office advances pile up.

And what of the man who could not raise a smile at his own antics with the monkey? The sense of melancholy at the daily business of living, the smell of hopes defeated, the pain of desire mocked or ignored underwrite everything Terry

Johnson has written. Sex is the key to his work. Mostly it's characterised as a relentless obsession which keeps people busy but miserable. The husbands in *The London Cuckolds* don't have sex with their wives because all their time and ingenuity is directed towards stopping their wives from having sex with other men. Benjamin in *The Graduate* is terrified of sex, then satiated with it, never satisfied. For Sid in *Cleo, Camping, Emmanuelle and Dick*, womanising is at best a reflex, a mechanism for coping with the passing of time, at worst the gate of a trap leading to the miseries of love. The most typically Johnsonian moment in this volume is the exchange between Sid and Barbara in Act Three of *Cleo, Camping, Emmanuelle and Dick*, when Sid reveals that he doesn't like the man he is when he's with his wife. Barbara is given the final word: 'I can't stop you getting old, Sid. If we were together I wouldn't be new any more. And all you ever want is someone new. If you feel old, Sid, it's because all you dream of is new.'

Sexual desire in Terry Johnson's plays is the great motivating spark; but as soon as the fire is burning, the participants are alive to the moment when only the ashes remain.

Stephen Jeffreys
December 2003

The London Cuckolds

by Edward Ravenscroft, Gent.

adapted by Terry Johnson

The London Cuckolds was first performed in the Lyttelton Auditorium of the Royal National Theatre on 13 February 1998. The cast was as follows:

Wiseacres	Robin Soans
Peggy	Kelly Reilly
Doodle	Anthony O'Donnell
Arabella	Caroline Quentin
Dashwell	William Chubb
Eugenia	Sharon Small
Ramble	Ben Miles
Townley	Nigel Lindsay
Loveday	Alexander Hanson
Aunt	Hilda Braid
Engine	Charon Bourke
Jane	Ysobel Gonzalez
Roger	Joseph Murray
Tom	Malcolm Browning
Coachman/1st Chimney-Sweep	Roger Swaine
Scullery Boy/2nd Chimney-Sweep	Morgan Symes
1st Watchman	Richard Addison
2nd Watchman	Simon Markey
Lamp Boy/3rd Watchman	Tom Peters
1st Servant	Virginia Hatton
2nd Servant	Kate Dyson

Directed by Terry Johnson
Designed by William Dudley
Lighting by Simon Corder
Music by Roger Skeaping
Sound by Colin Pink
Staff Director Charlotte Conquest
Stage Manager David Milling
Deputy Stage Manager Emma Gordon
Assistant Stage Manager Katy de Main
Assistant Stage Manager Michele Enright
Assistant Stage Manager Richard Reddrop

Characters

Wiseacres, *an Alderman of London*
Peggy, *bride to Wiseacres, an Innocent, and Country-bred*
Doodle, *an Alderman of London*
Arabella, *wife to Doodle, a Pretender to Wit*
Dashwell, *a City Scrivener*
Eugenia, *wife to Dashwell, a hypocrite*
Ramble, *a great Designer on Ladies, but unsuccessful in his intrigues*
Townley, *a Gentleman of the times, careless of women, but fortunate*
Loveday, *a Young Merchant, formerly a lover of Eugenia*
Aunt, *Governess to Peggy*
Engine, *Woman to Arabella*
Jane, *Eugenia's Maid*
Roger, *Footman to Ramble*
Tom, *Footman to Townley*
Lamp boy
Vendor
Two Chimney-Sweeps
Three Watchmen
Scullery Boy
Servants

Prologue

Spoken by **Arabella**

Well, now's your time, my masters of the pit
You that delights in women, wine and wit.
All things this evening jump for your delight
In mirth we wear the day, in love the night.
The theatre is open, and 'twould be to our cost
To strive and fail to please you most.
You gallants and you nymphs shall laugh
To see those struggle who have chose the married path
And those who sit with boosy husbands or with pinch-lipped
wives
Might look downcast should we dare criticise
The Mansion house of marriage, that never gives content
Like the convenient modish tenement
Of love, that's held by moderate lease or yearly rent.
But ladies, if with me you would your counsel join,
We'll make our tenants pay a swinging fine.
For if you drain your keeper 'til he's poor
And have the wit to lay it up in store
He must marry you in hope to mend his life
For what he lost to a mistress he must gain by a wife!
As for the rest, be not severe with us, but laugh;
For 'twould be folly to condemn what one glimpses in a glass.

(As for you critics, we are glad to see you in such number
And hope that in the least we do not disturb your slumber
Also praying we have had the wit
To sit you just precisely where you each prefer to sit.)

Act One

Scene One

The street before **Doodle***'s house.*

Enter **Alderman Wiseacres** *and* **Doodle**.

Wiseacres   Well, Mr Alderman Doodle, you promise to go along with me?

Doodle   Yes. I will dispense with business on this occasion. Who else goes?

Wiseacres   Only our neighbour Mr Dashwell.

Doodle   We'll be going as soon as the Exchange closes?

Wiseacres   Yes, and you shall then see the most simple innocent thing of a wife.

Doodle   What? Is she simple you say?

Wiseacres   Indeed she is silly. A mere infant in her intellects. But for her bigness you'd think her a baby.

Doodle   How old is she?

Wiseacres   But fourteen.

Doodle   An infant to you indeed; why, you are above fifty.

Wiseacres   What of it?

Doodle   But a discreet woman of thirty had been more suitable for you.

Wiseacres   But my intention is to marry a woman that will be young when I am old. I am convinced that an old man can never love an old woman. Age is a sore decayer and renders men backward in their duty, therefore I am marrying a woman so young that she might be a temptation to me when I am old. Perfumes, oils and oysters are nothing comparable to youth and beauty.

Doodle   So that's your drift.

Wiseacres   I have long lived a bachelor. I begin late, so would lengthen out my satisfaction as far as I'm able.

Doodle   But why do you marry one so silly; where's the satisfaction in that?

Wiseacres   Because a young wife that has wit would play the Devil with an old husband. Even the young husbands have trouble keeping them true nowadays.

Doodle   In this City, certainly.

Wiseacres   Therefore I chose a girl of four years of age that had no signs of wit. Her father and mother were none of the wisest either and, fortunately, dead. I placed the child in the care of her aunt, a somewhat decayed gentlewoman who was also a bit soft. I placed them in the country, at a lone house, and instructed her to bring the girl up in all simplicity and never to let her play amongst Boys. Now she's been moulded to my instruction I shall reap the fruits of my labour.

Doodle   But were there not fools enough of Heaven's making?

Wiseacres   Yes, but such grow wiser by experience and by the time they come to twenty years of age are quite another thing. This forward age ripens them apace. Thus I have bred a fool and marry her so young she never shall grow wiser.

Doodle   But should a wife not be a companion to a man? Would you have your wife a slave?

Wiseacres   Much rather than be a slave to a wife. A witty wife is the greatest plague on earth; she will have so many tricks and inventions to deceive a husband, he might never sleep for keeping watch upon his honour. From all which cares and troubles he is freed that has married a wife without the wit to offend.

Doodle   But if my wife was a fool I should always suspect *her* a whore, for 'tis want of wit that makes 'em believe the flatteries of men. I tell you, Mr Alderman; a woman without sense is like a castle without soldiers, to be taken at every assault.

Wiseacres   But I say still; wit is a dangerous weapon in a woman.

Doodle   I tell you, Brother Wiseacres, you are in the wrong.

Wiseacres   I tell you, Brother Doodle, I am in the right. You have a witty wife; much good may it do you.

Doodle   And much good to you and your fool!

Wiseacres   Better a fool than a wanton!

Doodle   Better a wanton than both!

Enter **Dashwell**.

Wiseacres   Your insistence provokes me!

Doodle   And your want of reason provokes me!

Wiseacres   I hope you will allow a witty wife may be a slut!

Doodle   And a foolish wife will certainly be one!

Dashwell   What has raised this heat between you?

Wiseacres   Oh, Mr Dashwell, in good time. You shall be judge now. We are in dispute here as to whether 'tis best for a man to have a laughing little giggling, highty, tighty, prattling, tattling, gossiping wife; such a one as he has married . . . ?

Doodle   Or a simple, sneaking, bashful, awkward, ill-bred country girl who wouldn't say boo to a goose, who can only answer ay *forsooth* and no *forsooth*, and stands in awe of her chambermaid! Such a one as Alderman Wiseacres here has taken pains to rear for his own proper use.

Wiseacres   What need my wife have wit to make her loud, talkative and impertinent when I have enough for her and myself too?

Doodle   Mr Dashwell; which of us do you think is in the right?

Dashwell   In the right?

Doodle   Ay.

Dashwell   Why, I think you both in the wrong.

Wiseacres   Both in the wrong!

Doodle   How can that be?

Dashwell   A wife that has wit will outwit her husband, and she that has no wit will be outwitted by those who wish to outwit him. So as to which will make her husband a cuckold first or oftenest; 'tis an even bet, if you would lay one.

Wiseacres   You are a married man, Mr Dashwell; what course have you taken?

Doodle   Ay; is yours wise or foolish?

Dashwell   Security lies not in the wise or the foolish but in the Godly wife.

Wiseacres   Oh, the Godly wife.

Dashwell   One that prays and goes often to church. Such a one have I.

Doodle   Sheer hypocrites all. How many cuckolds must there be in a parish whose bell tolls out their wives twice a day for assignations!

Wiseacres   Nor should my wife be taught catechism by some smooth-faced priest; Heaven knows what doctrine he may put into her!

Doodle   Much good may your Godly wife do you!

Dashwell   The world has never been of one mind since there was more than one man in it, and never will be so long as there are two. But to our business; I must go and acquaint my wife I'm going out of town, so shall meet you at Garraways coffee-house.

Doodle   The coffee-house.

Dashwell *exits*.

Wiseacres   Mr Alderman, you need not acquaint your wife with news of my marriage, for *my* wife shall be no gossiper nor woman of the times. I shall marry her tomorrow morning in private and in private she shall live.

Doodle   As you please.

Wiseacres   The coffee-house, then.

Doodle   The coffee-house.

Exit **Wiseacres**.

I dare not think what sport my wife would make of him should she have heard this odd humour.

He opens a door and **Arabella** *and* **Engine**, *who have been listening, tumble in.*

Arabella/Engine   Ha ha ha ha ha ha.

Doodle   Thou art very merry, wife.

Arabella   Ha ha ha.

Doodle   Prithee what dost thou laugh at?

Arabella   Lord, husband. If *your* wife was but a fool I am certain there would be no sense in the house!

Doodle   You overheard our discourse?

Arabella   He had a fling at me too, but I'll be revenged if ever I can come to speak to his silly wife. I'll read her a chapter of wisdom shall clear her understanding. How far off is this pattern of innocence?

Doodle   But a few hours from London.

Arabella   And you are to go upon this piece of gallantry to fetch the lady?

Doodle   He desired and I have promised.

Arabella   Are we to expect you home at dinner?

Doodle   No, we shall dine together in the city, then take the coach. Well, wife, you shan't see me again 'til tomorrow. There's a kiss to remember me. Adieu.

Arabella   Adieu, husband.

Exit **Doodle**.

Arabella   A kiss! Slender diet to live upon until tomorrow. I have a mind to feast in his absence upon lustier fare than a dull city husband. Engine, durst I pursue my inclinations with the man you have often heard me speak of?

Engine   A little variety, madam, would be pleasant. Always to feed upon an Alderman's flesh must be enough to cloy your stomach.

Arabella   He's so sparing with it, I'm never less than starving.

Engine   The better you're allowed to look abroad. Troth, madam, you must never lose your longing.

Arabella   Thou shalt go to him. Thou hast a pretty good way of speaking; I'll leave it to thy management.

Engine   I can assure you, if you like the gentleman, the gentleman will like you.

Arabella   Offer no assurances; love is a doubtful voyage.

Engine   Yes, if the venture be in a leaky rotten-bottomed boat such as your husband. But in such a well-built ship, so finely rigged, as that other you speak of, you run no risk at all.

Arabella   Well then go to my Lover and see if he has stowage room left for a heart. If so, contract for mine. But tell him, what foul weather soever happens, he shall preserve my cargo though he throw the rest overboard.

Engine   I have him in sight already; a tall stout vessel, well-manned, bearing up briskly, spreading all sails for haste, and pulling you on board. Methinks I see him lie across your hawser already!

Arabella   Come, wench, thy tongue runs and we lose time.

Engine   I'll regain it on my expedition!

Exeunt.

Scene Two

Ramble's *lodging.*

Enter **Ramble** *and* **Townley**, *in morning gowns.*

Townley   Prethee, Ned Ramble, what makes thee so early a riser, after so late a debauch as we made last night?

Ramble   Business, Frank.

Townley   What business can a Gentleman have to make him rise at ten, that went drunk to bed at four?

Ramble   I am of a mind to pursue an intrigue. A new mistress, Frank.

Townley   An intrigue! I never knew any of your intrigues come to anything.

Ramble   'Tis true, I have been unfortunate hitherto, yet perseverance will overcome destiny.

Townley   Prethee, Ned, I wish you would let women alone and learn to divert thyself with a bottle. Wine is cheaper bought, more easily opened, and quicker dispatched.

Ramble   If I should attend the playhouse once more with you, Frank Townley, and drink as we did yesterday, I should be fit neither for the company of women nor men, I am so squeamish today.

Townley   Custom will overcome that; come let's go and drink away thy complaints.

Ramble   I'll have no more, I thank you, this month.

Townley   But Ned, wine gives a certain elevation of spirit that a man half bowsy shall advance farther with a woman in one encounter, than a sober fellow as thou art in ten. Come, let us abandon this sober end of the Town, where a man can't reel into a Tavern after eleven a'clock, for sawcy Constables that will send him home against his will.

Ramble   Frank, I do decline.

Enter **Roger**.

Roger   Sir, here's a Lady's Maid desires to speak with you in private.

Ramble   Show her in! Did I not tell you, Frank, I had better business today than the bottle?

Townley   A Love Ambassadress?

Ramble   You must doubt it not, but step into the next room.

Townley   I scarce believe thy luck.

Exit **Townley**. *Enter* **Engine**.

Roger   There's my master.

Ramble   A good morrow to you, mistress.

Engine   I wish you the same, sir; and think to bring you such good news my wish will surely be successful.

Ramble   What is it I pray, and from whom?

Engine   From a Fair Lady, sir. Perhaps you will think me forward, should I go on . . .

Ramble   I could never think amiss of one that has such an auspicious countenance.

Engine   You flatter me, I protest I blush at my undertaking.

Ramble   Pray let me hear my fortune from those pretty Lips.

Engine   Sir, consider how accomplish'd a person you are, and how worthily you attract the eyes of the Ladies, and think it then no wonder at all that a certain Lady thinks you the most admirable person of your whole Sex. Since yesterday she spied you at the playhouse . . .

Ramble   At the Playhouse you say, and but yesterday?

Engine   Indeed, sir.

Ramble (*aside*)   Then this is not the invitation I expected.

Engine   My lady talks of you with so much delight and fervency, that I thought it injustice to you, as well as injurious to her, if I should not acquaint you withall, and each with the other.

Ramble   You have rais'd me to a wonderful expectation. Pray who is this Lady?

Engine   A rich Alderman's young wife, one that has been married only Six Months. One that speaks prettily in your praise . . .

Ramble   Good.

Engine   And has the tenderest sentiments in her thoughts for you.

Ramble   Very good.

Engine   And o'er whom you have such an Ascendancy, that could she be assur'd you were one with whom her reputation might be safe . . .

Ramble   She could Love me; is it so?

Engine   It is indeed. After such an assurance, it would not be in her power to refuse you any favour could be expected from a woman.

Ramble   Thou pourest harmony in my ears, that strikes upon my heart-strings, and makes it bound with joy. Take this Gold to encourage thee. Where is this obliging Beauty, when shall I see her?

Engine   Her husband is this day gone out of Town.

Ramble   Conduct me to her.

Engine   Not 'til night, that darkness may secure her reputation. Approach with caution and circumspection, as Misers do the hoard of Wealth they are afraid to lose.

Ramble   I'll think her a Mine of Gold, myself the Indian that has discover'd it, and imagine all other citizens Spaniards that would rob me of't, so secretly I will approach –

Engine   Announce yourself thus . . . (*She knocks the table.*) Such prudence will secure a lasting Joy. This notebook I took from her. Within you will find her name and where she might be found. But interpret not that my errand proceeds from any commands of hers.

Ramble   Not in the least.

Engine   I know the secrets of her heart, and took the liberty without her knowledge.

Ramble   Dear mistress, I am yours.

Engine   Your Servant, sir.

Exit **Engine**. *Enter* **Townley**.

Ramble   Roger! Bring my clothes that I may dress me.

Enter **Roger** *with clothes*.

Townley   Ned, if ever thou prove successful in an intrigue, it will be this.

Ramble   Of that I am inclined to have no doubt. But bless me, Frank, 'tis not the intrigue that I spoke of.

Townley   How say you?

Ramble *shows* **Townley** *a Letter*.

Ramble   This letter I did receive but yesterday.

Townley   A Woman's Hand!

Ramble   And a fair one, I assure you, to send such an invitation. And now I am tempted by another bold Challenger. But twice the chase must yield twice the quarry!

Townley   Are you better acquainted with this first Amour?

Ramble   I had but stood behind her, look'd amorously upon her, and sighed to her across the pew.

Townley   Ah, this is a church Lady then, some rich old widow, for whom thou dost intend with dry slavish lechery to raise thyself to the equipage of a stallion and drudge out a fortune.

Ramble   Have better thoughts, friend; she is neither old nor ugly, nor one whom fortune has yet blessed with widowhood. She is a wife; young, plump, pretty, and blooming as the spring.

Townley   What is her husband?

Ramble   A blockheaded city attorney. A trudging, drudging, curmudgeoning, petitioning citizen, that with a little law, and much knavery has got a great estate.

Townley   A lawyer! Cuckold the Rogue for that reason alone.

Ramble   By the inducement of her parents she married him against her will, and now made nauseous in his bed, rises every morning by six with a pretence to attend church. And loathing his company at home, pretends all day to be at Prayers, that she may be alone in her chamber.

Townley   'Tis strange a man should find a Mistress at Church, that never goes to one.

Ramble   'Tis true: till of late, I had never been at church since my father's funeral, and would not have gone then, but to conduct him thither and ensure he didn't return to take back the Estate I got by his death. Nor had I been since, but for a sudden shower of Rain that drove me inside, where came I by this miracle of a woman, who instantly wrought my conversion.

Townley   And have you said your prayers?

Ramble   I dare not pray against Temptation, lest Heaven should have taken me at my word, and spoil'd my intrigue.

Townley   Spoke like a Cavalier, e'Gad! If thy inclinations did but lie a little more to the Bottle, thou wouldst be an admirably honest Fellow.

Ramble   I must make haste.

Townley   But, Ned, what of the other pretty mackerel circling thy ardent sprat?

Ramble   Curse my luck, that one appointment should prevent the other.

Townley   If you are doubtful, toss a coin.

Ramble   No, I resolve to attempt this one first, because I know the person, and am sure she pleases me. What perfections this one has are yet unknown to me, therefore with more ease is she neglected.

Townley   Who is this morning's woman; what's her name?

Ramble   It is not like a Gallant, to reveal a kind Lady's name. It is here set down in fair characters.

Townley   Let me see that.

Ramble   Look no longer, she's not of your acquaintance.

Townley   Indeed that may be so. The notebook, however, once was mine.

Ramble   Thine! No, thou art deceiv'd.

Townley   Mine. I know it by the Clasps: pray look on the inside of the cover, and see if there be not a cupid drawn with a red-lead pen?

Ramble   Gad, Frank, thou hast guessed right, there is.

Townley   'Tis then the same.

Ramble   Ah.

Townley   The woman I gave it to is the person of all the world I most fancy.

Ramble   Is she very handsome?

Townley   I know not the charms of her face, 'tis her wit I admire.

Ramble   Has your intrigue then been carried on in the dark?

Townley   No, I have seen her often masked at plays. She has a delicate shape, and a pretty hand; she once showed me that as a Sample. Snow was never so white, nor alabaster half so sleek and polished. She is all air, mirth and wit. Roguish, but not impudent. Witty, but not rampant. You should hear her banter most excellently with those cockerels of the pit that come flirting at her. But she always leaves alone when the play is done.

Ramble   But how came she by your notebook?

Townley   But yesterday I was humming a new song in the pit, and she ask'd me if I could give it her. I had it written down, so I presented the book to her. She seemed the most faithful of women, who is revealed the most fickle.

Ramble   I am glad to hear her good character, but am now dissatisfied that one intrigue should cross the other.

Townley   Since it is so, give me the directions, and I will go in your place.

Ramble   Thank you for that, but no. I'll fear not to meet both fair inviters.

Townley   But you can secure only one to yourself.

Ramble   If any accident cross one design, I have the other lady in reserve.

Townley   Thou art ill natur'd, hard-hearted, and wouldst not part with one, hadst thou twenty. For punishment I wish thee the same curse I do to misers that hoard up gold, and would not save a man from starving, which is that you may be robbed of all, and after the loss hang thy self with grief.

Ramble   Alas, Frank Townley, I thought you could not love anything but a Bottle.

Townley   Farewell, churl.

Ramble   In spite of thy prophecy, meet me tomorrow morning, and I'll tell thee such pleasant stories of this night's joys, thou shalt for ever be converted from wine to women.

Women are Miracles the Gods have given.

That by their brightness we may guess at Heaven.

Exeunt.

Act Two

Scene One

A room in **Dashwell***'s house.*

An impressive supper table set. Enter **Eugenia** *and* **Jane**.

Jane   Madam, Mr Ramble awaits at the back door.

Eugenia   Jane, though I love this Mr Ramble, my inclinations are not so much at fault as your counsels. For had not you persuaded me, I should never have consented to his coming. Tonight. In my husband's absence.

Jane   Madam, when a man will press a woman to marry against her inclinations, he lays for himself the foundation of becoming a cuckold shortly after. Troth, madam, think no more of your husband, but of the man you love, who is this night come to your embraces. I'll warrant you you'll not repent tomorrow morning.

Eugenia   If unexpectedly my husband should return –

Jane   There is no fear of that.

Eugenia   Somebody knocks at the front. Run to the door.

Enter **Loveday**, *meanly habited, in black.*

Jane   Who would you speak with, sir?

Loveday   Is Mr Dashwell within?

Jane   He is out of Town.

Eugenia   Jane, who is it?

Jane   A gentleman, madam, to speak to your husband.

Loveday   Madam, I have letters for him from his brother at Hamburg.

Eugenia   Give me the letters, sir. I am sorry for my

husband's absence; our further acquaintance must wait upon his return.

Loveday   In the letters, madam, your husband's brother recommends me to him as a servant, and asks that I might be entertained in this house for a short time. With your indulgence, madam.

Eugenia   Jane, this is unlucky. What shall we do?

Jane   I could dispatch him to bed, do you but give the order.

Eugenia   Sir, my house is not well provided of beds at present, you must be content with a lodging in the garret. Jane, take care to see him lodged, I am sleepy and will go to my parlour. Jane, make haste, for I am not very well.

Exit **Eugenia**.

Jane   Come, sir, you have rid a long journey today, and must be weary.

Loveday   I came but from Canterbury today, but must confess to great hunger!

Jane   Because my Lady's not well, let me beg you be content with a little cheese tonight, which shall be brought up to you.

Loveday   And a glass of beer at least?

Jane   This is a house of some abstinence. Now, sir, pray follow me. I shall light your chamber.

Exit **Jane**.

Loveday   How fair Eugenia look'd. With how much joy in this short interview did I behold those eyes, whose wounds I have borne so long, whose influence felt at so great a distance! I wish she had not been indispose'd. What's this? A supper? Somebody is to come in the husband's absence! Eugenia pretends to be gone to bed, her indisposition is feign'd, my company was unseasonable, to lodge me in the Garret was policy. And so the girl I once knew has indeed become all of a woman.

Jane (*within*)   Please, sir, come hither.

Loveday   With all my heart, for I am very weary. 'Tis so; they are for posting me supperless to bed, to remove me out of the way. I'll venture to observe.

Exit **Loveday**. *Enter* **Eugenia** *and* **Ramble**.

Eugenia   Come, sir, enter here. Well, Mr Ramble, you see what influence you Gentlemen have over us weak Women.

Ramble   Oh my dear Life, my Joy.

Eugenia   I ne'er thought I should condescend to admit you to my house in my husband's absence thus, what will you think of me?

Ramble   I'll think thee the kindest, loving'st, the dearest, and the best of thy whole sex.

Eugenia   May I then trust, sir, your honour, and intentions?

Ramble   Let me not answer thee, but in this Language.

Eugenia   Jane!

Enter **Jane**.

Jane   Madam?

Eugenia   Is supper upon the Table?

Jane   As you can see, madam.

Eugenia   Come, sir, let us satisfy ourselves with meat and wine.

Ramble   Yet make but a hasty meal of it, that we may the sooner come to that more delicious Banquet, the feast that Love has prepared for us, that feast of Soul and Senses, and of all at once.

Eugenia   Come, sir, now you have said Grace, sit down.

Jane   Less the meat grow cold.

They sit down to Table.

Ramble   Jane, I am obliged to you.

Eugenia   Jane, have a care. Mr Ramble may seek to corrupt you to let him into my chamber after I'm in bed, anon.

Ramble   O sweet wished-for hour!

Eugenia   Be sure, Jane, you don't let him have the key.

Jane   No, madam, I'll be sure to put that in my pocket. When you are both lock'd in.

Ramble   Thank you, Jane.

Exit **Jane**.

Eugenia   I see you have corrupted my Servant already; fie upon you. Come, sir, will you carve?

Ramble   You if you please, madam.

Eugenia   Would you a leg or . . . otherwise? Do not look at me thus, sir; your eyes do tie my tongue.

Ramble   Then let us reserve our thoughts 'til anon, 'til I have thee in bed in my arms, where darkness will privilege thee to tell thy thoughts without a blush freely.

Eugenia   Use your conquest with discretion, and allude not to my blushes. Eat, sir! I confess I can deny you nothing, and 'tis too late now to retreat.

Ramble   Be not faint-hearted, nor ashamed, now Fortune has blessed us with the opportunity. Now let us be all rapture, all fire, kiss, hug, and embrace, and never have done.

Eugenia   Have a care, sir, of feeding too heartily on Love, 'tis a surfeiting diet, with which your sex is soon satisfied. That is the reason you men seek variety so much.

Ramble   Fear not that now, for thou art a dish of all varieties, like tapath. Like a Spanish table that contains the best of everything; all the charms of thy whole Sex are here in this one composition.

Knocking at the door.

Ramble   Who can it be thus late?

Eugenia   Pray Heaven it be not my husband.

Ramble   No no, fortune would not be such an enemy to Love.

Knocking without. Enter **Jane**.

Eugenia   Hark again. Jane! Run to the door and see who knocks.

Jane   I have seen from the window, madam, 'tis my Master!

Eugenia   What shall we do?

Ramble   Cursed spite, where shall I hide?

Jane   Go into the Closet, sir, there, there.

Ramble *goes in. Knocking.*

Eugenia   Heavens, how he knocks. Wait, sir. Thrust in the table and all.

Table and all is put into the Closet.

Eugenia   So, if it be my Husband, tell him I am at my Prayers and would not be disturb'd. Get him up to bed.

Jane   Yes, madam. He'll beat down the door.

Knocking.

Eugenia   Stay, where is my prayer-book?

Jane   In the parlour, madam.

Exit **Jane**. **Eugenia** *settles herself to read upon the couch.*

Enter **Dashwell** *and* **Doodle**, *with* **Jane**.

Dashwell   Jane, you grow slower of service the longer you remain in it. Is my wife in the parlour? We'll go into her.

Jane   She is at Prayers, sir, and would not be disturb'd.

Dashwell   Let her pray anon. . . I have brought Mr

Alderman Doodle to see her. Wife, come prethee. Wife, leave off praying, thou art always a praying, lay by thy book.

Eugenia   Oh me, husband, are you come home, indeed I did not expect you tonight. Mr Alderman, your humble Servant.

Doodle   Your Servant, good Mrs Dashwell.

Eugenia   I hope your wife is well.

Doodle   I left her well in the morning; she's not at her prayers, I'll warrant you, even a little of that suffices her.

Eugenia   Truly I think I cannot better spend my time.

Dashwell   Well, wife, prithee, what hast thou for our supper, we are very hungry, the fresh air has got us a stomach.

Eugenia   Truly, husband, not expecting you home, I provided nothing, we made shift with what was left at dinner, there is nothing at all in the house.

Enter **Loveday**, *with a Letter.*

Dashwell   Who is this?

Eugenia   O my dear, I had forgot to tell you, this young man comes from your Brother with recommendations to you.

Loveday   Here's a letter from him, sir. I was just going to bed, but when I heard you come, I slip'd on my clothes and made bold to know your pleasure.

Dashwell   Indeed, sir. Reach me a Candle from the closet, Jane.

Eugenia   Lord, husband, is it not a little late for business?

Dashwell   Jane, a candle!

Eugenia   How did it happen pray, that you all return'd tonight?

Doodle   Our Brother Alderman heard of a business at the Exchange today, which will require his presence there tomorrow, therefore he resolv'd to bring his Bride to Town tonight, and be Married early in the morning.

Eugenia   Is she come then?

Dashwell   We left her and her Aunt at the Coach-house.

Eugenia   The Marriage I suppose will be private? –

Doodle   Yes, there will be only the Aunt, your husband, and myself. Alderman Wiseacres has the oddest humours; he will have her call him Uncle.

Eugenia   She is very young, I hear.

Dashwell   My Brother gives you a very good character. I'll attempt tomorrow to gain you employment.

Loveday   I humbly thank you, sir.

Dashwell   He names nothing particular; pray what are you capable of?

Loveday   I have been bred a scholar, taken some degrees at the University. Indeed, whilst I was at Oxford, I studied a very Mysterious Art; and spent much time in the contemplation of Magick, which the vulgar call the Black-Art. For this I was expell'd. I can perform wonderful things, yet without danger. Any time when you and your Lady are at leisure, I will show something of my skill for your diversion.

Eugenia   Oh goodness, Husband! I would not see conjuring for all the world, it is a naughty wicked thing, and dangerous.

Loveday   Nay good Lady, you shall have no hurt from me. It is very useful sometimes. I can by my art reveal robberies, procure a wind for ships becalm'd and bring 'em to port, discover private enemies, and the like.

Dashwell   I beg your pardon, I believe nothing of all this.

Doodle   I would you could help us to a good supper, for I am damnably hungry.

Dashwell   Ay, with all the trimmings.

Loveday   That, sir. . . I'll do with all my heart.

Dashwell   Canst thou?

Loveday   In a trice, the easiest thing of a hundred.

Dashwell   Prethee do then.

Eugenia   O Lord husband! What do you mean?

Dashwell   Nay, nay, ne'er fright yourself. You'll see no such thing.

Loveday   I'll warrant you a Supper, sir.

Dashwell   Sayest you so. But let it be hot.

Loveday   Hot. Ay, sir . . .

Doodle   It must needs be hot if it comes from the Devil.

Jane   What does this fellow mean?

Eugenia   I hope he's not in earnest.

Loveday   Fear not, madam, but sit you down; and you, Sir, by your Lady.

Eugenia   For Heaven's sake, husband, let me be gone.

Dashwell   No, no, sit down; let us see it. Begin.

Loveday   Have patience, you shall see nothing to fright you. Silence I pray. Mephorbus, Mephorbus, Mephorbus. Thrice I have thee invoked my Familiar. Be thou assistant to my desires, supply what e'er a hungry appetite requires. By all the powers of the Zodiac, Aries, Taurus, Gemini, Cancer, Leo, Virgo, Libra, Scorpio, Sagittarius, Capricorn, Aquarius, Pisces. Assist ye Seven Planets too, Mars, Sol, Venus, Mercury, Luna, Dragon's Head, and Dragon's Tail. Shed your auspicious influences, and to my charm give efficacious strength.

Jane   Oh the Devil is coming, I smell Brimstone already.

Dashwell   Peace, you Baggage, you've already supped.

Doodle   Would I were under the Table, that the Devil mayn't see me. If he comes.

Loveday   Tacet . . .

Dashwell   That's hold your peace.

Loveday   Arom Gascodin Adelphon, Eus, Eusticon Olam amemnos.

After the charms, he stands with his Head as listening to an invisible.

Thanks, Mephorbus. Now, sir, you may prepare to tuck in.

Dashwell   Why, I see no meat. The Devil has failed you.

Doodle   I thought you could Conjure.

Loveday   Let your Servant open that door. . . and draw in the Table as it has been furnished by the Power of my Art.

Dashwell   As he commands, Jane. Do so.

Jane *opens the closet, draws out the Table.*

Dashwell   Ha! But 'tis wonderful, a table plentifully furnish'd! Sir, you impress me indeed. Good meat and wine; 'tis excellent. Wife, Mr Alderman, fall to.

Eugenia   Eat of the Devil's food?

Doodle   I warrant you 'tis but a Vision, 'twill vanish if you touch it.

Loveday   No, though it came by a supernatural means, yet it is no delusion; 'tis good substantial food, such as nature and the bounty of Heaven afford. To encourage you, see I will fall to and eat heartily.

Dashwell   Excellent fare, in faith. O rare Art; sir, you are an excellent caterer.

Eugenia   I could not have believed there was such power in Art, if my eyes had not seen it.

Doodle   Pray Heaven it digest well.

Loveday   I warrant you, sir.

Dashwell   Here, sir. Here's to you, and I thank you for our good cheer.

Loveday   Your Servant, sir. Come, Mr Alderman; the cook's good health.

Doodle   Auh! What mean you, drink the Devil's health?

Loveday   Will you eat of his meat and not thank him?

Doodle   'Tis somewhat uncivil, I confess.

Loveday   If you eat with a Tory, the money that bought his meat was the price of orphans' tears, and so came from the Devil too. And yet we eat with him, drink his health, and thank him.

Doodle   Ay, well. . .

Dashwell   If you can do this all the year round, I'll take you to be my book-keeper.

Loveday   My Art serves me only in time of extremity. If done for covetousness, my invocations have no strength.

Dashwell   That's a pity.

Doodle   Pray tell me, by what means was this table furnish'd; was it by the help of Spirits? I heard no noise.

Loveday   It was done by a Familiar that I have command of.

Doodle   Ah.

Loveday   If you please I will shew him in human shape.

Doodle   Oh, no.

Dashwell   Pray do, sir, that I may thank him.

Eugenia   O by no means, sir. What, husband, would you thank the Devil?

Dashwell   Why, is't not the proverb, *Give the Devil his due*? Fear not.

Loveday   I warrant you, Lady, it shall be no harm to you; he is hereabouts invisible already.

Eugenia   Oh.

Loveday   Set the door wide open, that his passage may be free.

Dashwell   Quick, Jane.

Loveday   Mephorbus, that lurkest here, put on human shape, and come forth in the likeness of a fine well-dress'd gentleman, such as may please this Lady's eye. Presto, I say . . . be gone!

Enter **Ramble**.

Loveday   Pass by, pay your reverence, and make your exit.

Ramble *bows and exits.*

Loveday   So, madam, how did you like the Familiar?

Eugenia   It had a frightful shape.

Dashwell   It look'd a fine gentleman.

Doodle   It was a mannerly Devil too, he bow'd as he pass'd by.

Eugenia   Hang a light outside the door to ensure the Devil does not return.

Exit **Jane**.

Dashwell   But pray, why was the door opened, could he not have gone through the keyhole?

Loveday   Yes, sir, but then he would have carried away part of your house; for Spirits are sullen and malicious.

Dashwell   I understand.

Doodle   Well, Mr Dashwell, I'll take my leave.

Dashwell   I'll to the door with you.

Doodle   Mr Conjurer, good night. I thank you for my good supper.

Loveday   Your servant, sir.

Doodle   Madam.

Dashwell *goes out with* **Doodle**. *Enter* **Jane**.

Loveday   Madam, I had not thought so familiar a Familiar would have frighted you.

Eugenia   Jane, help the Gentleman to a Candle.

Jane   Sir, will you please to take that?

Loveday   Madam . . .

Eugenia   Good night, sir.

Dashwell *returns*.

Loveday Good night, sir.

Dashwell   And a good repose to you, sir.

Loveday   Good night, madam.

Exit **Loveday**.

Dashwell   An admirable fellow this, wife.

Eugenia   Oh fie, a wicked man to conjure, and to raise a Devil.

Dashwell   A kind of Devil, but a gentle kind. Come, prethee let's go to bed now.

Eugenia   I could not sleep tonight without saying my prayers again. I have a prayer they say will make evil things fly from one. I'll make use of it tonight.

Dashwell   Should the Spirit return and reveal a devilish nature I'll warrant, wife, you're devout enough to lay him.

Eugenia   I'll say my prayers here below, then I won't disturb you.

Dashwell   Good night then, wife.

Exit **Dashwell**.

Eugenia   Good night. Jane, does Mr Ramble remain hereabout?

Jane   He hovers near the door. He begs you to contrive his admittance for one quarter of an hour.

Eugenia   Go you up, and give me notice when your Master is in bed. When he sleeps we shall once again consider Mr Ramble's suit.

Jane   Yes, madam.

Exit **Jane**.

Eugenia   That silly men conspire to deny each other what the other each doth sorely covet shall not deter me from *my* pleasure. I am now confirmed in my desire to bring this intrigue to a propitious conclusion.

Exit.

Scene Two

The street, before the houses of **Wiseacres**, **Dashwell** *and* **Doodle**.

Enter **Ramble** *in the street.*

Ramble   Well, here was a defeat of Fortune. I would tempt her once more, but think I shall see what luck I could have with my other Mistress. Indeed, I am confirmed in my pursuit.

Exit **Ramble**. *Enter* **Aunt**, **Peggy** *and a* **Lamp Boy**. *Enter* **Ramble**.

Peggy   Forsooth, Aunt, this is a most hugeous great place.

Ramble   Who goes yonder? Gad, a most pretty creature.

Peggy   Here be a number of houses, Aunt.

Aunt   Ay, Peggy, and fine houses, when you see 'em by daylight.

Peggy   Then shall I see them all tomorrow?

Aunt   O you can't see all London in a week.

Peggy   O Leminy! Not in a week, Aunt?

Ramble   A Country Girl.

Peggy   And does my Nuncle own all the town?

Aunt   All, Peggy? No, nor the King, God bless him, not half.

Ramble   She is so pretty, I cannot forbear speaking to her.
By your leave, old Gentlewoman. . .

Aunt   How now, sir, who are you?

Ramble   A Gentleman, and one that desires to be
acquainted with you and this little Lady here.

Aunt   Stand off, come away, child, don't let him be near
thee.

Ramble   Nay, I'll not part with this pretty hand yet.

Aunt   Shove him away, Peggy.

Peggy   O, but forsooth, Aunt, he's a Gentleman.

Aunt   Ay, but a London Gentleman. Come from him, or
he'll bite thee.

Peggy   Deeds, sir, will you bite me?

Ramble   Bite thee! Not for a thousand Worlds. Yet
methinks I could eat thee.

Aunt   Stand off, I say, stand off, come away, child, or he'll
devour thee.

Ramble   Believe her not, she's a lying envious old woman. I
would hug thee, kiss thee, give thee Gold and jewels, make
thee a little Queen, if I had thee.

Peggy   O dear Aunt! Did you ever hear the like?

Aunt   Believe him not, he's a lying flattering London
Varlet . . . he'll spirit thee away beyond the Sea.

Peggy   Oh la! I won't go beyond the Sea. Oh la, la!

Ramble   Thou shalt not, dear creature, be not afraid. Good
Gentlewoman, do not fright a young innocent thing thus . . . I
intend her no harm.

Peggy   See you there now, Aunt.

Ramble   I only offer my service to wait on you to your Lodgings.

Aunt   No, sir, let go her hand, we have not so far home, but we can go without your help. Get you gone I say.

Peggy   Nay pray, Aunt, don't beat the Gentleman, he does me no hurt, he only squeezes my hand a little.

Ramble   Oh!

Peggy   Sir, what ails thee?

Ramble   Thy innocence has jarred my heart.

Peggy   Indeed I have not done you no harm, not I?

Ramble   Thou art insensible of the wound thy eyes have made.

Peggy   Wound! Oh dear. Where do you bleed?

Ramble   Oh, 'tis inwardly!

Peggy   Aunt, I warrant you one of your pins has scratched him.

Aunt   Break from him, or he'll bewitch thee.

Enter **Wiseacres** *and* **Doodle**.

Wiseacres   I wonder they are not yet come.

Aunt   Yonder comes your Uncle. Odds me, he'll knock us all on the head. Come away, come away.

Ramble   Hau, let me kiss thy hand first; to part from thee is death.

Wiseacres   Hau! What do I see?

Ramble   Adieu, sweet Innocence.

Wiseacres   Men already buzzing about her, how comes this?

Doodle   Where there is meat in summer, there will be flies.

Wiseacres   I say how comes this?

Ramble   I'll step aside and watch where they go.

Aunt   This rude Royster here would stop us in the street whether we would or no.

Ramble (*aside*)   O you old Crony.

Peggy   Don't make my Nuncle angry, Aunt. He did but hold me by the hand.

Wiseacres   How? Let a man touch you? Did not I warn you not to let any man speak to you?

Peggy   Oh, but he was a Gentleman, and my Aunt told me I must make a curtsy to gentlefolks.

Wiseacres   This was a villain! He would have murther'd thee, and eat thee.

Peggy   Oh grievous! I am glad you came then, Nuncle, he said indeed he could eat me.

Wiseacres   O Monstrous!

Doodle   Be not so passionate; she could not help it.

Wiseacres   I must seem angry to make her afraid for the future.

Aunt   In London they get young folks and bake 'em in Pies.

Peggy   O sadness!

Doodle   What will this come to? Never did I see one so simple.

Wiseacres   What made you stay so long?

Aunt   It was so late we could not get a coach in Southwark, and were forc'd to come on foot.

Peggy   Oh, Nuncle, we came over a bridge where there's a huge pond.

Wiseacres   Lamp Boy, here's sixpence for you, put out your Light and go your ways.

Lamp Boy   Yes, Master.

Exit.

Wiseacres   Alderman Doodle, lead on. Peggy, come give me your hand, Peggy. Here . . . this way . . . so, so, get you in, get you in.

Exeunt as into **Wiseacres**' *house; he shuts the door.*

Ramble   The crafty Old Fox, he put out the lamp that I might not see where they went in. No mind; I have other skillets warming elsewhere if I can now but find my man Roger.

Exit **Ramble**. *Enter* **Townley**.

Townley   Ha, the Light's gone, and I can see nobody! Sure, 'twas Ramble I saw from the Tavern window; he's upon the scent of some new intrigue. If I could have met the Rogue, he should not have scap'd from me till he had drank his bottle. Hark, I hear a door open! It may be him bolting out of some little Cunny-burrough . . .

Enter **Jane**.

Jane   Sir?

Townley   Where is he?

Jane   Sir, you must whisper, for fear of being heard.

Townley   You resolve to determine the way is clear, I'll warrant.

Jane   Sir, where are you?.

Townley   Does the rascal skulk behind you?

Jane   No, sir. He is in bed.

Townley   God rest him!

Take hands.

Jane   My Lady bid me bring you in.

Townley   How say you?

Jane   Having dispatched him upstairs she has a mind now to your company.

Townley   Does she?

Jane   She sits upon the Couch in the dark, she'll have no light in the room.

Townley   Apt modesty indeed.

Jane   You must not stay long; therefore what you do, do quickly. Give me your hand.

Townley   Yes, but . . .

Jane   My mistress awaits, aroused by this night's unfolding all but beyond the bounds of decency.

Townley   Then I'll endeavour.

Jane   Come, sir, softly.

Townley   Here's a blind bargain struck up, but I cannot resist the temptation.

Exeunt, as into **Dashwell**'s *house. Enter* **Ramble** *and* **Roger**.

Roger   This, sir, is Alderman Doodle's house. I ask'd three or four innkeepers . . .

Ramble   Ha! A neighbourly intrigue! I have a signal that shall open this portal and conduct me to the mortal paradise within.

He knocks.

Ramble   Stand there at a distance and wait upon my coming forth.

Arabella *opens the door.*

Ramble   Madam?

Arabella   Who are you, sir?

Ramble   He whose heart has flown before him. Madam, do you see the stars?

Arabella   The stars?

Ramble   For each we see a thousand more unseen and

none to touch thy beauty, and each and every one conspires to bring us to a sweet embrace.

Arabella *closes the door.*

Ramble   Roger, you are sure you have not mistaken the House?

Roger   Ay, sir, there's no other great green door but that. They all told me at the great green door.

Ramble   Dolt! I seek an ocean of delight and you tangle us in a shallow backwater. Walk on and discover this Doodle's true abode!

Exeunt **Ramble** *and* **Roger**. *Enter* **Engine** *and* **Arabella**.

Engine   Indeed, he is the same man to whom I gave your token, and is known as Mr Ramble.

Arabella   And there is your mistake; for you thought I meant Ramble, when I ask'd who Townley was!

Engine   They are constant Companions, madam. And were then together at the Play.

Arabella   You must haste to tell him 'tis a mistake, and that he is not the person I did expect.

Engine   O, madam, by no means, lest for revenge he should discover to your husband!

Arabella   Do you think he would do so ill a thing?

Engine   Who knows how he may resent the disappointment; 'twould be such an affront you must suppose the worst.

Arabella   They are returned; make haste.

Exeunt **Arabella** *and* **Engine**. *Enter* **Ramble** *and* **Roger**.

Ramble   The Devil take this night; there is no other door it can be but this. My good friend Townley did assert this lady's fickle nature. But here is one could be trusted with thy heart. The door is fast. To knock is not convenient, to expect is painful, but a Lover must have patience, a little sufferance sweetens the delight. My trust is still in faithful Eugenia.

Jane *opens the door. Enter* **Townley** *and* **Eugenia**, *embracing.*

Jane   Step this way, sir, and swiftly.

Ramble   What is this?

Jane   Come, madam, do not detain him any longer, 'tis dangerous.

Eugenia   Yet is it not unmannerly that one should go so soon, that did come so suddenly?

Ramble   Hau!

Townley   Dear kind sweet creature, when shall I be thus bless'd again?

Eugenia   Often, if you be discreet.

Townley   I could live an Age in thy arms, this was so very short –

Eugenia   Ere long, we'll find whole hours of pleasure. Of all men, sir, it is you and you alone who . . . who in God's Heaven are you, sir?

Ramble   Have at thee, traitor; draw, and fight.

He draws, and runs at **Townley**. **Eugenia** *and* **Jane** *run in, and close the door.*

Eugenia/Jane   Ah, ah, ah!

Roger   Hold, hold, Master, hold, 'tis Mr Townley, 'tis Mr Townley.

Ramble   Ha, Townley.

Townley   Ramble! What a plague did you mean?

Ramble   To have kill'd you, had you not been my very good friend.

Townley   Short warning, prethee next time give me leave to make my Will.

Ramble   How came you here?

Townley   By the wheel of fortune, I can scarcely tell thee.
Prethee, who was this Wench, with whom I have had so sweet
a satisfaction?

Ramble   I perceive your innocence by warrant of your
ignorance. 'Twas one of my two intrigues. I beat the bush, but
thou has catch'd the bird.

Townley   Ned, I only took a potshot. And my aim was
untrue. Next time she'll be your game.

Ramble   A curse on all ill luck.

Townley   I told you in the morning, fortune would jilt you.
Come, walk off; I have company staying for me at the Tavern.

Ramble   Fortune is the wind and woman the tide; both turn
all ways to confound the steadfast voyager. I shall in future
make more haste and be not easily put off.

Exeunt.

Act Three

Scene One

A room in **Doodle**'s *house.*

Enter **Arabella** *and* **Engine**.

Arabella Engine; you have discovered him?

Engine On the steps of the Tavern, madam, and I have summoned him.

Arabella Is there no other remedy to keeping his counsel?

Engine None but the simplest, madam.

Arabella Indeed, I have no aversion to his person. And if I had never seen that Townley, I should have somewhat liked this Ramble.

Engine Resolve to go forward now, you'll like him better tomorrow morning, I warrant you.

Arabella Well, if he press very hard, and I find I cannot otherwise make sure of him . . .

A knock at the door, opened by **Engine**. *Enter* **Ramble**.

Ramble Madam.

Arabella I thank you, sir, for returning, and would beg your understanding. My rude dismissal of your tender suit being but the modest constraint of one unused to such endeavours.

Ramble Such discretion only serves to sweeten the dish. And one that is long in preparation commands an even greater appetite.

Arabella Your meaning escapes me, sir.

Ramble I mean to enquire, madam, why you are not yet in bed?

Arabella   Is it late, sir?

Ramble   Oh very late; and sitting up is pernicious to beauty . . .

Arabella   I have but little, and should preserve it. In order therefore to do so, sir, I beg your pardon, and take my leave.

Ramble   Ay to bed, to bed. Miss Engine, pray help me disrobe.

Arabella   What mean you, sir?

Ramble   Faith, to go to bed too . . .

Arabella   You'll go home first?

Ramble   Devil take me if I do. I mean to stay and sleep with you.

Arabella   With me?

Ramble   Even so.

Arabella   Whether I will or no?

Ramble   That's e'en as you please; if you are as willing as I, 'tis so much the better.

Arabella   Sure you are but in jest.

Ramble   Come, madam, I know how matters go; you are a fine, brisk, handsome Lady, and have a dull dronish husband without a sting; I am a young active fellow fit for employment, and e'Gad I know your wants. Therefore, madam, come. Your nightdress becomes you so well, and you look so very tempting . . . I can hardly forbear you a minute longer.

Arabella   I should chide you severely now, for your ill opinion of me, but I perceive you are beyond saving.

Ramble   I am not so stiff-necked a Sinner but I may be mollified by morning.

Arabella   No, I am very sleepy and must go to bed, therefore pray be gone.

Ramble   If I go tonight, I do deserve to be canonis'd!

Arabella   Sir, if you do hope . . .

Ramble   I have all hope, and faith, and charity. Hope that you love me, faith to believe you dissemble, and Charity enough to supply your wants in your husband's absence.

Arabella   Sir, I find you intend to be troublesome. I shall leave you.

Ramble   But I shan't leave you.

Arabella   Why, what do you intend to do?

Ramble   To follow you.

Arabella   Whither?

Ramble   To your Chamber.

Arabella   For what?

Ramble   To hug, kiss, and come to bed with you.

Arabella   You would not dare it.

Ramble   So I would.

Arabella   Since you are so resolute, I'll shall indeed retire.

Ramble   Perhaps you'll lock the door.

Arabella   I scorn to do so. I'll see what you dare do.

Ramble   I'll dare if I die for't.

Arabella   Take notice then, thou desperate resolute man, that I now go to my chamber, where I'll undress me, go into my bed, and if you dare to follow me, kiss, or come to bed to me; if all the strength and passion a provoked Woman has, can do't, I'll lay thee breathless and panting, and so maul thee, thou shalt ever after be afraid to look a woman in the face.

Ramble   Stay and hear me now: Thou shalt no sooner be there but I'll be there; kiss you, hug you, down with you, and as often as I down with you, be sure to give you the rising-blow, that if at last you do chance to maul me, 'Gad you shan't have much reason to brag in the morning. And so angry, threatening woman, get thee gone and do thy worst.

Arabella   And you, sir, do you your best. Adieu.

Exit **Arabella**.

Engine   Well here is like to be fearful doings. Here's heavy threatening on both sides.

Ramble   I long till the skirmish begins.

Engine   Pray, sir, do not tarry; she has nothing but her nightgown to slip off.

Ramble   I shall have her at my mercy. Think you she consents?

Engine   Oh, sir, have no mercy on her, she'll not complain of hard usage, I warrant you.

Ramble   Then, to the fray!

Exit **Ramble**.

Engine   Let me see, what has my pain-taking brought me in since morning. One–two–three–four guineas. This is a profitable profession. This employment was formerly named bawding and pimping, but our Age is more civilis'd and our Language much refin'd. It is now called doing a friend a favour. Whore is now prettily call'd Mistress. Pimp; friend. Cuckold-maker; gallant. Thus the terms being civilis'd the thing itself becomes more acceptable. What Clowns they were in former Ages.

Enter **Doodle**.

Doodle   Where are you here?

Engine   Ha! My Master.

Engine *runs to the chamber door and seems to speak as rejoicing.*

Engine   O Lord, madam, here's my Master, here's my Master, here's my Master, my Master's come . . .

Doodle   Why are the doors open at this time of night?

Engine   My Master, madam, my Master's come, O
lemminy.

Doodle   Well?

Engine   My Master. My Master.

Doodle   Are you mad? I say why were the doors left open
thus late?

Engine   I was standing at the door, and my Lady called all
of a sudden. I am so glad you are come home, Master.
Madam, here's my Master. My Master's here!

Doodle   Rogues might have come in and rob'd the house.

Engine   Indeed, sir! Madam; my Master's home.

*Enter **Arabella** in nightgown and slippers, runs and hugs him about
the neck.*

Arabella   Oh my dear. Dear . . . dear. Art thou return'd?

Doodle   I have been come to Town a great while.

Arabella   Oh my dear, dear. . . dear dear.

Engine   Hist.

*Beckons to **Ramble** to slip by – he comes stealing out. **Doodle** turns
and he slips back again.*

Doodle   Yes, wife, but I am very sleepy and must retire.

Arabella   Oh, you are a naughty hubby. You have been a
great while in Town, and would not come home to me before.
I won't love you now I think on't.

Doodle   I'll be going to bed then.

Arabella   Ay, but you shall kiss me first, your constant wife.

*She hugs him again, **Engine** beckons to **Ramble**, who comes out but
retreats.*

Kiss me. Kiss me heartily.

Doodle   So, so, wife. Prethee be quiet.

Arabella   Oh my hubby, dear, dear, dear hubby . . .

Engine   Hem – em . . . ah . . .

Ramble *comes out and retreats again.*

Doodle   I am so weary, and thou stand'st hugging me . . .

Arabella   Well, we shall remember this. You are come home and will make no fuss of me.

Doodle   Prethee, let me go to bed.

Arabella   Engine, let us go see what's in the house for your Master to eat.

Doodle   I have supp'd already, wife.

Arabella   And what had my dear for supper –

Doodle   A few oysters, and a young Partridge.

Arabella   And how far went dear today?

Doodle   A few Miles . . .

Arabella   And what time came you back?

Doodle   Prethee, wife, why stand'st thou asking me so many questions.

Arabella   Untie your Master's shoes the while –

Doodle   No no, leave your fussing, give me my Cap and Nightgown.

Arabella   Engine, run into the Chamber and fetch 'em.

Doodle   No matter, we'll go in . . .

Exit **Engine**. **Arabella** *sings.*

Arabella   I have a husband, but what of that?
    He neither loves me . . . nor my . . . little pussy Cat;
    Little Pussy gets a Mouse and with it does play.
    But my husband ignores me all the long day –

Doodle   Prethee, wife, do not be so troublesome.

Arabella   There was a Lady lov'd a Swine, quoth she.
Dear Pig-hog quoth she, wilt thou be mine? . . .
Hunh! quoth he . . . diddly di.
Husband, you lov'd to see me merry formerly.

Doodle   Yes, wife, but I am so sleepy tonight.

Enter **Engine**.

Engine   Sir, there's none of your gown in the Chamber.

Doodle   Stay, now I think on't, 'tis in my Counting-house.
Go to bed, wife, I'll undress me there, and come to you.

Arabella   There were some letters come today; you should
perhaps look over them.

Doodle   No, no, I'll come presently . . .

Exit **Doodle**.

Arabella   Fox! Come out of your hole. Make haste, lest he
returns.

Enter **Ramble**.

Engine   Madam, the door; my Master has locked it, and
taken out the key.

Ramble   Then which way shall I get out?

Arabella   Ah ha ha . . .

Ramble   Is all this a laughing matter?

Arabella   I laugh at your faint heart . . .

Engine   What shall we do, madam?

Arabella   You must take Mr Ramble into your chamber,
and let him sleep in your bed.

Ramble   What, within there?

Arabella   Even so, sir.

Engine   And thank your Stars.

Ramble   'Gad I sweat with the thought of it.

Engine   And well may you, sir, for my Mistress is given to walk in her sleep. And if in the middle of the night she should chance to come to your bedside, and take you betwixt sleeping and waking . . .

Ramble   Say, madam, would you be so kind?

Engine   That may easily be. My Master will soon be asleep, as you may know by his snoring.

Ramble   But, should he wake, and miss her?

Arabella   To prevent that danger, Engine, come you to my bedside. Softly, I'll rise, and you shall lie down in my place.

Engine   Methinks in this endeavour I am become a little too involved. What, madam, if my master awake and turn to me?

Arabella   He'll find thee a Woman, will he not?

Engine   Nay, now with your leave . . .

Ramble *gives her money.*

Engine   Rather than spoil a good intrigue, I'll venture.

Arabella   An excellent device.

Engine   Get you both in.

Arabella   This is likely such an unlucky project, I would not venture but that the very thought of it now demands its consummation.

Engine   Go, go, my Master's coming back.

Exeunt **Arabella** *and* **Ramble**. *Enter* **Doodle**, *in a cap and nightgown.*

Doodle   Is my wife in bed?

Engine   Softly, sir, she's asleep.

Doodle   So, so, good night, make haste to bed.

Exit.

Engine   Oh the vain imaginations of a husband, who thinks himself secure of a wife! I long to be married to show my wit. Indeed there is no distance between man and woman that the other will not cross; he crowing all the while, she travelling silent. My Master snores already. Now must I lie by that dull drowsy animal.

Enter **Arabella** *in her nightgown.*

Arabella   Softly, wench, softly . . .

Engine   I warrant you, madam . . . he snores like a Turk.

Arabella   Have a care of waking him.

Engine   You instruct me in mine own strict intention, madam. Have you a care to make good use of your time, and don't stay too long.

Exit **Arabella**.

Engine   So. Thus far all goes well. Now must I undergo the severe penance, to lie by a man and sweating for fear he should wake, and find me out. Or to the worse; wake and find me to his liking. But I must venture now, so happy go lucky and to bed go I.

Roger (*without*)   Fire! Fire Fire!

Engine   Hark!

Knocking at the door.

Roger (*without*)   Fire! Fire . . . Fire . . .

Engine   O Heavens . . . we are undone . . . they cry Fire!

Enter **Arabella**.

Arabella   O, Engine, don't you hear 'em knock, and cry fire!

Roger (*without*)   Fire, fire, fire!

Arabella   This will certainly waken him anon. Let us cry fire too, and say, I am just got up. Fire. Fire. Fire . . .

Roger (*without*)   Fire, fire, fire.

Engine Fire. Fire. Fire.

Enter **Ramble**.

Ramble Fire. Fi . . . !

Arabella/Engine Hist!

Ramble What must I do now?

Engine Don't stir out till my Master's gone.

Exit **Ramble**. *Enter* **Doodle**.

Doodle What's the matter, is the house on fire?

Engine Don't you hear 'em knock?

Doodle Open the door.

Engine Give me the Key.

Doodle Follow me. All follow me! Oh fire . . . fire . . . fire . . .

Exeunt **Arabella**, **Engine**, **Doodle**. *Enter* **Ramble**.

Ramble What must I do now, venture to be discover'd, or stay here and die a martyr to save a Lady's honour? A pox of luck still. My life or her good name? It takes but small consideration.

Enter **Engine**.

Engine Here is no smell of burning, nor any smoke. Be you mad? Hide thyself! Sure the fire is not in this house.

Ramble *hides beneath her skirts. Enter* **Doodle** *and* **Arabella**.

Doodle Why, here's no fire, nor nothing like it. Come, wife . . . come in again. They knock, and cry fire, as if they were mad, and yet there was nobody!

Arabella It was a false Alarm.

Doodle This was the roguery of some drunken fellows in their night frolics.

Arabella I am glad it was no worse.

Doodle   Mistress Engine, pray lock the doors.

Engine   Yes, sir.

Doodle   Pray then, do so.

Engine   Now, sir?

Doodle   At once.

Engine   Deeds, sir, I would not.

Doodle   How say you?

Engine   It does not take my fancy.

Arabella   Engine, do as thy master would instruct.

Engine   Indeed, madam, I would do whatever you will, were it not beneath me.

Doodle   You dare to reveal thy cheek in such abundance?

Engine   'Tis not my choice to do so, sure.

Arabella   Engine, what has got into you?

Engine   Nothing, madam, though 'twould not be my choice neither.

Doodle   Plague on thy disrespect; I say you; lock the doors.

He thrusts her to the door, revealing **Ramble***.*

Arabella   Husband, I swoon.

Doodle   Say you so?

Arabella   These cries of fire and sudden comings to and going fro have quite upset my humour. I do faint.

Doodle   Indeed I fear so.

Ramble *sneaks out of the door.* **Engine** *closes it.*

Engine   There, sir, I have locked the door. Here is your key, sir. The door is locked. As you did request me, so indeed the door is most securely locked.

Doodle   Well, well . . .

Engine   As you did request me to lock the door, sir, so have
I . . .

Doodle   Enough. Thy mistress swoons. Bring aqua vitae.

Engine   If you request it, sir, so it shall be done.

Doodle   Come, wife, to bed.

Exeunt **Doodle** *and* **Arabella**.

Engine   Now this night's intrigues surely must lie beyond
any success.

Exit.

Scene Two

The street before **Doodle***'s house.*

Enter **Ramble**.

Ramble   This is scarce worth believing! To come so near to
paradise but twice, deeds but thrice if Mistress Engine had
never locked her door. There is but little now left of this night
but to return home. Who's there?

Roger   'Tis I, sir. Your man Roger.

Ramble   Did I not send you home?

Roger   I'll tell you, sir, that you may know, what a piece of
service I have done you, and how fitly qualified am I to be
your servant.

Ramble   Well, sir, in what?

Roger   I guessed, sir, by your sending me home, that your
intention was to lay a better game than cards tonight, and
'twas a lucky thought, for you were no sooner indoors but I
perceived a man come plodding along, go in without
knocking, and shut the door. So this, thought I, is the
husband. And now thought I must my master be thrust into a
closet and remain in purgatory all night . . . unless I work his
deliverance.

Ramble   And so, sir?

Roger   So I cried out fire. And thundered and knocked 'til I raised the house and put the people in confusion that you might escape in the hurry. Now, sir, if you will speak your conscience, I do believe this piece of policy did bring you off. Your bare acknowledgement, sir, will be to me above any reward.

Ramble   It was you then that knocked and cried out fire?

Roger   Yes, sir; at your service.

Ramble   Lend me that stick in your hand.

Roger   This stick; for what, sir?

Ramble   Lend it me, I say.

Roger   Here, sir.

Ramble   Now will I reward your excellent piece of service.

Beats him.

Roger   Oh sir; what do you mean, sir?

Ramble   To beat you till you have no invention left!

Roger   Oh, oh oh, sir, will you be ungrateful, sir, will you be ungrateful?

Ramble   It was you, you dog, hindered me of the sweetest enjoyments man ever missed!

Roger   'Twas well meant! Indeed, sir, 'twas well meant!

Ramble   Be gone and come not near me this week, lest I beat thee to pulp!

Exit **Roger**. **Engine** *at the window.*

Engine   Sir. Mr Ramble.

Ramble   Here.

Engine   Spite of all, my Lady is still willing, but my master took the key again.

Ramble   Is there no window to creep in?

Engine   Just there below is a cellar-hole with a bar out. Try if you can get in there.

Ramble   I have found it.

Engine   Try if it be wide enough to get through.

Ramble   I believe it is.

Engine   I'll come down then and open the cellar door.

Ramble   Do. Do, rare creature . . . I'll go heels forward because I don't know how far it is to the bottom. So . . . hup. Hup. This hole begins to grow tighter. Hup. Hup. The reward of lovers has needs be so sweet for which they endure so much. Hup. Hup. 'Tis damnably narrow now, but I'll another squeeze . . . hup, hup hup . . . Oh, my guts. I can't get an inch further. What a spite this is. I'll have to come out again.

Engine *above at the window.*

Engine   Sir, sir . . . where are you?

Ramble   Where are you?

Engine   Here above. The cook has locked the cellar door. If you do get in you can't come upstairs.

Ramble   Then I must give this up for tonight, and think of a stratagem against tomorrow. Hup . . . Hup . . . Hup . . . I can neither get quite in nor out.

Engine   How, sir?

Ramble   I am stuck! Hup-a . . . hup-a . . . hup-a . . . There is some damned hook or staple on the inside has got hold of my clothes.

Engine   Ha ha ha.

Ramble   A pox on this.

Engine   Ha ha ha.

*Enter a **Vendor**, singing, passing by.*

Vendor   'Taters!

Ramble   Yonder comes company; now shall I be taken for a house-breaker.

Engine   'Tis none but a vendor. Be silent and he'll pass you by.

Vendor   'Taters!

As he passes **Ramble**, *stokes his fire, knocking out clinker.*

Vendor   Will you have a 'tater!

Ramble   Ahhh.

Vendor *exits.*

Engine   Sir; what is the matter?

Ramble   Son of a whore! He has thrown his clinker in my face!

Engine   Ha ha ha . . . excuse me, sir, I can't forbear . . . ha ha ha.

Ramble   S'death how it burns!

Engine   Hist, sir. Hist. You will waken the household.

A window opens above, and **Doodle** *throws the contents of a chamberpot upon his head as he looks up, then retires.*

Ramble   Augh!

Engine   What's the matter, sir?

Ramble   One rogue has set me on fire and another has quenched me with a stale chamberpot. Faugh, how it stinks.

Engine   My master Doodle is regular in habits.

Ramble   Never was a lover in such a pickle!

Engine   Truly, this is enough to cool anybody's courage.

Ramble   Hup-a . . . hup-a . . . hup-a . . . It won't do, I am as fast as if I were wedged in.

Engine   Be silent; here come some others.

Enter two **Chimney-Sweeps***.*

1st Chimney-Sweep   Hold, Tom, stay. I am damnably
grip'd in my guts. I must unfasten.

2nd Chimney-Sweep   Make haste then.

1st Chimney-Sweep   Oh, I am damnably full of wind.

Stands with back against **Ramble***'s face and untrusses. (Farts, surely.)*

Ramble   Faugh! Oh, you stinking cur. Away with you.

2nd Chimney-Sweep   Who's there?

Ramble   A friend.

1st Chimney-Sweep   Who are you?

2nd Chimney-Sweep   What are you?

Ramble   A gentleman. Pray help me here for I am stuck
fast; lend me your hands.

Engine   'Tis true, friends; help the gentleman out.

1st Chimney-Sweep   Hark you, Tom; a rare opportunity.
Take you hold of him by that arm . . . Hold, sir, we shall spoil
your hat and periwig . . .

2nd Chimney-Sweep   Give me your sword, sir, that you
may not do yourself damage . . .

Ramble   Thank you, sirs.

*They take off his hat and periwig, clap one of their sooty hats on his head,
blacken his face and run away.*

1st Chimney-Sweep   Now, Tom . . . Scour and away!

Ramble   What? Thieves! Thieves!

Engine   What have they done, sir?

Ramble   The rogues are run away with my new beaver hat.
And my periwig and sword.

Engine   Oh the rascals . . .

1st Watchman   Watch ho!

Engine   Sir, your crying out has raised the watch; what will you do now?

Ramble   Now? Now I shall be lodged in the jail, carried before a magistrate tomorrow, and talked of in every coffee-house by noon. Then the bards shall make my name a jest over all over the nation!

Enter **Watchmen** *with lanterns.*

1st Watchman   Here; this way they cried thieves! Follow!

2nd Watchman   Ay, 'Twas hereabouts.

3rd Watchman   Ha! Here's one lies upon the ground.

1st Watchman   Are you killed, sir? Speak.

2nd Watchman   Ay; if you are dead, pray tell us.

Ramble   No, friends; I am hardly hurt at all.

3rd Watchman   Hau, neighbours; he is halfway in at the grates. This is some thief!

2nd Watchman   Ay, come to rob the house.

Ramble   Pray help me out, friends, and I'll tell you the truth.

1st Watchman   Hold there; there may be more rogues inside; let us knock and raise the house.

3rd Watchman   Ay; knock hard.

2nd Watchman (*knocks hard at the door*)   Rise. Thieves here, thieves in your house!

Ramble   Now shall I further be disgraced.

Doodle *appears above.*

Doodle   Hold. Hold; are you mad? What's the matter there?

2nd Watchman   We have catched a thief creeping in at your cellar door.

Doodle   A thief!

1st Watchman   We believe there are some other rogues in the house already.

Doodle   Honest Watchmen, I thank you. I'll come down.

Ramble   Pray you honest Watchmen, help me out, for I am in a great deal of pain.

1st Watchman   Come, neighbours; we may venture to pull him out now.

2nd Watchman   Pull you by that arm.

3rd Watchman   Pluck hard!

Ramble   Oh . . . I would I were like an egg steeped in vinegar.

3rd Watchman   Nay; you must endure it.

1st Watchman   Come, neighbours; all hands to the work . . .

Ramble   Zounds, my guts!

2nd Watchman   So, 'tis done. Get up, sir.

Enter **Doodle** *in nightgown with headpiece, bandoleers and a musket charged and cocked.*

Doodle   Come, where is this thief, where are these rogues?

2nd Watchman   We suppose there are some in the cellar, that got in before.

Enter **Arabella** *and* **Engine**.

Doodle   Say you so? Say you so? If there be, I'll send 'em out!

Doodle *shoots the musket off into the cellar, and falls backward as if knocked down.*

Oh, neighbours. Neighbours. Oh.

1st Watchman   You han't hurt yourself, Master, I hope?

Doodle   Is my right arm on?

1st Watchman   Indeed, sir; stir it, sir. Do you feel any pain?

Doodle   No, not at all.

2nd Watchman   Get up then, Master; there's no harm done.

Doodle   Always was a damn obstinate piece.

2nd Watchman   Hold, sir!

Doodle   Is this the rogue?

1st Watchman   Whilst you examine him, we'll search below.

Doodle   Ay, pray do. Engine, go below with the Watchmen.

Exeunt **Engine** *and* **1st Watchman**.

Arabella   What's the matter here, husband?

Doodle   We have catched a thief, wife.

Ramble   Sir, I am a gentleman, and one that scorns such base actions. I'll tell you in short, Sir, how I came to be fastened in your window.

Doodle   Ay that, sir. Do so.

Ramble   . . . Walking down the street for a little air I was dogged by two or three rogues who came up behind me and began to rifle my pockets. Knowing I had this purse of gold about me, slid from them upon the ground, found my feet at the cellar window and crowded myself as far in as I could to secure my pockets.

Doodle   Then you cried out thief yourself?

Ramble   Yes; 'twas I.

Arabella   'Tis very likely, husband.

Doodle   Ay, so 'tis. And if nobody be found in my house, I'll release you.

Enter **Engine** *and* **1st Watchman**.

1st Watchman   We can find nobody, sir.

Engine   We have looked so much as in the oven, and the cistern.

Doodle   Well, sir, your servant then. Watchmen, see this gentleman home.

1st Watchman   What, must he be released?

2nd Watchman   Ay; he's an honest gentleman and has been robbed himself.

Ramble   Sir, good night to you. Your servant, madam.

Arabella   Sir, if your mistress was but here in my place to see you now, she could not choose but to love you for such a piece of gallantry, and take you about the neck, and kiss you.

Ramble   Madam, you are kind.

Arabella   Had you but first washed your face.

Doodle   Pray excuse her, sir; my wife's a merry prating wag . . .

Ramble   I like her ne'er the worse.

Doodle   Good night, sir.

Ramble   Your servant, sir. Good night, madam.

Arabella   Good night, sweep.

Doodle   Come, wife; you are a little too severe with the gentleman.

Arabella   What, should I have no revenge of him for raising us out of our beds?

Exeunt **Doodle**, **Arabella** *and* **Engine**. *Enter* **Townley** *and* **Tom**.

Ramble   Come, gentlemen, forward to my lodging.

Townley   Now you dog, am not I very merry? This 'tis to be drunk, you dog.

Tom   Sir, don't make such noise. We are near the watch.

Townley   Watch? Shew 'em me, that I may scour among 'em; I ne'er killed a Watchman yet.

1st Watchman   Who goes there?

Townley   You are the son of a whore!

3rd Watchman   Knock him down.

Ramble   No, be kind to him. He is a friend of mine. He's in drink.

Townley   Hold, a truce. Truce. A friend of thine? Who the Devil art thou?

Tom   By his clothes, sir, it should be Mr Ramble.

Townley   Ramble! Pox on't, hold up your light. Ramble! What the pox art thou doing thus, like the Prince of Darkness with these hell-hounds about thee, and in this pickle?

Ramble   Misfortunes, Frank. Misfortunes.

1st Watchman   The gentleman has been knocked down and robbed, sir.

Townley   No, neighbours, this comes of whoring.

Ramble   Hold your tongue.

Townley   And the husband came and you were forced to creep up the chimney to get away. This comes of your whoring still.

3rd Watchman   No, sir, indeed; there's been a burglary.

Townley   Burglary, Ned? Burglary? Worse and worse. This comes of whoring still. Hereafter, Ned, be ruled by me; leave whoring and burglary and fall to honest drinking.

Ramble   Watchmen, prethee go home; this gentleman and I lodge in the same house.

Townley   Look you, friends; I'll go home if you please, but for this wild man here, take a backroom for him at some great inn, hang out his picture, blow a trumpet, and show him for a groat a piece. I warrant you you'll raise a fortune.

1st Watchman   In company you will safely home. We'll go our ways. Good night.

Exeunt the **Watchmen**.

Townley   Well, Ned, to tell the truth, I am a little ashamed of your company at present.

Ramble   I curse my stars.

Townley   'Tis in vain. They will shed their malicious influence.

Ramble   Considering how my supper fell into your mouth earlier, you should thank the stars. I started the hare, gave her the long course, and you took her at the half turn.

Townley   Make your court to the bottle, Ned, to the bottle.

Ramble   I take your council and will forswear all womankind! But for the hope I have to bring one of these two designs to perfection.

Townley   Still wilt thou be mislead by hopes; hope is more flattering than women and less faithful than good fortune.

Ramble   Frank, you speak well. Hope is the whore that breeds all ill-luck. A pox on her, and on womankind also.

Drinks. Enter **Jane**.

Jane   Here's a letter, sir.

Ramble   Ha!

Jane   To be delivered to you with all speed.

Ramble   Let me see it quickly.

Exit **Jane**.

Ramble   From Eugenia!

Townley   Ay, the Devil's come abroad again to hinder your conversion.

Ramble (*reads*)   'Sir, my husband will be from home all tomorrow morning. I am very desirous to be informed of the particulars of last night's misfortune; curiosity forces me, in spite of blushes, to give you this invitation.' Yes!

Townley   Ay, the Devil dances again.

Ramble   Frank, is not here temptation now, is it to be resisted think you? Can flesh and blood forbear going? What can hinder now? Frank Townley, give me thy hand. If I fail now, I will from this time give over assignation and stratagems and be thy convert for ever. Let us go home. Tomorrow's return shall see me victorious!

Exeunt.

Interval.

Act Four

Scene One

Communal gardens behind **Wiseacre***'s,* **Doodle***'s and* **Dashwell***'s houses. A gate and summer house.*

Enter **Dashwell** *and* **Doodle**, *as from the wedding.*

Dashwell   Are the Bride and the Groom come from the church?

Doodle   Indeed, Mr Alderman. But why do we wait in the gardens?

Dashwell   It is our brother Wiseacres' wish that his coming home with his Bride be no public spectacle, and this rear entry thus becomes his married threshold.

Doodle   'Tis a shorter route also, and more suited to his years. Here come the happy couple.

Enter **Wiseacres**, **Aunt** *and* **Peggy**, *being carried by a* **Coachman**.

Wiseacres   In, sir; in. Make haste.

Peggy   Indeed, husband, this is a fine transport.

Wiseacres   Over the threshold, sir, deposit her thus. Cover thy head, wife; I would not have thee seen by neighbours all and sundry. Here's money for you, sir.

Coachman   None desired, sir; 'twas a light burden and a pretty one.

Wiseacres   Be gone, Scoundrel. Make thy way.

Exit the **Coachman**, **Aunt** *and* **Peggy**.

Dashwell   Methought it a fine ceremony, Mr Alderman, though the chapel be small, and the congregation no greater than could fill a single pew.

Wiseacres   I would not have a public marriage, sir, for all the town to pry and tittle-tattle after.

Doodle   Though our wives are like to protest at their absence.

Wiseacres   Let 'em, Mr Alderman. I would not have the wives in particular; lest they lay claim to friendship of the Bride and turn her head from her husband. Let marriage be man's business, I say.

Dashwell   And will you now be about it, sir?

Wiseacres   What, say you?

Dashwell   Your business, sir.

Wiseacres   Indeed, sir. I am inclined to wait upon it.

Doodle   Such may you be thus compelled, for as we came in at the gate a messenger did give me this; 'tis from the Master of the ship in which we all have great concerns and is come up the river today. He desires us to take a boat and go down this tide.

Wiseacres   No question, we must go.

Dashwell   Methinks it is very unlucky that business should fall out thus on your Wedding day, and force you to leave your Bride unbedded.

Wiseacres   Indeed, but business is more pressing. I shall never be much concerned at anything that calls me away, knowing what security I have of my wife in her simplicity.

Doodle   So you have said, sir, but I shall not be converted without a Miracle.

Wiseacres   We have time afore the tide; I will now shew you an example that shall convince you of your error. Ho, Wife . . . Peggy . . . Pray sit and observe; you shall behold and wonder.

Enter **Aunt** *and* **Peggy**.

Aunt   Here, and please you is your Bride . . .

Wiseacres   There's my dainty Peggy. Peggy. Come to me, Peggy.

Peggy   Yes forsooth.

Wiseacres   And pray, Aunt; fetch me from the house the fine gilt cap and halberd that stands in the hall. And my nightcap, also.

Aunt   If you will, sir. Peggy, where's your Curtesie to your Nuncle and the Gentlemen?

Exit **Aunt**.

Wiseacres   Indeed; your Curtesie . . .

Peggy *curtsies*.

Wiseacres   So, that's as I am your Uncle; another now as I am your husband . . . So, now stand before me. You know, Peggy, you are now my wife.

Peggy   Yes forsooth, so Naunt tells me.

Wiseacres   And that is a happiness for which you are to thank Heaven, that you have married a discreet sober person.

Peggy   Yes forsooth.

Wiseacres   Now tell me, Peggy, do you know what love is?

Peggy   Love, it is to give one fine things.

Wiseacres   How know you that, Peggy?

Peggy   Because, forsooth, Nuncle-Husband, Naunt said you lov'd me, and therefore that you gave me this Petticoat and Manto, and these Ribbonds, and this, and this . . .

Wiseacres   Indeed, indeed.

Doodle   Oh, she'll learn well in time . . .

Wiseacres   But now you are my wife, Peggy, and the love of a wife to her husband is to do all things that he desires and commands.

Peggy   Yes, forsooth.

Dashwell But, beside the love of a wife, Peggy, there is the duty of a wife, do you know what the duty of a wife is?

Peggy Duty, Nuncle, what's that?

Wiseacres I have not time to instruct you now in the whole duty of a wife, because business calls me away . . . I will therefore only inform you at present part of the duty.

Peggy Yes forsooth.

Enter **Arabella**, *looking from a balcony.*

Arabella I have heard all so far, but now I'll venture to peep, and see a little.

Enter **Aunt** *with cap-and-feather, a halberd and nightcap.*

Wiseacres That duty, Peggy, is to be done in this manner; here, put this on so . . . and now take this halberd in your hand . . . so. Now you shall be thus amply attired a great part of the night, for to watch while your husband is asleep is the duty of a wife here in London.

Peggy Yes forsooth, Nuncle. Oh dear Aunt, are not these very pretty things?

Arabella The fool's pleased. Oh, simplicity.

Wiseacres And though I shall not be present tonight,upon my pillow will I leave my nightcap, which is the emblem of me, your husband; and you must show all duty and reverence to that nightcap as if it were myself. So make your low curtsie to my nightcap.

Peggy Yes forsooth.

Arabella Oh, ridiculous.

Doodle Was there ever such a piece of simplicity as this?

Wiseacres Aunt, I commit Peggy to thy care; keep you the key of her chamber. About break of day go in and put her to bed. Let her sleep 'til noon. Then put her to bed in the afternoon again, and let her sleep 'til evening. Keep my doors shut all day and let her remain thus in ignorance. So now;

help to unharness her. There's my best Peggy. I wonder what kind of caution you give your wife; and what security you'll have of her in your absence.

Enter **Arabella**.

Arabella   A little better I hope than you have of your Mistress Ninny there.

Doodle   Wife!

Wiseacres   Is she here?

Arabella   I'll give her a lesson shall make her wiser.

Wiseacres   Go, withdraw . . .

Arabella   No, pray stay a little. These are not manners fit for city folk to show one so countrified.

Doodle   But, wife, we have business.

Arabella   But, husband; so do I. Look at me, husband.

Doodle   What frolic now, wife?

Arabella   You are going out of town, husband?

Doodle   Yes, wife.

Arabella   Do your duty then and come and kiss me.

Doodle   Oh. Ay, with all my heart, wife.

Arabella   Nay, nay; come not round, but over the bench. Nay, jump. Husband. Jump.

Doodle *jumps over.*

Doodle   So, there, wife.

Arabella   So, now back again this way; for the kiss you have earned, and another.

She goes round the bench and he jumps back again.

Doodle   Thou art such a wag, wife. So.

Arabella   Now there's a husband for you. Look you, little gentlewoman, your husband has taught you your duty, now do you teach him his, and make him do this every night and morning. You must teach your husband to come over and over, again and again, and make him glad to jump at it. I'll tell you another . . .

Wiseacres   Good neighbour, take your wife indoors!

Arabella   You teach your wife to reverence your nightcap. Look ye, Mistress Peggy; take his greasy nightcap thus and throw it downstairs, and him after it!

Wiseacres   Away, Peggy, away. This is a madwoman. See how she flings about; away or she will tear ye to pieces.

Peggy   Oh la! Aunt! Aunt!

Aunt   Ay, come away, Peggy, away . . .

Wiseacres   So, so. Lock her up in a room 'til we are gone.

Exeunt **Aunt** *and* **Peggy**.

Doodle   So, so enough, wife; thou hast had thy frolic.

Arabella   You are a fine man indeed; marry a woman to make a fool of her? You shall learn her more wit, or every wife in the parish shall be her schoolmistress.

Wiseacres   Well, your husband here may do what he please with you; let me alone to give my wife what instructions I see fit. I'll fain see what course he'll take with you now.

Doodle   Why, I will admit my wife has a forward wit . . . but needs little admonition.

Wiseacres   Pah.

Doodle   As you please; you shall hear now what I shall say to my wife. Well, dear . . . I would let you know that I am going and shall take my leave of you.

Arabella   Thank you, husband.

Doodle   Now, wife, I need give thee no instructions how to behave yourself while I am gone; I trust all to thy own discretion.

Arabella   I warrant you, husband; I have wit enough not to do myself any harm.

Doodle   Hear you this . . .

Arabella   And for any I do you, I have wit enough not to let you know it.

Doodle   My wife will have her jest, you see.

Wiseacres   And this, brother, you call her waggery.

Doodle   Ay, ay.

Arabella   Husband, business calls you from me, but you shall carry the key of your treasure with you. Though I bid you to make haste back again since every man has a key that will fit the same lock.

Doodle   Wife, I durst trust thee among all the picklocks in England . . . but I have only one thing to request of thee.

Arabella   What is that?

Doodle   Only this; that till my return, to all impertinent men, that ask you any questions, answer 'em with No. Let 'em say what they please, let your answer still be No.

Arabella   Husband, 'til I see you again I shall be sure to sing no other tune. All that I answer to any manner of man will be no and nothing but no, no no.

Doodle   You promise me?

Arabella   Yes. Sincerely.

Doodle   What will you forfeit if you break your word?

Arabella   The locket of diamonds you promised to buy me.

Doodle   Good. Bear witness, Mr Alderman. I have done, wife.

Wiseacres   And this is all the surety you take?

Arabella   A wiser course than you have taken I hope, that leaves your wife to walk about your chamber all night in armour, like an enchanted knight upon a fairyground.

Wiseacres   We must make haste or we'll miss the tide.

Doodle   Then, wife, adieu.

Arabella   Ta ta, husband.

Exeunt **Wiseacres** *and* **Doodle**. *Enter* **Ramble** *and* **Townley** *over the wall.*

Arabella   So, no is the word. We shall see what can be made of this no. But hold, what's this strange entrance?

Ramble   As we counted them in, so they have gone out, Frank. Give me your hand.

Townley   The inn step is kinder to a man's breeches, Ned.

Arabella   'Tis my mistaken lover, and the man I did mistake him for! I'll observe, and unobserved.

Arabella *hides.*

Townley   Why do you pursue a face but glimpsed in the street when in your pocket you hold a sure note of promise?

Ramble   'Tis true the fair Eugenia awaits my coming to port, but this little Peggy veers me off course. E'en with a bird fast in the hand, methinks it foolish to pass by another's bush.

Townley   Shall we not make our way to the inn; this chase is more suited to country half-wits. Did you not swear your own misfortune and my counsel had converted thee?

Ramble   Indeed, and I shall never more make love my business, beyond this evening. You must wait here, concealed, and watch for their return. I shall make my entrance in the Italian style . . . and thus . . .

He climbs an ivy but is deposited back on the ground.

Upon reflection, Frank, I concur the fair Eugenia offers an easier entrance, the joys of which I shall forthwith avail myself.

Exit **Ramble**.

Townley   No good can come of this. This is no task for a sober gentleman. I shall conceal myself, but would have this venture fast concluded.

Townley *discovers* **Arabella**.

Townley   Madam. Forgive your most humble servant.

Arabella   No.

Townley   God's truth but I am, and would have you do so.

Arabella   No.

Townley   Madam, my trespass was not intended. I shall take my leave.

Arabella   No.

Townley   You give me leave to stand and talk with you a little?

Arabella   No.

Townley   Then, Lady Contrary, farewell.

Arabella   No.

Townley   There is no question but this is a Wife. Madam, is your husband at home?

Arabella   No.

Townley   Then, madam, would you be hard-hearted if there was a man that desired you?

Arabella   No.

Townley   By Jove, I would kiss thee for that, but that I fear 'twould put you out of humour.

Arabella   No.

Townley   That was kindly said. Would you refuse to accept this ring from me?

Arabella   No.

Townley   And shall I wait on you to your door?

Arabella   No.

Townley   Ah, that spoils it again. Let us steal in unseen, my pretty little rogue.

Arabella   No.

Townley   Must I then be gone and leave you?

Arabella   No.

Townley   No, no, and ever no. Now, Lady, answer me at your peril: are you a maid?

Arabella   Ha, ha, ha!

Townley   Would you refuse a bed-fellow in his room tonight if you like the man?

Arabella   No.

Townley   If I took your hand, would you demur?

Arabella   No.

Townley   If I embraced you, would you thrust me away?

Arabella   No.

Townley   Or if I kissed thee, turn thy head?

Arabella   No.

Townley   Madam, is there any such liberty you would deny me?

Arabella   No.

Townley   And any time better than this present hour for us to so consort.

Arabella   No. No. No, no, no.

Exit **Arabella** *to the summer house, laughing.*

Townley   Here's a fair opportunity for an afternoon's diversion.

Exit **Townley**.

Scene Two

Eugenia's room in **Dashwell***'s house.*

Enter **Eugenia** *and* **Jane**.

Eugenia   Jane, did you deliver my letter to Mr Ramble?

Jane   Yes, madam, last night; I caught him in the street.

Eugenia   I wonder at his absence. Jane; be you at the door below and watch for his coming.

Jane   Yes, madam.

Exit **Jane**, *enter* **Loveday**.

Loveday   Madam, good evening to you.

Eugenia   What mean you, sir, to come hither uninvited?

Loveday   Nothing, madam, that one so virtuous might not assume. All day I have watched your husband's going out to get an opportunity to speak with you in private. Nay, blush not, madam, at anything that passed last night; what knowledge I have gathered of your secrets lies buried in this breast. The frolic I played last night was harmless, and I would not have proceeded so far, but to clear the house of a rival.

Eugenia   What mean you, sir?

Loveday   I mean an intruder to your affections, one that invades my right.

Eugenia   I understand you not, sir.

Loveday   Marriage has entitled you your husband's, your duty and obedience are his, but if you have any love to spare besides, I claim it as my due.

Eugenia   I confess you know my secrets, therefore may think to make me comply . . .

Loveday   No, lady; I scorn that.

Eugenia   And keep me in thrall by threatening to discover last night's transactions to my husband! That is a poor design.

Loveday   I have better intentions and a nobler claim. Look well on me; though in disguise, do you not know me?

Eugenia   Know you?

He offers his moustache, which she supposes an insect.

Loveday   Am I not like the one that loved you, and to whom you so often kindly said you could never love any other man? Is Loveday so lost in your remembrance? Have seven years so altered me?

Eugenia   Loveday? Is it you? Forgive my excess of wonder; your growth and the smallpox have so altered you. I scarce know you in anything but your voice, and even that is altered too.

His accent changes.

Loveday   You see, Eugenia, how subject we are to change. But my heart is still the same, and I wish yours were so too.

Eugenia   Be assured, Loveday, I can never hate the man I once lov'd so much.

Loveday   How young and innocent we were in our first loves; and all our vows sincere. But time and absence has effaced them quite, and your heart has taken new impressions. Oh, Eugenia, 'tis death to me to see you, and not to see you mine.

Eugenia   Speak not too much, my Loveday, lest you again raise the flame which was never quite extinct, for still it lies hot and glowing at my heart. But tell me; why came you in this disguise?

Loveday   When I returned from travel I heard the fatal news of your marriage, but excused you, because your friends deceived you.

Eugenia   Alas, they told me you were dead!

Loveday   That was our parents' plot to divide our affections. They writ the same to me of you.

Eugenia   Had I known you were living . . .

Loveday   Eugenia, say no more of that. Though you are married I claim a share in your affections. I cannot live without your kindness, and since you incline towards a gallant; I claim that title.

Eugenia   I confess I once loved you. Nor have my affections ever abated; the sight of you revives them again. Be you discreet, and I cannot be unkind.

Loveday   Blessed Eugenia!

Eugenia   My dear Loveday. How shall I recompense thy constancy?

Loveday   Love is the best reward of love. The hour is now inviting; your husband abroad, nobody to observe or restrain our desires . . . Say; shall we now? Blush not, nor turn thy head into my bosom, but to thy bed, my dear.

Eugenia   You have prevailed, and I have power to refuse you nothing. Wait. Jane! Stand there awhile and keep you silent. I must give some necessary orders to my maid.

Enter **Jane**.

Jane   Madam, I have spied Mr Ramble in the garden. By his many gestures he would gain admittance.

Eugenia   No matter for his coming now; my mind is altered.

Jane   Will you not see him then?

Eugenia   Not now. I will tell you my reasons another time.

Jane   As you wish, madam. I shall leave him to his pantomime.

Eugenia   Where are you going?

Jane   To make your bed.

Eugenia   No, no. Stay. I'll go to bed again for an hour.

Jane   I'll lay it smooth then for you.

Eugenia   Hold. Don't come in, go down, and remain below until I call you. Dismiss Mr Ramble and watch my husband's coming.

Jane   Yes, madam.

Exit **Jane**. **Loveday** *unbuttoned.*

Eugenia   Come, dearest, we must make . . . haste.

Loveday   Come to my arms, dear kind creature, and let me gaze upon thy charms, before the curtains are drawn round us, and day is shut from our sight. Thus I could look, and kiss, and hug, for ever. Oh, I am in an ecstasy of joy.

Eugenia   Came you hither to talk, my dear?

Loveday   Oh dear soul, such benevolent a reprimand. Come, now to bed. To bed, that we may plunge in bliss, and dive in the sweet ocean of delight.

Eugenia   Proceed where you will; I durst may follow.

A knock on the door.

Jane (*without*)   Madam, my master is below, and just coming up to you.

Eugenia   Oh, good wench, run down and stop him a little.

Jane   He's coming upstairs now.

Loveday   Where shall I hide myself?

Eugenia   Cover yourself in the bed.

She covers him in the bed, shuts the curtains, and sits upon a cushion by the bedside, as reading. Enter **Dashwell** *and* **Jane**.

Jane   Pray, sir, don't go in there, I am just going to make the bed.

Dashwell   Well, I shan't stay . . . what is your mistress doing?

Jane   What she is always doing, sir. Praying I think . . .

Dashwell   Oh, yonder she is . . . come wife, prethee lay by thy book. I did never see the like of thee, thou art always reading one good book or another.

Exit **Jane**.

Eugenia   I had just done, husband, and was coming down . . . that Jane might clean the room. Come, will you go below?

Dashwell   Stay a little, wife, I came only to tell thee I must go down-river. And to tell thee the news . . . the Bride and Bridegroom are come from church. What luck Mr Alderman will have in the marriage, I know not. Methinks the Bride is more fit to play with a doll than a husband. God's teeth, a Cock Sparrow would be too much for her.

Eugenia   How you talk, husband . . .

Dashwell   Wife . . . come hither, wife.

Eugenia   And who was there at the Wedding?

Dashwell   Only Alderman Doodle and myself, and an old woman the Bride calls Aunt. Come hither, wife.

Eugenia   Jane!

Eugenia   Prethee, husband, let us go down.

Dashwell   Prethee, wife, to bed!

Enter **Jane**.

Jane   Madam?

Dashwell   Jane, go down and prepare your mistress's . . . porridge.

Jane   Sir, 'tis nearly supper-time.

Dashwell   Eh? Then fetch me coffee, and my tobacco-box . . .

Jane   Lord, sir, you won't offer to take tobacco here, in my mistress's chamber?

Dashwell   Hark, somebody knocks.

Jane No, sir, no . . .

Dashwell Eh? Pouh, pish. Here, take the Key of my counting-house and fetch the packet of Letters that lies in the window.

Jane You know, sir, I could never open that scurvy door in my life.

Dashwell Go, say I.

Jane Yes, master.

Exit **Jane**.

Dashwell Now, wife . . . Pox on that dull wench . . . she has put me off. I shan't have such a mind again this month. Well, wife, I'll leave thee, I must catch the tide and see to business. Fare thee well, I'll come and see you before night.

Eugenia As you please, husband.

Exit **Dashwell**.

His absence never was more wish'd . . . are you not in a sweat, sir?

Loveday I am almost smother'd. If he had proceeded in his kindness to you, I should have had a fine time on't.

Eugenia Jane's coming was very lucky.

Loveday Would he not have been put off?

Eugenia Yes, he's never very troublesome.

Loveday Eugenia, let us bed with all the eager haste that ever Lovers made.

Jane (*within*) Hold, sir, hold, you must not go in.

Ramble (*within*) You are mistaken, Mrs Jane.

Jane (*within*) My mistress charg'd me to the contrary.

Ramble (*within*) You brought me a letter from her, she sent for me . . .

Eugenia   Hark, I think I hear him coming upstairs again.
Shut the Curtain.

Enter **Ramble** *followed by* **Jane**.

Eugenia   Who is it, Jane?

Ramble   'Tis I, your humble servant.

Jane   Madam, I did open my window to dismiss the
gentleman and he would not have me close it again until he
had secured his entrance.

Ramble   I received your letter, kiss'd it a thousand times,
and made what haste I could to obey your summons.

Eugenia   Things are alter'd since, my husband . . .

Ramble   He's safe, madam, I saw him go out.

Eugenia   He's gone but across the street, I am sure he will
not stay long, let me beg you therefore to shorten your visit.

Ramble   You seem to drive me hence. But yet you sent for me.

Eugenia   By that you see my kindness, were it convenient. I
dare not run too great a hazard, it imports me, sir, to be wary.
Wherefore if you love me, or ever hope for my kindness, go
away now for fear of a mischief.

Ramble   We have not yet talk'd half enough . . . you have
given me no account of the mischief you made last night. You
should know that other gentleman is my intimate friend and
acquaintance.

Eugenia   I am apt to believe you thought more than was,
and that he spoke more than he ought. We have not the time
to come to a complete understanding, therefore I beg you
would leave me at present.

Ramble   I dare refuse you nothing, but methinks so fair an
opportunity should not be lost, your husband gone abroad,
you undress'd, your bed there, I here . . .

Dashwell (*without*)   Jane, Jane, where are you?

Eugenia   Undone, that's my husband's voice, coming upstairs.

Ramble   I'll under the bed . . .

Eugenia   You can't, it's too low.

Ramble   I'll into't then.

Eugenia   Hold, no. No, my husband's come home to bed, he's not well.

Ramble   What shall I do?

Jane (*without*)   Have a care, sir, have a care . . .

Eugenia   Draw your Sword, be angry . . . threaten. Swear you'll kill . . .

Ramble   Who, your husband?

Eugenia   Anybody . . . no matter . . . hunt about as if you look'd for somebody.

Enter **Dashwell** *and* **Jane**.

Jane   I say have a care . . . have a care . . .

Dashwell   Have a care of what, you silly ninny. Wife, what makes you tremble?

Eugenia   O Lord, husband, I am so frighted . . .

Dashwell   Hau! A drawn Sword . . . what's he there? Who are you, sir? What would you have, sir?

Ramble   Have, sir . . .

Eugenia   Indeed, sir, he is not here. Pray be pacified . . .

Ramble   I'll be the death of him; his blood shall pay for the affront.

Dashwell   Know I not thy face, sir?

Eugenia   Indeed, sir, he is not here.

Ramble   Come, come, down on your knees all of you and confess.

Dashwell   What means this, wife?

Ramble   Down on your knees, sir.

Dashwell   Knees, sir?

Eugenia   He is not here upon my word, sir . . .

Dashwell   He is not here indeed, sir . . . Who is't, wife?

Ramble   He must be here, I follow'd him.

Jane   Indeed, sir, he went out again.

Ramble   No, he must be hereabouts, I'll not leave a corner unsearch'd . . . Hau . . .

He counterfeits a rage, throws open the curtains, pulls off the bedclothes and discovers **Loveday** *in the bed.*

Loveday   Hu!

Ramble   Ha!

Eugenia   Ah! I swoon!

Dashwell   A man in my bed.

Eugenia *screeks . . . runs to* **Ramble**, *catches him on his arm and swounds.*

Jane   Oh hold, sir, for Heaven's sake, my mistress swounds. She'll die away.

Ramble   Madam, be not frighted, I'll not meddle with him now for your sake.

Dashwell   What means all this?

Ramble   Your house shall at present be his Sanctuary, and protect the man that hath done me such injuries, but when I meet him abroad, let him guard well his throat, had he twenty lives he should not live one hour after.

Dashwell   Pray, sir, let me know the meaning of this, and how the young man has offended you.

Ramble   I cannot think on't without rage, let them tell you.

Dashwell   What have you done to the Gentleman to provoke him?

Loveday   Done to him, sir . . . no great matter . . . but that . . . a . . .

Eugenia   I'll tell you, husband . . . Jane being in the street and seeing this Gentleman pass by, was so foolish to shriek and cry out, the Devil! The Gentleman pressing to know her meaning, she told him she saw the Devil in his shape last night; and how one in this house rais'd him in his likeness; upon this the Gentleman being incens'd rush'd into the house to look for the young man, who, hearing him threaten, slip'd away and ran in here for shelter; and had not Jane and I hid him in my bed he had certainly been murther'd.

Dashwell   You silly baggage.

Jane   Truly, sir, it was my fright, the Devil last night and this Gentleman were so alike . . .

Dashwell   Nay he was very like him, that's the truth on't.

Ramble   Sir, now you know the reason, I hope you'll excuse my intruding into your house, and I beg your pardon, madam, for frighting you . . . as for that Conjuror, let him beware how he stirs over your threshold. Your servant, your servant . . . Oh, false, damn'd false woman!

Exit **Ramble**.

Dashwell   Jane, go down and lock the door after him.

Exit **Jane**.

Eugenia   How happen'd it that you return'd so luckily, husband?

Dashwell   By especial providence I think, the Master of the Ship having come to us on his initiative. And I am glad it fell out so, since my coming sav'd a man's life, for ought I know.

Eugenia   Indeed so am I, husband.

Loveday   And I.

Dashwell   And you, sir. I have received news for you. My correspondent in Bristol, to whom I recommended you, has sent word he is happy to employ and entertain you, and has promptly provided for your journey. You are to travel tomorrow and he says you must go very early.

Loveday   I thank you, sir, for your patronage.

Dashwell   Well then, all's done. I have writ a short note for you to travel with, and will fetch it.

Exit **Dashwell**.

Loveday   Oh, unlucky accident. He has cut off all my hopes. I cannot think of parting from you.

Eugenia   But you must go from hence.

Loveday   Not to gain one hour's privacy, one minute's enjoyment of my love. Both to be resolved and willing, and yet to be disappointed. Dear Eugenia; I am almost mad.

Eugenia   Despair not, Loveday, for now I shall try my art in spite of fortune. The cards are now in my hand, and I'll deal once more in hopes of better luck.

Loveday   Kind, dear woman, but how?

Eugenia   I hear him. Hide you there, but make no noise.

Exit **Loveday**, *enter* **Dashwell**.

Dashwell   Where is our visitor?

Eugenia   Husband, I sent him to his room.

Dashwell   How so? I must give him my letter so he may be gone early in the morning.

Eugenia   But I think it not appropriate you should recommend him to any friend, or entertain him further yourself. He is not the person you take him for.

Dashwell   What mean you?

Eugenia   I mean he is an impudent rascal, and only fit to be kicked out of doors.

Dashwell   What has he done?

Eugenia   I know not whether he made a false construction of my extra-ordinary care to hide him in my bed, but he had the impudence e'en now when you were gone to tell me that his coming here was for my sake, and that it would break his heart to leave the house 'til he had accomplished his design.

Dashwell   A rogue. So much I had begun to suspect!

Eugenia   And said he hoped, since time allowed him not further opportunities of courtship, I would without ceremony consent to steal out of bed from you when you were fast asleep, and slipping on my nightgown, meet him in the summer house.

Dashwell   The dainty rogue.

Eugenia   To be revenged of him for his insolence; I would have you dress yourself in a nightgown and cap, and go down in the dark, take a good cudgel in your hand and drub him soundly, then turn him out of doors. You may let Jane be with you to help you.

Dashwell   That shall be his punishment! I would not for a hundred pounds I had sent him where I intended, the insolent dog. Lose his labour? I'll give him the fruits of his labour.

Eugenia   Here is a nightgown.

Dashwell   Let me put it on quickly.

Eugenia   No, no. Go downstairs and dress you there, and hide yourself in the summer house 'til he comes.

Dashwell   I'll baulk him for making assignations! The rogue, the dog. The son of a cur. . .

Exit **Dashwell**.

Eugenia   Come, sir, come from your post.

Loveday   Dear creature; thou witty rogue.

Eugenia   An hour is our own by this invention.

Loveday   Let us retire, Eugenia, and make the best use on't we can.

Eugenia   But how shall it end?

Loveday   I can think of nothing but thee at present, and the Heaven I am going to enjoy. Now we shall fly to it and plunge into bliss and be nought but rapture, all ecstasy. Already I am all on fire, my soul is in a blaze. And whilst we talk I burn in vain.

Eugenia   All talk is vain when opportunity requires performance!

Scene Three

A bedchamber in **Wiseacres'** *house.*

Enter **Ramble***, dishevelled, as from the balcony.*

Ramble   This may be beyond the remit of a gentleman, but my daring is born of a noble and virtuous desperation. Someone comes. To be sure 'tis too heavy a step for a lady, nor a husband either.

Peggy *enters in armour and walks by the bedside.*

Ramble   What monster is this haunts a pleasant household?

Peggy *has difficulty with her duties, and removes her helmet.*

Ramble   Pretty creature . . . do not start.

Peggy   You are that same gentleman.

Ramble   What art thou doing at this time of night?

Peggy   I am a wife an't please you, this is the duty of a wife here in London.

Ramble   Oh, simplicity.

Peggy   Are you here, sir, to visit my husband?

Ramble   No, indeed to visit thee.

Peggy   I did so believe you to be a kind gentleman.

Ramble   How long have you been married, pretty miss?

Peggy   I was married this morning betimes.

Ramble   And who dressed you thus prettily?

Peggy   My Uncle-Husband.

Ramble   Your Uncle-Husband?

Peggy   Yes, my Uncle-Husband.

Ramble   And to what end did he dress you thus?

Peggy   Indeed, that I might watch whilst my husband sleeps.

Ramble   Sweet thing, you have been sorely imposed upon.

Peggy   'Tis but my duty.

Ramble   And is this all you know of the Duty of a Wife?

Peggy   This is as far as I have learned yet, but Uncle will teach me more when he comes back.

Ramble   Pretty Peggy, would you not thank a man that would teach you your lesson perfect before he comes?

Peggy   Oh, yes!

Ramble   Then first, Mrs Peggy, you must lay by this halberd, and these things, and come to your bed.

Ramble *sets about opening the armour.*

Peggy   Indeed; what is to be learned there?

Ramble   The most significant schooling.

Peggy   Oh, sir.

Ramble *drops armour on his foot.*

Peggy   Oh, sir, are you injured?

Ramble   'Tis of no consequence.

Peggy   But can you walk, sir.

Ramble   Indeed I can, Miss Peggy, but I have no plans to do so, for I shall stay with you tonight and take pains to instruct you in the entire duty of a wife.

Peggy   Will you indeed? But sir, they told me last night that such a one as you would eat me.

Ramble   Nay, Peggy, but we must pay special tutelage to thine own appetite.

Peggy   But my Uncle-Husband said I was to wear these things and not go to bed 'til morning that Aunt came to me, and that I was to do so all night, and he will be angry, and Aunt told me God won't bless me if I anger my husband.

Ramble *takes fire tongs to the armour.*

Ramble   But your Uncle-Husband came to me and told me he was mistaken, and your Aunt most heartily agreed and bid me come to you and teach you the right duty and which I was at prayers this morning I could swear God himself bid me tell you that you must go to bed and do as I'd have you do.

Peggy   Oh then indeed, I'll to bed and you shall teach me.

Ramble   Ay! Ay! Do dear pretty Peggy, and make haste. Never was there such a little fool as this. Now, my little sweet dear piece of innocence, thou little simple pretty foolish thing. What first lesson shall it pleasure us to undertake? I am almost out of my senses with joy.

A cry of 'fire' off.

Peggy   Hark, sir; the house is on fire.

Ramble   No. No indeed, it is not.

Peggy   Did you not hear 'em cry 'fire' in the street just now?

Ramble   Yes, but they cry a great many things here in London, as 'Hot 'Taters' and such.

Peggy   I have heard them, 'tis so, and 'Oranges and Lemons' too.

Ramble   Ay, Oranges and Lemons also.

Peggy   Then, sir, the fire must be for sale and you may commence thy teaching.

Enter **Aunt**, *with a pan on fire, with* **Scullery Boy**.

Scullery Boy   Fire!

Aunt   Fire!

Scullery Boy   Fire!

Aunt   Fire!

Ramble   Fire!

Peggy   Deeds, Aunt; have you bought some?

Aunt   This pan has took blaze and catched hold of the kitchen chimney . . .

Peggy   Oh, naughty fire.

Ramble   Old dame, be still!

Aunt   The Devil! The Devil has been upon thee!

Ramble   Do you decline to have the fiend extinguish thee?

Aunt   This is a righteous fire; no Devil's. Out, sir; out! I shall singe thy tail.

Ramble   Madam, I . . . farewell.

Aunt   Foolish child. Low wretched man.

Exit **Ramble** *pursued by* **Aunt** *and* **Scullery Boy**.

Peggy   To be sure London is a quite livelier place than the country. Though I would not have been so disappointed in my education.

Enter **Townley**, *unbraced, as from the balcony*.

Townley   I heard a cry of fire.

Peggy   Yet another visitor!

Townley   And thought to rescue my good friend and thee.

Peggy   Sir, there is no fire worth your fears, and your friend has departed, hurriedly.

Townley   Then, madam; you are safe.

Peggy   But disappointed, sir. Your friend was about to instruct me in my married duties for the benefit of my husband.

Townley   Indeed. A noble enterprise.

Peggy   Now he has rushed off and I shall learn nothing 'til another day.

Townley   Sweet Lady, to be in despond does not become thee. There are perhaps other tutors.

Peggy   But, sir, are you familiar with the subject?

Townley   I have been of recent study, madam. And I have a growing reputation.

Peggy   And might I be your special pupil, sir?

Townley   Hey ho. I'll forswear another bottle. (*Aside.*) Is it not a fine thing to grant horns to the cuckold and cuckolder both! – I'll mouse thee and touse thee and tumble thee 'til morn.

Act Five

Scene One

Communal gardens behind **Wiseacres**', **Doodle**'s *and* **Dashwell**'s *houses.*

Enter **Ramble** *on fire, pursued by* **Aunt** *and* **Scullery Boy**.

Aunt (*off*)   Vile seducer! Lewd villain!

Ramble   Not to be outwitted by old women and potboys, I have doubled back to where they will not have the wit to look.

Scullery Boy (*off*)   He came back this way with thought to outwit us.

Ramble   Oh, rats to 'em.

Ramble *hides.*

Aunt   I'll beat his wits from his skull ere he escapes me.

Scullery Boy   This way, missus. All vermin run for cover.

Aunt   I'll cut off his tail and more besides.

Exit **Aunt** *and* **Scullery Boy**. *Enter* **Doodle** *and* **Wiseacres**. **Ramble** *hides up a tree.*

Doodle   It was very well the master of the ship came up as he did and saved us from a fool's errand. It would have vexed you to have lost the first night's lodging with your Bride for a cold voyage of no purpose.

Wiseacres   Indeed. Now will I go to my little wife, whom I shall find upon duty, taking short turns around my bedside. Aunt!

Wiseacres *knocks.*

Doodle   I think it a great deal of cruelty in you so to torment a poor innocent. I will go home to my wife and set her tongue at liberty.

Aunt (*within*)   Who's there?

Wiseacres   'Tis I.

Enter **Aunt**.

Aunt   Oh, indeed. I did not expect you back tonight.

Wiseacres   What smell is this about the door?

Doodle   Here's a smell of soot and burning.

Aunt   Alas, after you went a pot caught the kitchen chimney on fire. I was frighted out of my wits.

Wiseacres   How, fire?

Aunt   Thank providence it was quickly out. It did no great harm, but to interupt Peggy as she . . . went to bed.

Wiseacres   Peggy? To bed?

Aunt   Indeed, sir.

Wiseacres   Contrary to my orders, going to bed?

Aunt   But without my knowledge, sir.

Wiseacres   Into bed in contempt of my commands! Monstrous!

Doodle   Now where's your caution?

Aunt   Nay, I told her you would be very angry.

Wiseacres   And what said she to that?

Aunt   She said no, you would not be angry.

Wiseacres   Bid her slip on her nightgown and come down to me to acknowledge her fault! I'll turn you out of doors for this, and for such another I'll send her out after you. Go call her down to me!

Aunt   Yes an't please ye, sir.

Wiseacres   Leave your ducking and dropping and tell her quickly.

Exit **Aunt**.

Aunt (*off*)   Peggy! Mistress Peggy!

Doodle   Nay, nay, Mr Alderman; hear the business before you are so angry.

Wiseacres   You must know I think severely on this; for a wife who would not obey the temperate and agreeable instructions of a devoted and concerned husband may not be trusted either in those things of greater consequence.

Enter **Townley** *above, hurriedly*.

Doodle   Whilst I would never trust a simple wife, I am indisposed to believe even the simplest could have erred so already.

Townley *leaps to the ground and discovers* **Doodle** *and* **Wiseacres**.

Doodle   Ha!

Wiseacres   God's teeth!

Ramble (*aside*)   For one so fond of an inn, I observe my friend Frank Townley does greatly frequent ladies' chambers.

Wiseacres   And who are you, sir?

Townley   Um . . . Where is the fire, sir?

Wiseacres   The fire?

Townley   And what knave has stole away my ladder?

Wiseacres   What mean you, sir?

Townley   To put out the fire I saw when I heard the cry of fire and climbed the wall to bring aid to any endangered by the fire that . . . was on fire.

Doodle   Good citizen, I thought the fire was done before we came.

Townley   Ay, sir, some time, but I have had experience in the fortitude and insistence of that element and would take all pains to be sure it was out before I went on my way.

Wiseacres   This sounds a considerate citizen.

Doodle   I smell other than cinders and soot. What think you now sir, of your simple wife?

Wiseacres   You may think as you please of this man's jumping from the balcony, and make false conjectures, but you are mistaken. I am assured by this gentleman's honest demeanour he did but commit an act of great courage.

Ramble (*aside*)   And will needs find greater courage ere I confront him.

Doodle   Nay, if this man's tumbling out of your wife's chamber window is no argument, I find you are wilfully resolved to maintain your error or have lost thy wits.

Wiseacres   By your leave, I am not yet convinced I was in the wrong.

Doodle   Good night, sir. Wife! Whoever is awake; come down and open the door! 'Tis not your wife who is a fool, sir, but you yourself.

Wiseacres   Say you so, sir? Doubt you the word of this good gentleman! He did come to my house to put out a fire!

Doodle   Methinks to light one, more likely, by putting a taper to your wife.

Townley   Sir, I do object to your lewd conjecture. Indeed, sir, I was otherwise engaged before the cry of fire and thus could not have approached this Gentleman's wife so rudely.

Wiseacres   Hear you this? Expand upon your explanation, sir!

Townley   Now I think on it, 'twas such an unusual adventure to tell it you would convince you both most surely, for nothing so unlikely could be thought of in aid of an excuse.

Doodle   Pray what was it, sir?

Townley   Well, if we be gentlemen . . . earlier tonight it was my good fortune to offer my service to a lady. One other than your wife, sir, be assured. I began to make some little courtships to her, but to everything I said she answered nothing but No.

Wiseacres   No, sir?

Townley   Yes, sir. Not a word could I get from her but no, no, no.

Wiseacres   Nothing but no?

Townley   Whatever I asked her was no.

Doodle   Hum . . . So, sir . . .

Wiseacres   Pray, sir, continue.

Townley   I asked her if I should be her servant; she said no.

Doodle   Such a response would be to the honour of a lady.

Enter **Arabella** *above.*

Townley   Indeed, sir, but then, perceiving she had taken up an odd humour to say nothing but no and had resolved to give no other answer, I studied to ask such questions, that if she answered no, it would please me well.

Wiseacres   Very good, sir. Hear you this, Mr Alderman?

Exit **Arabella**.

Doodle   What of it?

Wiseacres   Well, sir, and how then?

Townley   I asked her then if she would not be angry if I went indoors with her, and she said no.

Wiseacres   No, Brother!

Townley   If she would refuse me as a bed-fellow; no.

Wiseacres   No, she said again.

Townley   If that I embraced her, would she thrust me away? She said; no.

Wiseacres   No.

Townley   If there was any such liberty she would deny me? No!

Wiseacres   No. No. She said no, Brother!

Doodle   No, well . . . I observe that . . . humph.

Ramble (*aside*)   What stars conspire round Frank Townley's head that he does make such easy acquaintance with these women?

Townley   So now I tell you, Gentlemen, I led her to this very summer house . . .

Enter **Engine** *with wine.*

Engine   Sir, my mistress sent me out with this wine that you might take a nightcap.

Doodle   It is late, certainly. Let us go inside.

Wiseacres   Pray listen, sir; let him go on.

Townley   In ran she, in ran I. Onto the bench she throws herself, onto the bench throw I myself by her . . .

Engine   Pray drink, sir . . .

Townley   Or upon her as you may guess.

Engine   'Tis a special vintage.

Wiseacres   And not a word but no said the lady all this while. No was the word, Brother.

Doodle   Ay, yes, yes. So I hear.

Engine   Drink, sir! Drink to that kind lady's good health, and that it may continue.

Townley   To the health of the Negative Lady. Long life indeed.

Doodle   Long life.

Ramble (*aside*)   And a short one to you, Frank Townley, and the gout along with it.

Townley *drinks and discovers his ring in the glass.*

Townley   Ha. A ring in my mouth, and my ring.

Enter **Arabella**.

Arabella   Gentlemen, husband. It grows late; will you gossip all night? Am I of your acquaintance, sir?

Wiseacres   Well, sir?

Doodle   Well, sir?

Townley   . . .

Arabella   I had overheard your story from the window.

Wiseacres   Come sir; let us have the rest of your story.

Ramble (*aside*)   Indeed I would hear it too.

Townley   Well . . . To make my story short . . . As I prepared to . . .

Wiseacres   To tumble this jade . . .

Townley   To share affections with this innocent creature I had thus outwitted . . . for 'tis certain she should be pitied for my cruel usage . . .

Wiseacres   Hang it all, sir; continue.

Townley   . . . I did fall off the bench and strike my head against a large stone. And with such a fall I waked out of my dream.

Wiseacres   Wha?

Doodle   Why then, this is all but a dream?

Townley   Yes, sir.

Wiseacres   How! A dream?

Townley   Ay, sir; a dream.

Wiseacres   You have not said it was a dream.

Townley   Could such a strange encounter be other than

such? To be sure, it could not happen with credence e'en in the Playhouse.

Ramble (*aside*)   It is a wonder to observe such wit from one so ordinarily witless.

Doodle   This is wonderful. A dream it was, for certain.

Arabella   But is it not strange, husband, that this gentleman should dream a Lady who would behave so alike as to how you instructed me?

Wiseacres   I would warrant that's odd, would you not, Alderman?

Arabella   Truly, sir, I wondered all the while where the story would end. It was so pat to our intrigue.

Doodle   Truly, wife, I knew not what to think on't, 'til I heard it was but a dream.

Arabella   Well, sir, I must beg your pardon if I have made you a cuckold . . .

Doodle   How, madam?

Arabella   But 'twas in a dream, sir.

Townley   So sweet a dream I could wish to dream it a thousand times o'er.

Arabella   I can almost fancy but that I am in a dream still.

Townley   Methinks this feels more like a dream than the other.

Enter **Aunt** *and* **Peggy**.

Aunt   She is here an't please you.

Townley   I'll bid you all good night.

Wiseacres   No sir, stand by. I would speak to you further concerning this unlikely dream. Wait while I must chastise my wife, then we shall take a drink together. Peggy; come hither.

Peggy   Welcome home, Nuncle-Husband.

Wiseacres   Peggy, how durst you neglect your duty to me your husband and go to bed?

Peggy   But I did not neglect my duty.

Wiseacres   Why, went you not to bed? Hau?

Peggy   Yes, but I went to bed to learn my duty.

Wiseacres   Did I not teach you what you were to do?

Peggy   But he taught me a better duty than that you showed me; a great deal.

Wiseacres   He? What he?

Doodle   What he is this?

Peggy   He that came before the fire and asked me why I walked so and when I told him he said that was but the first duty and he would show me all the rest of the nightly duties of a wife, and that you had sent him so to do.

Wiseacres   The Devil he did. Stand, sir!

Wiseacres *draws upon* **Townley**.

Tempt me not. I shall run you through.

Ramble (*aside*)   Now might my friend be judged harshly, wrongly, and justly and all at once!

Townley   Have a care with your weapon, sir, for a gentleman such as I does easily bleed.

Peggy   Nuncle, husband, do not threaten so.

Wiseacres   Continue, Peggy; what next occurred.

Peggy   Why nothing, for there was a cry of fire, and the man rushed away.

Aunt   Indeed it is true, sir; discovering the rogue I did chase him off.

Wiseacres   And this is the man did promise you these . . . lessons?

Peggy   Why no, sir; it was not he.

Townley   You hear this, sir? The man did nothing and was not me neither.

Wiseacres   Be sure and tell me the truth, Peggy.

Peggy   No, sir, certainly. This is the man who came to save me from the fire.

Wiseacres   Ha! Hear you that, Alderman.

Doodle   Indeed.

Wiseacres   It is as he says; he came to give assistance.

Townley   Ever your servant, sir.

Peggy   This man made no promises, but gave great assistance, and taught the very things the other had promised.

Wiseacres   Wha!

Peggy   I could not think the other could have been a better teacher neither.

Ramble (*aside*)   Here's proof; my former friend has sprung another snare I was at pains to set!

Doodle   Pray, Peggy; what did he teach you?

Peggy   Nay I can't tell you, but I have learned a great deal and, Uncle, if I were in bed I could show you!

Wiseacres   You are a baggage!

Peggy   Indeed, Uncle, I had forgot you told me I must call you husband, but Uncle-Husband it was ten times a better duty than that you taught me.

Wiseacres   Very pleasant.

Peggy   Yes, yes. So pleasant I could do such duty all night long. Though after he taught me my lesson two or three times, I fell fast asleep.

Wiseacres   Hahhh!

Ramble (*aside*)   Lay on, sir; do your worst. Another blow, surely, would be just.

Peggy   But Nuncle, do not treat him so. When I share with you all I have learnt, I'm sure you will be best pleased.

Townley   Peace, sir; the lady has confused herself. I have imparted to her no such knowledge, nor had any of her. This, would you but give me respite, could I prove to your satisfaction.

Wiseacres   I shall hold, sir, but only that you might lie with your last breath and thus speed to hell upon it. And then send her swiftly after.

Aunt   Oh, mercy.

Peggy   Aunt, is it something I have done has made Nuncle-Husband angry?

Townley   When I did enter the lady's room to search for fire, she was asleep.

Aunt   'Tis true. Have patience.

Wiseacres   Were you sleeping?

Peggy   Indeed, sir; when Aunt woke me to say you were come home, and the man was gone.

Townley   As I stood close she did toss in her sleep and briefly open her eyes to me.

Wiseacres   And it was this man you did see?

Peggy   Indeed it was he but methought . . .

Wiseacres   You did think?

Peggy   Methought I know not what.

Wiseacres   This may answer it. You only thought 'twas so. 'Twas all but your thought.

Doodle   How's this?

Wiseacres   Your glimpse of this man was midwife to a dream.

Doodle   Impossible.

Wiseacres   There was no teacher, nor no lessons.

Peggy   But there was though . . .

Wiseacres/Aunt/Townley   No there was not.

Peggy   But indeed . . . and indeed . . . Uncle-Husband, there was.

Wiseacres   Peace I tell you; there was not. 'Twas all but a dream.

Townley   A dream.

Doodle   A dream?

Arabella   Well, to be sure, Gentlemen, there has been so much dreaming I would swear this was more likely a dream that we do now walk in and talk in and make but little sense of.

Doodle   Hark you, Brother Alderman, what think you of a fool for a wife now?

Wiseacres   What think you of a witty one?

Townley   What's the meaning of all this, madam?

Arabella   They don't know themselves.

Ramble (*aside*)   My enforced seclusion does bring on the cramp. I would they'd all retire. I must adjust my purchase, thus.

Peggy   Methinks it was a very strange dream had quite so many strangers in't. For, Nuncle-Husband, there was surely another man . . .

Wiseacres   Be silent! There were no other men but that morpheous commanded.

Doodle   No other men and be done. Let us be agreed that he talks nonsense who would have it that all wives are faithless, that *are* not.

Wiseacres   Or that rakes and seducers fall from the very trees, that *do* not!

Ramble *falls from a tree into an ornamental pond.*

Ramble   Aaarhg!

Doodle   Ha!

Wiseacres   Servants, hither! What Devil are you, sir?!

Arabella   My unlucky lover.

Doodle   God's truth, it is the Devil indeed. I have seen him conjured once before! Come not close to me, thou fiend!

Servants *enter and take* **Ramble**.

Wiseacres   Hold him for a rogue! He is a fiend, you say?

Doodle   Ay, sir, and haunts your tree!

Wiseacres   Pish.

Doodle   Or can live in cupboards too.

Ramble   Good sirs, I am neither a rogue nor fiend nor any rough sort of man, but a gentleman who has found himself through no ill deeds . . . up a tree.

Wiseacres   Wretched cur! Explain thyself.

Townley   If you had been asleep and dreamt much, 'twould be beneficial to you.

Ramble   If you had been to Dover and enlisted thyself, 'twould be beneficial also.

Wiseacres   If your explanation be not fit, you shall be trounced as a hooligan or hanged as a thief! Speak, blackguard!

Peggy   Oh, Nuncle-Husband, do not hang him, for he stole nothing that I saw.

Townley   That's true, I'll warrant.

Peggy   This is the man who proves it was no dream at all!!

He did nothing but offer to teach me the duty of a wife; didn't you, sir?

Ramble   No. No.

Wiseacres   Go, wife; go. You are in a dream still.

Peggy   Oh but it was no dream though. This is the gentleman that offered theory and this is the gentleman in practice.

Doodle   Ha, ha, ha. There's simplicity for you.

Arabella   Well, Mr Alderman, is your foolish wife so very innocent?

Doodle   Methinks, sir, you are neither a spirit nor a figment, but one who hides in cupboards and up trees awaiting opportunity.

Townley   Indeed, and in cellar-holes too, disguised as an African.

Ramble   Mr Townley, you have kept better company than I tonight and I would so beg your silence!

Wiseacres   In cellar-holes? Then, Alderman Doodle, he has laid siege to your property also!

Doodle   Let's have done with further conjecture and turn him in for a common thief!

Wiseacres   Do so!

Ramble   Kind sirs, desist. Do not arrest me for I am neither thief, spirit, African, seducer, Devil nor dream.

Wiseacres   Then, sir, what are you?

Ramble   I am, sir . . . a catcher of rats. An employment which does oblige me to seek my quarry in the strangest quarters, such as cellar-holes, cupboards, and up trees . . .

Doodle   Up trees?

Ramble   Indeed, sir, the rat chased from one place will make ingenious use of another.

Townley   So much is evident.

Ramble   And in the course of my endeavours, gentlemen, have been spied by my lady thus and put into a dream, and by this honest gentleman and mistook for a thief, and in pursuit of half a dozen verminous creatures of no mean aspect, by you all this night for a man of no virtue. My profession is a mean one, but honourable, as I hope you now will find me. For to grant honour to one who deserves it is to claim honour for oneself, and for one's wife too, if ever it had been in doubt.

Wiseacres   I would believe you speak honestly, sir.

Doodle   Ay, and wisely too.

Peggy   But be there rats in trees?

Wiseacres   Shush.

Enter **Dashwell**, *in his wife's attire, and* **Jane**.

Dashwell   Hark you, Mr Alderman, and Mr Alderman there.

Townley   Heaven! What foul fiend is that?

Arabella   Neighbour Dashwell!

Doodle   Turned Coquette!

Wiseacres   What means this?

Dashwell   You'll see anon. But pray in the interim leave your disputes of a witty wife or a foolish wife, and learn by example presently that you are both in the wrong, as I told you before. And now be convinced what 'tis to have a zealous wife.

Wiseacres   Why I pray, what hast to say as to that matter?

Dashwell   A villain has tempted my wife to meet him in the summer house to commit his felonious purpose against my honour. She has proved herself a virtuous, good woman, and has acquainted me with the wicked machinations, and has advised me to entertain him here in the dark.

Ramble   Hark you, Frank Townley, is this an endeavour of yours or an intrigue of mine?

Townley   I know not.

Jane   Hark, sir; the garden door unlocks. The traitor is coming.

Dashwell   Hist! Then be silent all, I pray. Put out your candles and conceal yourselves. But do not help the rogue, though he cry out never so, for it will be I that do caress him.

Doodle   Brave sir; lay him on.

Wiseacres   Lay him on soundly.

All conceal themselves as **Loveday** *enters with a hunting whip.*

Dashwell   Jane, I hear him come. Stand close; be ready.

Jane   I warrant you, sir.

Loveday   Oh, sweet heaven? Earthly beauty? Where hide thee?

Dashwell   Hem, hem.

Loveday   The Cuckold hems. Little thinks he how he is counter-plotted. Hist. Where are you?

Dashwell   Hem, here.

Loveday   Where?

Dashwell   Hist, here, here. Hist.

Loveday   Oh my dear, art thou here? Let me prepare my arms to embrace thee, and give thee the sweet enjoyment of my love! Discover the immodest vigour of my passion. Receive thou the full might and bold expression of my ardour, thus . . .

He whips **Dashwell**.

Dashwell   Ah! Hold. Hold. Hold.

Loveday   I'll take down your courage!

Dashwell   Hold! Help! Help!

Loveday Make appointments in the dark!

Jane Wrong my Lady!

She beats him also. Enter **Eugenia** *with a light.*

Doodle They swinge him unjustly.

Dashwell Oh, murder. Murder! Murder! Oh!

Doodle Desist, sir!

Loveday Do you think it could be my intention ever to wrong so worthy a gentleman as your husband?

Dashwell Oh hold, hold; you're deceived.

Loveday No, lewd woman, 'tis you are deceived in your expectation. Now I will go to your husband, and acquaint him with what a chaste good wife you are.

Dashwell Here, here; bring the candle. I say you are deceived.

Eugenia Well, husband, have you met with him handsomely?

Loveday Ha! Madam Eugenia! Who then have I been handling all this while?

Dashwell Oh wife, I have been lashed and beaten here most unmercifully.

Loveday Oh Lord, sir; is it you? It was not my intention to thus abuse you, but to punish the lewd behaviour of your wife.

Eugenia How have you been beaten? Sirrah, I'll have you hanged. First tempt me, then beat my husband!

Loveday Oh misfortune; have I been injuring you, sir, all this while?

Eugenia I acquainted my husband with your intentions, and sent him in my place to be revenged of you for your insolence.

Dashwell Nay, nay, wife; 'twas a mistake. Nay, nay; I am convinced it was well meant.

Wiseacres   Well, well, Mr Dashwell, you have certainly paid him off; ha, ha, ha.

Dashwell   Well, well; talk no more of it.

Doodle   'Tis very suspicious.

Dashwell   He meant no hurt; he did it but to try my wife, for my sake.

Wiseacres   And I fear he has indeed tried her for you, neighbour.

Dashwell   Well, well . . . censure as you please. This misfortune is a great satisfaction to me. I heard your stories from within, and would not yet change my wife for her that a man leapt from her window, nor the Lady No of whom that Gentleman dreamed such a fine dream there, nor one who would have him clamouring at her cellar-hole, ha ha.

Doodle   Nor one who would hide him in her cupboard and cry Devil, forsooth.

Dashwell   What say you?

Doodle   Do you not recognise this apparition?

Dashwell   Who's this? The Devil indeed.

Doodle   Indeed the Devil. Ha!

Dashwell   I'll warrant you a thief, sir, of property or persons, and if the law will not trounce you there are husbands surely shall.

Doodle   Aye, and a ratcatcher should have no complaint when a rat is caught.

Wiseacres   Nor killed neither.

Loveday   Gentlemen, desist. Do not treat him so unkindly as already bears such wounds.

Ramble   I thank you, sir. 'Tis often neighbours want compassion, that the traveller more easily affords. But wait; who's this? Valentine? Valentine Loveday, my friend. How long have you been come from Hamburg?

All (*variously*)   How? Valentine Loveday? And from Hamburg?

Loveday   I am discovered.

Dashwell   My wife's former suitor. Nay then, I fear there's something more in this business than I yet apprehend.

Townley   I fear you have made mischief, Ned.

Dashwell   Pray, sir, how came you to use this trick to get into my service?

Loveday   Sir; the truth is honourable, yet harsh. Some friends of mine, having come to Hamburg, did report to me that Eugenia, since she had married you, had lost her virtuous inclinations. They supposed her disgusted with her marriage.

Dashwell   Ha!

Eugenia   I am neither beholden to them for their opinion, nor you for your belief.

Loveday   Madam, the truth of this slander I resolved to know, purposing never to marry, nor put trust in womankind if she was false. But now I am assured of her virtue and shall not return to Hamburg, but will remain in this City to look myself a wife.

Arabella   He has a quick invention.

Loveday   And now, sir, I hope you are satisfied, and give me your pardon.

Dashwell   Ay, ay. I must be satisfied. Have no thought you could design upon my wife, for it must be remembered you have the assets of but a single man. And she is married, sir, to an Alderman of the City and is thus secured. She has, sir, of her own, not one pound. And must needs be satisfied.

Doodle   Ay, ay Mr Dashwell. You may well scratch your head. For all your wife's virtue you'll see the fruits of her zeal upon your forehead ere long.

Dashwell   I would not yet change my wife's virtue for your wife's wit, Mr Alderman!

Doodle   But neighbour, I think, *consideratis considerandis*, the witty wife is the best of the three.

Dashwell   To that I answer in your own wife's dialect; No.

Wiseacres   Let all be settled then, and let's retire.

Peggy   But Nuncle-Husband . . . In London, dreams are dreams, I know. And gentlemen are not, you say, and so shall I. But Nuncle-Husband rats, I know, will not go up no trees.

Ramble   Here's trouble at its prettiest.

Peggy   So this gentleman is no rat-catcher, and if he be no gentleman neither, I can scarce believe he is a dream, 'cos there he stands and there he is.

Wiseacres   Child, listen now and listen well. I spoke to a conjuror before I went, to conjure up something before your eyes on purpose to make you think as you thought, and to conjure you asleep, and make you dream as you dreamt, and the face of this gentleman, who you had seen at his business in the street entered the dream as you fell sleeping, and the face of this gentleman entered the dream as you were roused. I tell you it was all but a dream, and the conjuror's doing.

Peggy   Then Uncle-Husband, speak to him to conjure up such a thing every night. And let me dream whenever I'm asleep.

Wiseacres   How she torments me.

Peggy   Indeed Uncle-Husband it seemed to me just for all the world as if I had been awake.

Wiseacres   Go. Get you into bed.

Peggy   Yes. But might the conjuror conjure so again?

Wiseacres   No. No, he has taught me now. I'll come and conjure myself.

Peggy   But can you conjure as well as he did?

Wiseacres *strikes* **Peggy**.

Wiseacres   Get you in! Take her away or I'll break your bones.

Aunt   Ah woe. We shall all be hanged. All hanged.

Exeunt **Peggy** *and* **Aunt**.

Dashwell   Now, Mr Alderman I hope you are convinced. This is what comes of a silly wife.

Wiseacres   Pray concern yourself with your zealous wife over there, who has been above at her devotions.

Doodle   Oh ha, ha, ha.

Wiseacres   And you, Brother Alderman, concern yourself with your witty wife who has done No disloyal thing and therefore has made you No cuckold!

Dashwell   I will not be moved to change my opinion. I have business in the morning. Wife. Good night, Gentlemen.

Doodle   Nor shall I be otherwise converted. Come wife. Good night.

Wiseacres   I shall never more trust a wife's simplicity, but from henceforth I'll keep her under lock and key.

Exeunt **Dashwell**, **Doodle** *and* **Wiseacres**.

Arabella   Sirs, I find you are the charitable men who have instructed the innocent.

Ramble   Madam; he is the man.

Arabella   And so he is. And Eugenia, I now spy the hypocrite under the veil of devotion. I always had too good an opinion of your wit to believe you were in earnest. Let us meet tomorrow, each confess the whole truth, and laugh heartily at the folly of our husbands.

Eugenia   With mine you see how smoothly matters went. He is a cuckold. Cudgelled yet content.

Arabella   And what will you with the fine Loveday?

Eugenia   He has my heart, and shall keep it always.

Dashwell (*within*)   Wife!

Loveday   Come, fair Eugenia. Let us take this chance and fly.

Eugenia   To where, my love?

Loveday   Where'er the sun shall rise each day, or every evening set its gleam upon our union.

Eugenia   Loveday, though I do cherish thee, my life is of this City, and this good house. Whilst your figure is fine, it is but paltry clothed. Love may embrace but ne'er sustain our lives. You must live thus; alone, yet in my heart.

Exit **Eugenia**.

Ramble   Now I find I have lost all my mistresses. Eugenia repulses me e'en more curtly than she did thee, Loveday. And you, Frank, have leapt into that lady's saddle before me. But I am sure of my pretty fool when e'er I can come at her.

Townley   'Til then, Ned, to the bottle?

Ramble   Ay; lead on. Madam . . .

Arabella   Struggle not for a fine farewell, sir. Take you your cue from the able Eugenia.

Ramble   Madam, as you would have it.

Exeunt **Ramble** *and* **Townley**.

Arabella   Think you, sir, that love is a greater thing than barter? Think you we women prize our hearts more cheaply than our determined lives?

Loveday   I do love the fair Eugenia.

Arabella   If you would play the game further, sir, it must be a solo hand.

Loveday   Your servant, madam, and ever hers.

Exit **Loveday**.

Epilogue

Spoken by Arabella.

And so, rouse up, ye drowsie cuckolds of our isle.
We see your aching hearts behind your forced smiles.
Haste hence like bees, back to your little hives
And drive away the hornets from your wives.
And like the noble deer does carry antlers high,
Be proud of the chase you would deny.
For what all men in their hidden tender hearts discern
Is the route they would travel, their wives have also learned.
And for each bold encounter in which men loudly glory
In some more secret place a gentler tryst plays out the
woman's story.
And what provoked the poet to this fury?
Perhaps his wit springs not from wisdom but from injury.
All lovers fall to earth that first seemed Heaven sent.
Passion, faith, devotion; all are quickly spent.
All's one; our sins upon us, we'll never be content.

End.

**Cleo, Camping,
Emmanuelle and Dick
(Cor, Blimey!)**

Cleo, Camping, Emmanuelle and Dick was first performed in the Lyttelton auditorium of the Royal National Theatre on 4 September 1998. The cast was as follows:

Sid	Geoffrey Hutchings
Kenneth	Adam Godley
Barbara	Samantha Spiro
Sally	Jacqueline Defferary
Imogen	Gina Bellman
Eddie	Kenneth MacDonald

Directed by Terry Johnson
Designed by William Dudley
Lighting by Simon Corder
Costumes by Nettie Edwards
Music by Barrington Pheloung
Sound by Adam Rudd

Characters

Sid, *forty, eventually late fifties.*
Kenneth, *late thirties, eventually early fifties.*
Barbara, *twenty-five, eventually late thirties.*
Sally, *eighteen, eventually mid-thirties. Petite, intense, in denial of herself.*
Imogen, *nineteen, eventually late twenties. Attractive.*
Eddie, *early thirties/late thirties. Huge East-Ender.*

Setting

A caravan, circa early sixties.

Act One

Cleo. 1964.

A spanking new caravan with all mod cons, including shower and toilet. A telephone line comes in through the window. Beyond, the austere prison camp walls of the Pinewood Studio buildings.

*Enter **Sally**, eighteen years old. She takes off her coat, drops her large bag, and looks around her. Sees a pile of a man's clothing and sets about tidying. Hanging the trousers she breaks off to smell the jacket, imagining the man. Then hesitates to pick up the crumpled underwear. Uses two fingers and holds the pants at arm's length. Enter **Sid**, broad-featured, big-nosed, about forty years old, costumed as Mark Antony.*

Sid   Afternoon.

Sally   Oh, hello.

Sid   If you want to fiddle about with my pants I'd be very grateful if you'd wait 'til I've got them on.

Sally   Sorry.

She offers them to him.

Sid   I don't want them; I know where they've been.

She puts the pants on the table.

Burning question is: where have *you* been?

Sally   What?

Sid   All my life.

Sally   Um. . .

Sid   I wish I'd met you sooner; a girl with your fearless attitude to underwear.

Sally   I'm Sally.

Sid   Saluté.

Sally   Pardon?

Sid   That's Shakespeare that is. That's Roman for 'Hello sweetheart'. I'm giving me Mark Antony.

Sally   I know. I'm your new dresser?

Sid   You'll be seeing a lot of me, then.

Sally   Oh . . . probably.

Sid   Definitely. You're in the nick of time too.

Sally   Am I?

Sid   There's a rip in me toga.

Sally   Oh, whoops.

Sid   Second-hand tat.

Sally   I'll take it to wardrobe, shall I?

Sid   No, it's not that bad. Just put a safety pin in it or something.

Sally   Right.

She rummages in her bag. He drinks some bourbon and dials the phone.

Sid   Long as it fits. I'm not a silk purse sort of performer. I'm more at home in a pig's ear.

She kneels in front of him to tack-stitch the skirt.

Sid   (*phone*) Freddie? Sid. I missed the third at Aintree, mate; check my accumulator, will you? What's a nice girl like you doing in a place like that?

Sally   Oh, it's Richard Burton's.

Sid   Is it? I've been using it for years.

Sally   The toga. Gwenda just said; she got a job-lot off *Cleopatra*. He probably tore this fending off the Egyptians.

Sid   Fending off the missus, more like. (*Phone.*) Freddie? Oh for fu . . . crying out loud. I'm going to take a contract out on that bloody Edridge. Do me a shilling each way on Twice Nightly, will you?

Sally   It could do with a good clean, I know that.

Sid   I beg your pardon?

Sally   The toga.

Sid   (*phone*) You what? Oh come on, Freddie; it's only a couple of bob. All right, all right. I'll send the girl round with it. Well, half an hour; she's got her hands full at the moment. Freddie, you're a gent. Whose missus, my missus? What did you tell her? Good thinking. I'll catch you later.

Puts the phone down.

While you're down there, could you do us a favour?

Sally   I've only got two hands.

Sid   So what's the problem?

Sally *stops, embarrassed.*

Sid   That's a lovely shade of pink. I could live with that.

Sally   I was warned about you.

Sid   Lies. All lies.

Sally   I took the job anyway because I was quite intrigued.

Sid   All true then. Every word of it.

Sally   I'm disappointed.

Sid   Vicious falsehoods, unfounded fabrications, vile, malicious rumours . . .

She bites the thread.

Whoop . . .

Sally   Finished.

Sid   One blinding moment there I'd have put five grand on the existence of God.

Sally   I'm your third dresser since Monday, aren't I?

Sid   I've been the victim of a strange lesbian conspiracy. I hope you're not one of them.

Sally   No, I'm not.

Sid   How'd you get the job then?

Sally   I wrote to the studios? Got the usual 'we'll put you on file'. I never really dreamed I'd really be here.

Sid   It's not that surprising. I seem to get through dozens of you.

Sally   Production office gave me your mail.

Sid   Dump it. Have you got a boyfriend?

Sally   Um . . . no.

Sid   Do you live on your own?

Sally   I live with my mum.

Sid   That's lovely. How is she?

Sally   Dead. Um . . . she died. (*She laughs a little hysterical laugh.*) She died in April. I'm sorry. I live on my own.

Sid   What about your dad?

Sally   My dad?

Sid   Your dad.

Sally   I don't know my dad.

Sid   That's a shame.

Sally   What should I do with this?

Sid   Oh, just chuck it away. (*Phone.*) Bernie? Sid. Can you lend me fifty quid? Don't get philosophical about it; I want to get a little present for Val and I've left me wallet at home. Good man. I'll send the new girl over. *Arrivederci.*

Puts down the phone.

Sally   You want me to just . . . throw it away?

Sid   That's right. Now I need you to get fifty quid off Bernie in dressing-room six and give Jim in number two the thirty I owe him.

Sally   Don't you read your fan mail?

Sid   Never; it's all from mad people. Then nip the twenty round to the Plough. Look for a blimp on a bar-stool.

Sally   And give him two shillings?

Sid   Give him the twenty.

Sally   Mmm?

Sid   Ten quid's a shilling. Two and six is twenty-five quid. Give him a couple of bob.

Sally   Twenty pounds.

Sid   Bright girl. Get going.

Sally   I don't think this is in my job description.

Sid   It's very short, your job description. Three words. Keep. Sid. Happy. That's not difficult to understand unless you're a lesbian.

Sally   I'm not a lesbian.

Sid   What are you doing tomorrow night, then?

Sally   Nothing. I mean no. Don't.

Sid   I'll never understand women your age. When I was *your* age I never understood women your age. Now I'm *my* age I don't understand women any age. Do you play poker?

Sally   Have done, why?

Sid   It whiles away the hours.

Sally   I'd better get your bet on.

Sid   No hurry. Freddie gets a bit jumpy, but he always lays the bet.

Sally   You gamble a lot?

Sid   Naaah.

Sally   What about the poker?

Sid   That's not for money. That's for fun. C'mon; couple of hands.

Sally   I'm supposed to be working.

Sid   Uh, uh; Keep Sid Happy.

Sally   But I've got this list of things to do.

Sid   You're probably right. We'd barely get started. Well, not barely enough, anyway.

Sally   Pardon?

Sid   Nothing.

Sally   I'd better get on then.

Sid *can't let her go.*

Sid   Would you like one of these?

Sally   What is it?

Sid   Passion fruit.

Sally   Looks horrible.

Sid   It's tropical. You can only get these down Covent Garden. Very exotic. Go on; have a taste.

Sally   No thanks.

Sid   You want to live for ever? Go on.

Sally   Oh, all right. If you insist.

Sid   Careful.

Sally   Ooh. Whoops.

Sid   Not like that.

Sally   All down my chin.

Sid   Here; let me show you. You can't just bite into it because the skin is very bitter. The flesh on the other hand is very sweet. So before you can eat you have to make a little incision like this, then open it up like this . . . there you go.

Sally   Oh.

Sid   Nice?

Sally   Lovely. Mmm. That is nice.

Sid *wipes a drip from her chin with his finger and tastes it.*

Sally   It's true, isn't it?

Sid   What about?

Sally   You.

Sid   Every word. Especially the rumours. You going to give us a kiss then?

Sally   I've only just walked through the door.

Sid   And I bless the moment. It's the watching you walk out again I'm having trouble with.

Sally   Well, I'll be back.

Sid   Not necessarily. Some of you I never see again.

Sally   Are you surprised?

Sid   I'll tell you what; give us a kiss and then we decide what sort of kiss it was. Quick hello, long goodbye, or the first of a few.

Sally   Yes, but then what?

Sid   But what but then what?

Sally   You have to think about the consequences.

Sid   I was. I do. I am.

Sally   No, but it's not . . .

Sid   What?

Sally   Just don't.

Sid   I can't help it. It's something about that little bit right there.

Sally   Stop it.

Sid   Shadowy little curve just there.

Sally   Don't.

Sid   Why not?

Sally   Because you mustn't.

Sid *leans forward to kiss her. Enter* **Kenneth**, *taller than* **Sid**, *fine-featured, aquiline nose, dressed as Julius Caesar.*

Kenneth   This is an absolute disgrace.

Sid   Gawd strewth.

Kenneth   I don't mind telling you I am OUTRAGED.

Sid   Gawd strewth.

Kenneth   I have been hostage to this bloody profession for more years than I care to remember but this takes the biscuit, this does. And I'm not talking your common old Rich Tea. I'm not talking mere Custard Cream. I am talking your full Garibaldi!

Sid   Don't bother to knock.

Kenneth   If I bothered to knock every time there was a danger of finding you *in flagrante* with some witless polony I'd have the door off its hinges.

Sally   We weren't doing anything.

Kenneth   Well, it's a first, dearie. You half his age and both of you vertical.

Sid   Keep your filthy innuendos to yourself.

Kenneth   Well then, you keep *your* filthy in-your-end-os off the unit.

Laughs like a machine-gun.

Sid   There's a lady present, shut your gob.

Sally   I'll see you later.

Sid   No, no, no. You stay put. You shove off.

Kenneth   No, I've got a bone to pick with you. And I'm not talking clavicle, I'm not talking metacarpal here, I'm talking ilium and scapula. I'm talking the sort of bone you give a Rottweiler and NEVER GET BACK. I don't know who you are but I'm sure you've got better things to do than stand there gawping at me.

Sid   She's not gawping at anyone.

Kenneth *flashes* Sally.

Sally   Oh.

Kenneth   Didn't see that then, did she?

Sally   Excuse me.

Exit **Sally**.

Sid   I'll see you later, sweetheart. You know what you are?

Kenneth   Completely disinterested in your opinion, for a start. You should know I've spoken to my agent, I shall speak to Peter at the wrap and I shall scream blue murder at Gerald the next time I vada his 'orrible eek. First A.D. said it was a tatty old caravan and more fool you but it's not, is it? This is not a tatty old caravan, this is a Merry Traveller.

Sid   Correct.

Kenneth   It's a Merry fucking Traveller.

Sid   It's my Merry Traveller.

Kenneth   That dressing-room block is falling to bits.

Sid   I know.

Kenneth   It's damp, it's drafty, the plaster's coming off the walls . . .

Sid   I know.

Kenneth   And there's no hot water!

Sid   Piping hot in here, mate. Ascot boiler, TV, all mod cons.

Kenneth   There's a Nubian handmaiden just sprained her ankle trying to get her black off in the sink.

Sid   Coloured boyfriend?

Kenneth   Yes, and that's about as witty as it gets with you, isn't it? Peurile double entendres.

Sid   That's twice as witty as a single entendre, mate, which is more your mark.

Sid   phones.

Kenneth   And that's a toilet. There's me 'olding it in all day and they've given you your own toilet. What have you ever done to deserve a toilet? Stupid question.

Sid (*phone*) Supporting Artists, mate.

Kenneth   And you've got a shower.

Sid (*phone*) Female, you twit.

Kenneth   They've given a shower to a man whose idea of personal hygiene is opening the window a snidge. This is an absolute disgrace. This is my ninth.

Sid   This is my ninth.

Kenneth   I was in the first. I was in Constable.

Sid   I was in Cabby.

Kenneth   Cabby was unadulterated shite.

Sid   I see; if I'm in it and you're not, it's shite.

Kenneth   Perfectly reasonable supposition.

Sid (*phone*) Hello, it's Sidney. Hello, poppet. I hear there's a Nubian slave in a bit of trouble. Hand her the phone, will you?

Kenneth   And how much are you on?

Sid   I knew that was coming.

Kenneth   I'm no longer prepared to prostitute my incandescent talent to this unspeakable tat if it's no longer favoured nations. Working for a pittance is only bearable if you're working for a pittance too.

Sid   They've always treated me very nicely. (*Phone.*) Hello, sweetheart, this is Sidney. I hear you're having trouble with your ablutions.

Kenneth   Hawtrey's so incensed he almost sobered up.

Sid (*phone*) I know, it's a right pit; that's why I've got my own facilities which include a Super Spa shower unit which is entirely at your disposal.

Kenneth   She's not that daft.

Sid   Right then. See you in a couple of minutes.

Kenneth   You know it's a short step from seducing the walk-ons to eating the props.

Sid   Never bothered me, mate; I hate to see either go to waste.

Kenneth   Don't think I don't know what you want this for.

Sid   Bit of peace and quiet as befits the temperament of a creative artiste.

Kenneth   Creative artiste? There's only one thing you ever create which is probably why they've given you the toilet. I know what you want this for.

Sid   Do us a favour and fall on your dagger.

Kenneth   There'll come a lunchtime you'll be busy in here, I'll pull your wheelchocks out and you'll bounce all the way to Sound Stage Four.

Sid   I watched the rough cut of *Spying*.

Kenneth   Yes?

Sid   That new girl. The blonde.

Kenneth   You'd be so lucky.

Sid   She seemed like a nice girl.

Kenneth   I thought *Spying* reached a level of cinematic sophistication hitherto unwitnessed in this neck of the woods. A sort of farce-noir, I thought. A genuine 'omage. And some real comic chemistry between the characters for once. What did you think?

Sid   I wasn't in it.

Kenneth   We noticed.

Sid   What's she like? The new girl?

Kenneth   Fluffed her first line. I made some vaguely caustic remark and she gave me a right bleeding mouthful. When we did the snog she said me beard was like Fenella's minge. I was quite taken with her.

Sid   She's got a lovely screen presence. Very good on camera. Very good delivery, good diction. Intelligent interpretation. And the sort of backside you can put your beer on as you walk past.

Kenneth   I'm sure I wouldn't know.

Sid   She'd have *you* beat in a mincing contest, mate. More's the bleeding miracle. How was the snog?

Kenneth   Well, I wouldn't confide this to a reprobate like you were it not bound to frustrate you beyond all reason, but from a purely objective point of view she was a good enough kisser to give me the half-hard.

Sid   You're joking.

Kenneth   Yes, the perverse pneumatics of desire never cease to astonish. Hasn't happened to me since Jim Dale went down the stairs on that hospital trolley.

Sid   Is she fixed?

Kenneth   She's getting married on Saturday.

Sid   What's today?

Kenneth   Thursday.

Sid   That's a bit tight.

Kenneth   Even for you.

Sid   Have you got her number?

Kenneth   Why would I want her number?

Sid   Those knockers. Man to man, or near-as-damn-it, are they real?

Kenneth   How's your wife, Sidney?

Sid   She's fine.

Kenneth   Doesn't it strike you in the least bit hypocritical, posing as a devoted family man whilst incessantly propositioning these poor girls?

Sid   Not my fault, mate; long as they keep giving me the Romantic lead, I'll keep doing the research.

Someone knocks on the door.

Imogen   Hello?

Sid   Now make yourself scarce. *Entrez-vous.*

Enter **Imogen**. *Tall, attractive, half blacked-up.*

Sid   Step right up.

Imogen   Hello.

Sid   Watch your step there; it's a bit perilous.

Kenneth   Yes, you can say that again. Leave your knickers at the door if you're coming in here, dearie.

Imogen   I'm Imo.

Sid   I'm Sidney.

Imogen   Hello.

Sid   This is Kenneth; he was about to leave.

Imogen   Oh, hello, Kenneth. I think you're *really* funny.

Sid   Well, that makes two of you.

Imogen   No, you make me laugh, you really do. You're my favourite. (*Pause.*) And you are too. You're both my favourites. You really make me laugh. I only have to look at you. Both.

Kenneth   Your immaculate taste is matched solely by your critical discernment.

Imogen   Thank you.

Sid   Make yourself at home.

Imogen   Thank you. Ooh. It's a very amusing script, isn't it?

Kenneth   I'd say its overt humour resonates in inverse proportion to its inherent dramatic qualities, yes.

Sid   You're right; it's a clever script.

Imogen   Saluté.

Sid *laughs with her.* **Kenneth** *silent.*

Imogen   Infamy, infamy . . .

She laughs again, **Kenneth** *sneers approval.* **Sid** *silent.*

Kenneth   Yes. He nicked it, of course. Gets all his best gags from old radio scripts. Denis Norden should sue.

Sid   I'll catch you later then.

Kenneth   If you think I'm being fobbed off just so you can get your end away, you've another thing coming.

Imogen   Get your what away?

Sid   Take no notice. (*To* **Kenneth**.) Shove off.

Kenneth   I want to know how you got ensconced in a Merry Traveller.

Sid   Don't mind us. Professional banter.

Kenneth   Quite frankly, this favouritism is a fucking disgrace.

Sid   Would you like a little something to ward off the chill?

Imogen   Oh, no thank you. I don't drink.

Sid   Dontcha? That's . . . me neither.

Imogen   Bit of a health freak, I'm afraid.

Sid   Very wise.

Imogen   Vegetarian too.

Sid   That's amazing; so am I.

Imogen   Really? What a coincidence. What sign are you?

Kenneth   A406 Chiswick Roundabout.

Sid   Shuddup. What sign are *you*?

Imogen   I'm Libra.

Sid   I don't believe it.

Kenneth   Neither do I.

Sid   It's not often you meet a fellow librarian.

Imogen   I'd really like to get all this off.

Sid   Likewise, I'm sure. We'll give you a bit of privacy here; *voilà*.

He cantilevers the wardrobe doors to partition the interior.

Imogen   Oh, that's very clever, isn't it?

Sid   Shower's through here. On and off. Hot and cold.

Imogen   Fabulous. This is really sweet of you.

Sid   Can't have you going home like that.

Imogen   See you in a while, then.

Sid   Take your time, sweetheart.

She shutters herself into the ablution compartment.

Kenneth   Vegetarian?

Sid   I've eaten vegetables.

Kenneth   Lambs to the slaughter with you, isn't it?

Sid   You've got a mouth like a sewer and I couldn't care less, but when there's a lady in the room you keep your filthy gob shut, all right?

Kenneth   Are you even slightly conscious that your urge to protect that poor girl's honour is somewhat at odds with your shameless desire to shag her?

Sid   Lovely backside.

Kenneth   I thought not.

Sid *looks at his watch.*

Sid   Strewth. I'm missing the four o'clock.

Turns on a portable TV.

It amazes me, a bloke like you. How you can't appreciate a bird like that is beyond me.

Kenneth   Spare me the pity. Those sporadic pleasures of the flesh I do enjoy I have no intention of sharing with anyone else.

Imogen *cries out orgasmically, off.*

Sid   What's up?

Imogen   It's cold.

Sid   Turn the dooh-dah.

Imogen   I have turned the dooh-dah.

Sid   You have to turn the electric on; I'll show you.

Imogen   No, wait!

Sid   Close your eyes and I'll come in.

Kenneth   Under starter's orders.

Imogen *in bathtowel, pops her head round.*

Imogen   You have to what?

Kenneth   And they're off.

Sid   Little switch just there. Little red light. It has to heat up. Come and have a drink while you're waiting.

Imogen   No, that's all right; I've got to . . . um and er – all sorts of things. I'm going to the premiere of *Dr Zhivago* tonight.

Sid   That's nice, who with?

Imogen   Oh, I never know 'til I get in the limo. Lovely.

She shutters herself in.

Kenneth   Not exactly your intellectual equal, is she? Which about puts her on par with a jellyfish.

Sid   Number six. On the rails.

Kenneth   It's not the money. I'd be mortified to take a penny more for peddling this sort of tosh.

Sid   Come on, you stupid sodding mare.

Kenneth   It's the tacit acknowledgment of one's contribution . . .

Sid   Don't go round, go through, go . . . Oh, Jesus.

Kenneth   A bit of appreciation, that's all I'm asking. A bit of gratitude.

Sid   You hopeless bloody mare. That's not a racehorse, that's three hundredweight of bleeding catfood, that is.

Punches the TV and turns it off.

Kenneth   Spending any time whatsoever in your company leaves one with a giddying sense of *déjà vu*.

Sid   Can you lend us a pony?

Kenneth   You see what I mean?

Sid   Please?

Kenneth   You already owe me fifty.

Sid   Well, you're daft enough, then.

Kenneth   If you ever won, I'd understand it.

Sid   If every bird you tried to shag said yes, there'd be no point chasing 'em, would there?

Kenneth   If every bird you tried to shag said yes, you wouldn't be able to chase them; you'd be in a rest home.

Sid   I can't help it; I love those little gee-gees. Go on; lend us a hundred and fifty.

Kenneth   No.

Sid   I thought we were mates.

Kenneth   I'm nobody's mate, thank you.

Sid   We go back a long way, you and I.

Kenneth   That's as maybe, but we've nothing in common.

Sid   Nonsense.

Kenneth   Name me one thing.

Sid   Well . . .

Kenneth   You see.

Sid   Hawtrey. We've both been goosed by Hawtrey.

Kenneth   Yes, but you punched him.

Sid   He's thrown up on both of us.

Kenneth   That's your definition of 'mates', is it? Fifteen years verbal abuse, then five minutes rinsing chow mein off each other's trousers? Hardly the Musketeers, is it?

Sid   We never fancied Hawtrey, *but* . . .

Both   . . . we both got screwed by Hancock.

Kenneth   True.

Sid   Bastard.

Kenneth   All for one and every man for himself.

Sid   I only need a monkey.

Kenneth   No.

Sid   No wonder he dropped you.

Kenneth   He dropped you too.

Sid   He dropped you before he dropped me.

Kenneth   But he told me to my face.

Sid   I passed him the other day. I was driving down Piccadilly. He crossed the street ahead of me. Looked as if he hadn't slept for a week. Unshaven . . . he looked dreadful, quite dreadful. So full of liquor he didn't see me. I got the car parked but he'd gone.

Kenneth   Serves him right.

Sid   Have you no compassion?

Kenneth   Yes, and I'm saving it all for myself.

Barbara (*off*)   Hello-oh? Anybody home?

Sid   Gawd blimey.

Barbara   Kenneth?

Kenneth   Who is it?

Sid   It's her. Double-O whatsit.

Enter **Barbara**. *Short, blonde, buxom. Outrageous wardrobe accentuating her wiggle. Twenty-five years old.*

Barbara   It's only me.

Kenneth   Oh, hello.

Barbara   Just popped in to say hello. Am I interrupting?

Kenneth   I can't imagine what.

Barbara   Give us a snog, then.

Kenneth   Off camera? I should cocoa.

Barbara   Mmmmwha!

Kenneth   Charmed, I'm sure.

Barbara   Hello. You're Sidney.

Sid   Yes.

Barbara   I'm Barbara.

Sid   Yes.

Pause. **Sid** *is besotted.*

Barbara   It's really nice to meet you.

Sid   Yes.

Barbara   Thirty-six C.

Sid   What?

Barbara   You'll get used to them. Have a good butcher's. I don't mind a good ogle, it's all those surreptitious glances drive me mad. I get double vision just trying to establish eye contact.

Sid   Right.

Barbara   Am I stopping you getting undressed?

Kenneth   Chance'd be a fine thing.

Barbara   He's got good knees, hasn't he?

Kenneth   I don't wish to venture an opinion.

Barbara   You've got good knees.

Sid   Thank you.

Barbara   You can tell a lot about a man from his knees. Only good reason for getting his trousers off.

Kenneth   Good God in heaven, he's blushing.

Sid   Shut your face. Would you like a drink?

Barbara   That'd be nice.

Sid   Have a sit down.

Barbara   I can't stay long. I only popped in to give Kenny an invite.

Kenneth   You should paint the walls that colour.

Barbara   Leave him alone.

Kenneth   I hadn't expected to see you here. I heard they offered you Second Slave Girl and you told them to shove it.

Barbara   I did n'all. Only three lines and two of them were feeds. No, they're doing some re-recording on *Spying*. I had to pop in to dub me 'buttocks'.

Kenneth   I told 'em they'd have to dub your 'buttocks'.

Barbara   I had to say 'bottom' instead. You'd think that would lip-synch, wouldn't you, but it was a real sodding effort.

Kenneth   Buttocks.

Barbara   Bottom.

Kenneth *mouths 'Buttocks' as* **Barbara** *says:*

Barbara   Bottom.

Kenneth *mouths 'Bottom' as* **Barbara** *says:*

Barbara   Buttocks.

Barbara   Bollocks. That'd fit. But 'bottom', honestly.

Kenneth   I told Gerald he wouldn't get his 'buttocks' passed, in or out of context. But he rattled on about comic integrity. I told him, it doesn't matter how funny buttocks are, if Rothwell insists on rubbing our noses in 'em every five minutes the Lord Chamberlain is fully justified in his opinion of us as purveyors of utter filth.

Sid   Here we go.

Kenneth   Yes, well, I'm sick to death of serving the fantasies of that inefficient hack! For all our expertise we're producing culture far cruder than the bloody Tudors. Our entertainments echo our dilemmas. Permanent values are being utterly neglected, and the devouring grasp of the cheap gag has strangled the spirit.

Barbara   Oh, don't bang on, Kenny. Have an invite. It's not a big do or anything; it's just nip in the registry and pop down the boozer afterwards.

Sid   Can I come?

Barbara   Er . . . yes, if you like. You can come to the pub.

Sid   I love a wedding.

Barbara   It's not really a wedding. Haven't got time for all that palaver. It's just a way of saying, you know; me and him.

Sid   No honeymoon then?

Barbara   Sod off; he's not getting away with no honeymoon. Can't decide where to go though.

Kenneth   Madeira's nice, apparently.

Barbara   Where the cake comes from?

Kenneth   It's where Kenneth Horne goes. Round the Horne to Maderia.

Barbara   Can you drink the water?

Kenneth   I don't know. I don't do foreign. I did foreign in the war; I shall never do foreign again.

Barbara   That's why you're so pasty.

Kenneth   I'll have you know men of this complexion built the Empire.

Barbara   You could do with a bit of sun.

Kenneth   On this pittance?

Barbara   Ronnie deserves a nice holiday after Wandsworth nick.

Kenneth   How's he settling?

Barbara   Oh, not bad. I met him at the gates, you know. We got a taxi back to the flat. I'd had the whole place newly redecorated.

Kenneth   Did he like it?

Barbara   Well, he liked the bedroom ceiling.

Sid   What was he in for?

Barbara   He was fitted up. Receiving. I ask you. Ronnie; receiving. Doping greyhounds is about his mark. I daren't use anything out of the bathroom cabinet, and I've got a fridge full of mince.

Sid   I've just realised who we're talking about. He knocks about with the Krays, doesn't he?

Barbara   No, he doesn't. I do.

Sid   Oh.

Barbara   And they're not up for discussion, all right?

Sid   Fair enough.

Barbara   Co-ercion my arse. The only bit of coercion I know about was the premiere of *Sparrows* when they coerced five hundred people to cheer me all down the Old Kent Road, so I'm having no one knocking 'em, all right?

Sid   I wasn't knocking 'em.

Barbara   Good.

Sid   You can tell 'em I wasn't.

Barbara   Right.

Sid   Don't tell 'em I was 'cos I wasn't.

Barbara   All right.

Sid   Don't mention me at all, in fact.

Barbara   Oh, give over. Are you married, Sid?

Sid   Married alive.

Barbara   Long time?

Sid   Seventeen years.

Barbara   Ahh.

Sid   And a few before that.

Barbara   Years?

Sid   Wives. Take my advice; don't get married. Just find someone you don't like and buy them a house.

Barbara (*laughs*)   No, don't. Ronnie's been married before. He was married when I met him. I was with him nine months before I found out; he was working us in shifts.

Sid   This is the man you're going to marry?

Barbara   I went berserk. Have you ever been unfaithful, Sidney?

Sid   Naah.

Sound of running water off, and a sensual sigh from **Imogen**.

Kenneth   And her backside's more impressive than her timing.

Barbara   You cheeky devil; you've got a girl in there.

Sid   I'm doing her a favour.

Barbara   Is that what your wife would think?

Sid   My wife trusts me. You trust yours?

Barbara   He won't mess around again.

Sid   A leopard cannot change its spots.

Barbara   No, but it can have its balls cut off.

Phone rings, **Sid** *answers it.*

Sid   (*phone*) Hello? Yes, I'll tell him. Your presence is required in the Holy Temple of the Vestal Virgins. And a lot of good it'll do 'em.

Kenneth   Oh, it's all utter pap.

Sid   What about that two bob?

Kenneth   I haven't got two bob.

Sid   Come on, mate, I'm in deep manure.

Kenneth   Don't mate me.

Sid   Val's going to kill me.

Kenneth   I shouldn't worry; she's bound to be acquitted. Come on. I wouldn't advise you to plant your derrière here; you're not safe.

Sid   She's safe as houses in here.

Kenneth   Safe as houses in Dresden. If you stay here he'll have his hand in your purse in thirty seconds, and that'll be the hand nearest daylight.

Sid   Have another drink. Put your feet up.

Kenneth   Up where he likes 'em, keeping his ears warm.

Sid   Will you shut it!

Barbara   Oh, don't argue. I've got to go anyway. It was very nice to meet you.

Sid   *Enchanté*, I'm sure. Come again, any time.

Barbara   Thank you. You're a sweetheart.

She pecks him on the cheek.

Barbara   Bye, then.

Sid   Bye.

Kenneth *and* **Barbara** *leave the van and cross the lot.* **Sid** *gazes after them, prancing from one window to the next. Still hidden,* **Imogen** *starts to sing 'For All We Know'.*

Kenneth   Evening, ladies.

Kenneth *lifts his skirt. Some girls out of view scream and giggle.*

Barbara   Oh, put it away, please.

Kenneth   Beauty is in the eye of the beholder, so one feels beholden to give 'em an eyeful.

Kenneth *laughs his machine-gun laugh, and they disappear.* **Sid** *listens until the phone rings.*

Sid   (*phone*) Yeh? Hello, Bernie. Well . . . why not? No, no, mate; she's new; she's got the wrong end of the stick. She's going to Freddie to pick up some winnings. I need a bit from you 'cause I want to get a little present for Val. Bernie, would I lie to you? All right, but listen, mate; it's a dead cert and when it comes in I'm gonna get Val something really special. What do you mean, a divorce? Bernie . . . !

He puts the phone down and drinks. He seems pressured. **Imogen** *finishes singing and emerges.*

Imogen   Hello.

Sid   Hello.

Imogen   Everyone gone?

Sid   Yep.

Imogen   You've got lipstick.

Sid   Whoops.

He wipes off **Barbara***'s lipstick.*

Imogen   She's nice. She gave me a lovely smile earlier.

Sid   Yeh. She's got a nice smile.

He folds the tissue carefully and puts it in his pocket.

Imogen   She's very friendly for a short person. She's not a real blonde though. Although that's quite a good thing, because real blondes are usually much stupider than artificial ones; had you noticed that?

Sid   I had as a matter of fact.

Imogen   And far less aggressive in my experience. You like her, don't you?

Sid   . . . I'm very affable.

Imogen   Is that your type? Short blondes?

Sid   Absolutely. Unless there's an r in the month.

Imogen   It's May.

Sid   Or a y. That was a very nice song you were singing.

Imogen   My father used to sing it.

Sid   You get on well with your father?

Imogen   Daddy's dead. He died.

Sid   Oh, I'm sorry. Did you love him?

Imogen   Um . . . well, yes. I loved him very much.

Sid   That's nice. Do you like fruit?

Imogen   Yes.

Sid   Want some?

Imogen   Um . . .

Sid   Have some.

He offers her a different exotic fruit.

Imogen   Thank you.

Sid   That's a passion fruit.

Imogen   Is it?

Sid   That's right.

Imogen   Why?

Sid   I've no idea. Try it.

Imogen   I've never had a passion fruit.

Sid   Well, you can't just bite into it because the skin is very bitter. The flesh on the other hand is very sweet. So before you can eat you have to pull back the skin like so, and there's the flesh, look.

Imogen   Wow.

Sid   Those taste buds tingling?

Imogen   It's beautiful inside.

Sid   Isn't it? In you go.

Imogen   Mmm. Wow.

Sid   Use your tongue.

Imogen   I am.

Sid   How's that?

Imogen   It's . . .

Sid   Mmm?

Imogen   Delicious. Mmph; I'm all wet.

Sid   Stay that way; it gets better. Move over.

Imogen   Do you want some?

Sid   No, you enjoy yourself.

Imogen   Here.

Sid   You temptress. Cor.

Imogen   Good?

Sid   That's good, isn't it?

Imogen   That's very good.

Sid   Here; let me.

Imogen   No, no; you.

Sid   No no, after you.

They feed each other. He wipes the corner of her mouth with his finger and tastes her.

Imogen   Ooh. I'm all sticky.

Sid   You taste good.

Imogen   Have you got a tissue?

Sid   Who needs tissues? Here.

He turns her head towards him and leans towards her. **Barbara** *enters.*

Barbara   Are you decent? I suddenly remembered I'd forgotten something.

Sid   What was that then?

Barbara   I can't remember. Oh, hello.

Imogen   Hello.

Barbara   Are you Imogen?

Imogen   Yes, hello.

Barbara   There's a driver looking for you.

Imogen   Oh, heavens. I'm late. All sticky.

Barbara   Whoops.

Imogen   Thanks for the shower and the thingy.

Sid   Any time.

Imogen   Bye, then.

Barbara   Bye, love.

Imogen   Bye, Sid.

Sid   Bye bye.

Imogen   Byyye.

Exit **Imogen**.

Barbara   Now. Keys.

She finds them in her hand.

Barbara   Oh, here they are. Silly me.

Sid   You're jumping to conclusions.

Barbara   You're old enough to be her father.

Sid   Precisely; I was taking a paternal interest.

Barbara   You were taking a liberty. Poor girl's got enough stars in her eyes; she doesn't need one in her knickers.

Sid   Does your husband-to-be mind?

Barbara   Mind what?

Sid   You practising on other men.

Barbara   Cheeky sod.

Sid   Mind your language.

Barbara   Mind your own bloody business.

Sid   I can't abide a woman cursing.

Barbara   I can't abide a womaniser.

Sid   It's come to something when a bloke can't have an intelligent chat with a girl . . .

Barbara   A girl can't have an intelligent chat with two tongues in her mouth!

Sid   This is tragic. A lovely woman like you. Put a ring on your finger, suddenly you're every man's missus.

Barbara   One man's missus.

Sid   God help him.

Barbara   I'll drink to that.

Sid   I've got whisky, vodka, gin . . .

He opens a wardrobe to reveal an extraordinary selection.

Barbara   Fucking hell.

Sid (*winces*)   Oy.

Barbara   I mean; my, my, what a marvellous selection of beverages.

Sid   How about a Martini?

Barbara   Does anyone get out of here vertical?

Sid   You've got the wrong idea about me.

Barbara   That's me and the entire British Isles then.

Sid   No no no; you're mistaking the man for the screen persona! I may come across as lewd and licentious, but in actual fact I'm very respectful of the opposite sex.

Barbara   Pull the other one.

Sid   I was trying to.

Barbara   I know you were!

Sid   I ask you; is this the face of a reprobate? Secret of a good Martini is to make it relatively dry. Good measure of gin, nice little olive, then make sure it's had a good look at the other bottle. Cheers.

Barbara   Oh, all right. Just the one. I do know what you mean; people take one look at me and make all sorts of presumptions.

Sid   All of 'em insulting, all of 'em wrong. It's a disgrace.

Barbara   You're right. I'm sorry.

Sid   God help him.

Barbara   God help him. He'll need it. When he went inside I wasn't as well known as I am now, and he finds that hard. We've tried going back to the old places, but there's always someone with a grudge along the bar. One bloke asked me to sign a ten-bob note then blew his nose on it. That was the end of his nose. Be warned. Ronnie's sense of justice is always strictly anatomical.

Sid   I've told you; if you're fixed up I respect that. If you're getting married I'm not interested. Would you like some fruit?

Barbara   No, I'm fine.

Sid   Have a piece of fruit; it's good for you.

Barbara   I'm not really bothered.

Sid   I'm not talking Coxes here; I'm talking serious fruit.

Barbara   What sort of fruit?

Sid   Ever tried one of these?

He offers her yet another type of exotic fruit.

Barbara   What is it?

Sid   Passion fruit.

Barbara   Where's it come from?

Sid   Tahiti.

Barbara   I don't think I'd like it.

Sid   Well, you won't know that 'til you've tried it, will you?

Barbara   Oh, go on then.

Sid   You can't just bite into it because the skin is very bitter. The flesh on the other hand is very sweet. So before you can eat you have to pull back the skin like so, and there's the flesh, look.

Barbara   Oh, it's all pink.

Sid   If it could talk it'd be saying eat me.

Barbara   Give me the knife.

Sid   No, no.

Barbara   I want to cut a bit off.

Sid   You can't do that. That'd be sacrilege. Watch. Do as I do. Like this. Then like this.

Barbara   Oh, I see; like cunnilingus.

He chokes. She gets up, passing the fruit bowl.

And when you've finished that . . . have a banana.

And leaves him holding one.

Blackout.

Act Two

Scene One

Camping. 1969.

The caravan is a little the worse for wear; cluttered with years of use. It now stands in the middle of a field near Ruislip. It's raining heavily. **Kenneth** *and* **Sid** *sit miserably in front of a single-bar fire.*

Kenneth   We're never going to get out of this field.

Sid   Count your blessings.

Kenneth   We're going to sink without trace.

Sid   Go sit on the bus, then.

Kenneth   No longer welcome. I irritate the lesser mortals.

Sid   You irritate me and all. Get back to the bus.

Kenneth   I would if you didn't owe me three hundred quid.

Sid   If I didn't owe you three hundred quid you'd have to, mate. You wouldn't be here in the first place. If everyone I owed money to took this sort of advantage, we *would* bloody sink.

Kenneth   They're fools to themselves.

Sid   And don't disparage my generosity; it cost me a fiver to get Horace to run a cable from the genny.

Kenneth   My fiver.

Sid   Not your fiver.

Kenneth   Someone's fiver.

Sid   Your fiver's long gone, mate. You couldn't lend us five hundred, could you?

Kenneth   Five hundred?!

Sid   I've had a bit of a dodgy run.

Kenneth   That's half your entire fee

Sid   There's a dead cert at Newbury.

Kenneth   You had a dead cert at Aintree last week. It fell at the third and they shot it. Don't come much deader than that.

Sid   Come on, mate, I'm desperate.

Kenneth   It's the lavatory gets up my nose.

Sid   Here we go again.

Kenneth   You'd think with my arse I'd be the one to get given me own lavatory.

Sid   You're not the only one with an arse.

Kenneth   Bitter bloody misery it is, my fundament.

Sid   How big are they, these legendary haemorrhoids of yours?

Kenneth   I can't imagine what possible concern that's ever going to be of yours.

Sid   Me neither, mate.

Kenneth   I shall survive without your concern and can certainly do without your curiosity.

Sid   Then stop banging on about them.

Kenneth   Bum trouble's just a dirty joke to the likes of you, because you've never suffered. You wouldn't know and haven't the wit to imagine the abject creeping horror of an ailing anus.

Sid   Will you give it a rest!

Kenneth   The agony of it, the endless suffering, the wretched torment . . .

Sid   You don't know what suffering is, mate; I've had piles the size of tomatoes for twenty bloody years.

Kenneth   First I've heard of it.

Sid   That's because I don't dish 'em up every bloody mealtime. Unlike you I don't feel the urge to bring every conversation round to my backside. I've got piles'd put yours right in the shade, mate.

Kenneth   You are quite unbelievably competitive.

Sid   Five hundred quid.

Kenneth   What?

Sid   Five hundred quid I've got twice as many as you, and half as many to the pound.

Kenneth   This is all part of your pitifully desperate desire to prove yourself somehow superior to myself. So demonstrably hopeless a quest it was inevitable it would come down to arseholes eventually.

Sid   You want a butcher's?

Kenneth   I most certainly do not.

Sid   Then let's change the bleeding subject.

Kenneth   Didn't have you down for bum trouble. Who are you under?

Sid   How's that?

Kenneth   Which consultant; Berry or Hadfield?

Sid   Me GP.

Kenneth   Your GP? You can't trust some GP off Gunnersbury Avenue with your anus. You want your bum in the hands of a Harley Street man. You need Dr Berry. Berry's the man you need. I've gone off Hadfield.

Sid   Why?

Kenneth   One tends to go off bum doctors very suddenly. For reasons it's scarcely necessary to go into. How bad are they?

Sid   Torture.

Kenneth   Eleven in the morning?

Sid   Living hell. And purgatory about . . .

Both   . . . four o'clock.

Kenneth   I know.

Sid   Why is that?

Kenneth   The bowel moves in mysterious but predictable ways. You shouldn't do breakfast.

Sid   I can't not do breakfast.

Kenneth   And curry! God in his heaven, you eat curry.

Sid   I can't not eat curry.

Kenneth   I daren't even glance at a dhansak. A chilli con carne, possibly, at lunchtime, with plenty of yoghurt.

Sid   Yoghurt? I'd rather be dead.

Kenneth   Eat another vindaloo and you might be.

Sid   I've had some worrying mornings, admittedly. I have to admit it can get a bit lonely.

Kenneth   You had the elastic bands?

Sid   I don't want to talk about it.

Kenneth   The deep icy probing . . . the sharp prick of that horrible hypodermic.

Sid   Yes, thank you. That's enough.

Kenneth   The twang of rubber as it grips the doomed fillip of your mutating organ . . .

Sid   Will you shut your face!

Kenneth   Then he says keep an eye out for them! I should cocoa. I've not looked down a toilet for forty years and I don't intend to start now.

Sid   Please, let's change the subject. Do you want a gin?

Kenneth   Don't mind if I do. Have you got a bitter lemon?

Sid   No, I just had a shower.

They laugh.

Sid   To suffering.

Kenneth   Yes.

Sid   In silence.

Kenneth   I'd always believed you and I had nothing in common. One of the touchstones of my very existence has crumbled to dust. All the Greeks had 'em you know. All the great philosophers.

Sid   That's because they spent too much time with their heads up their arses.

Kenneth   Hancock had 'em.

Sid   You don't kill yourself because your backside hurts.

Kenneth   Well, it would be pretty ridiculous.

Sid   I wish I'd caught up with him, that day in Piccadilly.

Kenneth   Wouldn't have made a blind bit of difference.

Sid   Don't you believe it; things like that, chance encounters, change people's lives.

Kenneth   But to do it in Australia. Why Australia?

Sid   You ever been?

Kenneth   No.

Sid   Makes perfect sense. See Venice and die, see Melbourne and top yourself.

Kenneth   The man was mediocre. He slammed the door on everyone responsible for his success, and when he realised what he'd done, he slammed it on himself.

Sid   You know what you are; you're a misanthrope, that's what you are.

Kenneth   Define misanthrope.

Sid   You.

Kenneth   But what's it mean?

Sid   I don't know.

Kenneth   I didn't think you did.

Sid   Bernie said you're a misanthrope and Bernie's a scholar.

Kenneth   Well, he's right. I've never met anyone who wasn't running around trying to make sense of their lives by inflicting their sexual organs on everyone else. Or mewling in despair at the realisation they're nothing more than a rotting bag of bones.

Sid   I'll put you out in the rain again.

A knock on the door.

Barbara   Kenneth, are you in there?

Sid   He's always in here.

Barbara *enters in mac and bikini with green feet.*

Barbara   They've had to stop; they found a fish in the gate. Look at my feet.

Sid   Impossible.

Barbara   There wasn't any grass in the field, so they've sprayed the mud green. There's four props boys in sou'westers up an elm tree sticking leaves on. One of them fell out; he looks like the Jolly Green Giant. I'm dying for a wee.

Sid   I wouldn't go in there if I were you.

Barbara   Why not?

Kenneth   Sidney's left possibly his greatest performance in it.

Barbara   Oh, charming.

Sid   Well, for God's sake; it's my toilet.

Barbara   You could have flushed it.

Sid   The little flap's stuck.

Barbara   Do you think it's like this at Universal Studios?

Kenneth   I'm still damp from this morning.

Sid   You wouldn't be damp if you'd stop messing about and got on with it.

Kenneth   I was enjoying myself.

Sid   Acting's not something you enjoy. It's something you do and go home.

Barbara   What's got up your nose?

Kenneth   I corpsed him.

Sid   You did not corpse me!

Kenneth   You grinned.

Sid   I did not grin, I grimaced.

Kenneth   He had a bet on with the clapper-loader he wouldn't go to a second take all week.

Sid   I don't need a second take.

Barbara   Unless it's snogging.

Sid   And you call yourself a professional!

Kenneth   I certainly do.

Sid   A professional does not mug on his reverses.

Barbara   He always mugs on his reverses. Sends me right up.

Sid   It's undisciplined.

Barbara   It's funny.

Sid   Which is more than I can say for his close-ups.

Kenneth   There's nothing wrong with my close-ups. There's a laugh in every one of them; I make sure of it.

Sid   I've noticed. Never mind the sense of the scene.

Kenneth   Oh bugger the sense; it's the delivery they laugh at.

Sid   I'm an actor, mate.

Kenneth   You're a cheap vaudevillian, whereas I'm a classically trained thesbian. I have worked with Orson Welles.

Sid   So have I.

Kenneth   I have played Shakespeare.

Sid   Well, so have I.

Kenneth   I have read a book.

Sid *sniffs*. **Kenneth** *wins*.

Kenneth   I have sat on the steps of the Coliseum and debated the nature of man with Sophocles, I have.

Kenneth   farts.

Barbara   Kenny.

Sid   Bloody hell.

Barbara   Honestly. How you expect to maintain a decent working relationship with people I have no idea.

Kenneth   Rudolph Valentino was a farter. His leading ladies never complained.

Barbara   They were silent films.

Kenneth   I consider it one of my more singular accomplishments that I can display an uncommon degree of eloquence . . . (*Another little fart.*) . . . from both ends simultaneously.

Barbara   Oh, take it outside, for heaven's sake!

Sid   And don't come back.

Kenneth   I'm not leaving you two alone.

Barbara   Why not?

Kenneth   You ought to watch it. In and out of here all the time. People are beginning to talk.

Sid   What people?

Barbara   Who?

Kenneth   The entire unit, that's who.

Barbara   Well, not that it's any of their business, but I happen to be a happily married woman, all right?

Kenneth   That why you blubbed all the way to the registry, muttering you'd rather be shot?

Barbara   I might have had a decent marriage if I hadn't had a lousy honeymoon.

Kenneth   Wasn't my fault you had a lousy honeymoon.

Barbara   How do you know I had a lousy honeymoon?

Kenneth   I was there.

Barbara   Precisely. If you hadn't been there, Kenny, perhaps it wouldn't have been so lousy. Perhaps if your mother hadn't been there I might have had a few hours alone with my husband. Perhaps if you and your mother and your sister hadn't been there, there might have been a moment's silence during which we might have heard a parrot or something.

Kenneth   You had a lousy honeymoon because you booked us all on a cheap package flight which dumped us next to nowhere so we had to get a packet boat from hell to Funchal in a force eight gale from which I for one have never recovered!

Barbara   You shouldn't have eaten your dinner with the boat at forty-five degrees.

Kenneth   I paid for it, I'll bloody well eat it.

Barbara   There were fifty-year-old sailors threw up just watching you.

Kenneth   And it rained all bloody week. I wish I'd never invited meself.

Barbara   I thought you might distract us from the slow realisation we'd actually done it.

Kenneth   It smells in here. It smells of rot. I'm going to see if the caterers are still afloat.

Kenneth *leaves.*

Barbara   Christ, I'm cold. Give us a Scotch.

Sid   I dreamed about you last night.

Barbara   Did you?

Sid   No, you wouldn't let me. Whenever you walk in the room . . .

Barbara   Don't start.

Sid   I can't help it.

Barbara   I can't handle it.

Sid   I know I'm old, I'm out of condition, I've never been a looker . . .

Barbara   Stop it.

Sid   Self-pity, I know, that's not attractive in a man.

Barbara   Do you have to jump in the deep end every time there's only two of us. Couldn't we talk about the weather or something?

Sid   It's raining. I love you.

Barbara   No you don't. You fancy me and I'm having none of it and that's the end of the matter.

Sid   I love you.

Barbara   Sidney, how old are you?

Sid   Fifty-two.

Barbara   Fifty-six. How old am I?

Sid   Seventeen.

Barbara   I'm thirty-two. Now what's that about, Sidney?
Why can't you fancy someone your own age?

Sid   Have you seen the women my age? Have you kissed
one? Their lips go all furry. The back of their thighs go all
puddeny.

Barbara   Sidney.

Sid   I like 'em young. It's a sexual whatsname, innit?
Preference. You don't go around telling Ken and Charlie to
find a good woman, do you? But you treat me like a dirty
old sod.

Barbara   You are a dirty old sod.

Sid   Is that why you don't fancy me?

Barbara   Sid, I don't not fancy you . . .

Sid   You don't not?

Barbara   I love you to bits; you know that.

Sid   So you do fancy me?

Barbara   I didn't say that, I said I didn't not.

Sid   Well, you do or you don't.

Barbara   No, Sid, I will or I won't and I'm not going to.

Sid   You said if I stopped fooling around you'd think
about it.

Barbara   I did not. I said you'd be more attractive and
you would.

Sid   I haven't looked at another woman for months.

Barbara   Sid, you're married. So am I. And Ronnie's got
a sniff of this, you know.

Sid Has he?

Barbara He's given me a driver.

Sid That big bloke?

Barbara Yeh, so watch it.

Sid Thing is . . .

Barbara Sid, will you please change the subject!

Sid It's still raining. I still love you.

Barbara It'd be the end of our friendship.

Sid All your objections are clichés.

Barbara This whole thing's a cliché.

Sid First time I clapped eyes on you . . .

Barbara You had a woman in your shower.

Sid (*suddenly shouts*)   I'm not interested in anyone else!
Why do you insist on treating me like this . . .

He grabs a script and yanks it open.

. . . arsehole, this lecherous leering fucking . . . bastard!!

He tears up the script with surprising violence. **Barbara** *shocked to
silence.*

I don't want anyone else. It's you I want.

Barbara (*genuinely sorry*)   Oh, Sidney.

*She touches him and he takes immediate advantage, embracing her.
Suddenly they're kissing; a mutual passion. She pulls away.*

Barbara You're a good kisser, I'll give you that.

Sid I'm good all over.

Barbara Are you? I bet you are.

Lights fade.

Scene Two

Camping (continued).

Later in the day. The partitions are closed. No one's to be seen, but the caravan is rocking gently with an unmistakably rhythmic rattle and squeak. **Sally** *appears in a hurry, staggering through the mud in huge wellingtons, carrying a suit and a selection of trilbys. She stops when she recognises the motion. Turns back, looks at her watch, dithers, then shouts.*

Sally   Sid!

Various noises off announce a sudden uncoupling and a bruised shin.

Sid (*off*)   Gawd, strewth.

Imogen   Sssh!

Sid *stumbles into the main part of the van as* **Sally** *goes round the outside and enters.*

Sally   They've rescheduled, Sid; they want you in ten minutes.

Sid   Gawd blimey.

Sally   Nice lunch?

Sid   I was just learning me lines.

Sally   You've only got one line and you know it off by heart. So do the rest of us.

Sid   For one terrible moment I thought you were her.

Sally   Serve you right if it had been.

Sid   Sally; the thing I admire most in a woman is discretion.

Sally   No, Sid; the thing you admire most in a woman is yourself. This is for Barbara.

Sid   What is it?

Sally   Fishing-line. These trousers, that jacket. Hat's not continuity so choose one, I've got to see to Bernie. I'll be back in five minutes. Be ready, all right.

Sid   Sally; mum's the word.

Sally   No, Sid; wanker's the word.

Sally *leaves.* **Sid** *goes to the partition.*

Sid   All right; she's gone. You'd better get a move on before anyone else barges in.

Imogen *enters from behind the partition. She's drunk and not as vivacious as when we first met her. She finds her scattered clothes.*

Imogen   I'm sorry.

Sid   What for?

Imogen   Causing an argument. I'm always causing arguments. If there's a man and there's me and then someone else there's usually an argument.

Sid   Take no notice. Sally's a bit repressed. She doesn't understand the liniments of healthy desire.

Imogen   I'm surprised you even remembered me. I'm flattered. I mean, who was I then? I was out and about, I know, but I'd barely left LAMDA and honestly I knew nothing. I was nothing. This is such a strange business. You get a job, you meet someone, you like them, you maybe sleep with them, the job ends, then you never see them again even though you always say you will. I made some really good friends on *When Dinosaurs Ruled the Earth*, except Raquel of course, but she doesn't make friends she just takes the odd hostage. Thing is I haven't seen anyone since. Except there was a particularly persistent caveman who I did see once but his wife was pregnant and he just cried all evening. Everything's so . . . temporary. That's what's nice about working with you lot; you're one big happy family. I'd love to work with you lot again.

Sid   I'm gonna be needed soon.

Imogen *carries on drinking.*

Imogen   Oh, that's all right; I only popped in to say hello.
You know what I wish? I wish I had smaller breasts. Then
I'd get to play some women with small breasts, and they're
always the best parts. I'd really like to play women with no
breasts at all, you know, like in Ibsen. I should never have
done the centrefold. I'm actually very versatile. 'An
impressive multifaceted performance'; that's what they said
about me as Jenny Grubb in *Loving*. And that wasn't just
taking off the glasses and letting my hair down, that was
acting actually. I was *acting* her repressed sexuality. What I'm
saying is, I'm not just some stupid girl from Elmhurst with a
fucked knee, you know.

Sid   Right.

Imogen   I'm not just the Countess of Cleavage.

Sid   Absolutely.

Imogen   It's so hard to convince people I'm a serious
actress, but I really think it's beginning to happen. I've got
an audition for the Royal Shakespeare Company? And last
month I did *The Persuaders*. Only the pilot but both Roger
Moore and Tony Curtis were very complimentary and said
there was a very good chance my character could become
a regular.

Sid   I'm glad it's going well for you.

Imogen   Oh yes.

Sid   I'm glad you popped in.

Imogen   I'm glad too.

Sid   Thing is, um. . .

Imogen   Imogen.

Sid   Imogen. What we just did . . .

Imogen   I know, I know. I don't know why we did that I
mean I know you had a Royal Flush but I mean why so

suddenly I mean that's not why I came I don't want you to think I'm a complete tart or anything I always liked you.

Sid   Well, these things happen.

Imogen   Yes they do; it's just a spontaneous thing and nothing to be ashamed of an expression of one's sexuality I hope you don't think I do this a lot.

Sid   I'm sure you don't.

Imogen   Because I don't. It's not why I came. I came because I wanted some advice.

Sid   What's that then?

Imogen   Well, you see, if I get the job with the Royal Shakespeare Company it's going to clash with *The Persuaders* if *The Persuaders* goes into a series, which it should, I mean it's got Roger Moore *and* Tony Curtis in it, but it's not definite and I'm not sure if I should do it. I'd rather be in the Royal Shakespeare Company but the problem is it's not a huge part, in fact I don't speak and I have to take my clothes off, but it is the RSC and Stratford's lovely. Anyway; you've done a bit of everything so I thought you might advise me. What do you think I should do?

Sid   *Persuaders*.

Imogen   But that's not definite.

Sid   Shakespeare then, definitely.

Imogen   But I haven't actually been offered it.

Sid   I'd take The Persuaders, then.

Imogen   But I don't want to act in rubbish, I want to act in really good stuff.

Sid   Then if I were you, I'd hang out for the Shakespeare.

Imogen   The money's not very good.

Sid   That's why I'd tend towards *The Persuaders*.

Imogen   Of course, I might not get offered either.

Sid   In which case, take the other one.

Imogen   I *need* a job. A proper job. I don't mean to sound desperate but this not working; it's driving me mad.

Sid   I tell you what. I'll see what I can do.

Imogen   Oh, I didn't mean that you should . . .

Sid   No no no. No trouble.

Imogen   That's not what I . . . would you? I mean I hope you don't think that's why I came.

Sid   What are friends for?

Imogen   Hmmmm.

Sid   I'm going to have to get going.

Imogen   Daddy was on the board. Of LAMDA. I've never told anyone that. Anyway I mustn't be negative mustn't be negative mustn't be negative. Things can just turn right round, can't they? Round and round. Tonight even. I'm meeting Michael Winner for a drink at L'Escargot. Just for a chat, but you never know, do you?

Sid   That's right; you never know.

Imogen   I wouldn't mind doing a smallish part again if I was working with really good people.

Sid   I'll see what I can do.

Imogen   And what happened between us is a separate thing.

Sid   That's right.

Imogen   So if it happened again, well . . .

Sid   It mustn't happen again.

Imogen   Absolutely. That's what I . . . I mean if that's what you . . . that's fine.

Sid   You see, I'm being strictly monogamous at the moment.

Imogen   Oh, I'd hate to harm your marriage.

Sid   My marriage has nothing to do with it.

Imogen   Oh. Well, this was . . . we both know what this was, this was . . .

Sid   This was lovely.

Imogen   I feel a bit woosy. I think I'd better lie down.

Sid   You what?

Imogen   Room's going round.

Sid   Well, you'd better get some fresh air then.

Barbara *appears through the drizzle with* **Sally**, **Kenneth** *plodding on behind.* **Sid** *hears them approach.*

Barbara   What's it doing in the van?

Sally   I thought you were with Sid.

Barbara   I'm not always with Sid.

Sid   Second thoughts, perhaps you should have a little lie-down.

Imogen   Thank you.

Barbara   Why does everybody presume I'm with Sid?

Sally   Well, you usually are sometimes.

Sid   A nice quiet lie-down.

Imogen   I think you're right.

Imogen *retires.*

Barbara   Come on, Kenny; I want your honest opinion. I don't want to humiliate myself.

Kenneth   You shouldn't have signed the contract then.

Imogen   I usually come round in about half an hour.

Barbara   Sidney.

Sid   Who is it?

Barbara   Only us. You don't mind if we do a bit of wardrobe in here do you?

Sid   Umm . . .

Barbara   It's not something I can do on the dining bus.

Sid   Well, what does he want?

Kenneth   Dry trousers, if you don't mind.

Sid   I do mind.

Kenneth   I don't care.

Sally   They're all under a tree, Sid; you've got another ten minutes.

Barbara *finds the fishing-line.*

Barbara   Bert still insists it's props. I said if it's sewn to my bra it's costume.

Sally   Give it here.

Barbara   If Bert does it it'll be thirteen takes.

Sally   I'll do it.

Sid   What you doing?

Barbara   Rehearsing. I just don't want to make a complete tit of myself.

Kenneth *laughs. She joins in.*

Barbara   No, stop it.

Sally *sews the line to* **Barbara**'s *bra.*

Sid   You should tell Gerald to stuff his nudity clause right up his nose.

Barbara   I know; Ronnie's going to do his nut.

Sid   If I was your husband I wouldn't let you do it.

Kenneth   But you're not, are you?

Sid   Don't start.

Kenneth   Well, I for one have always held the state of matrimony in the highest regard.

Sid   That is rich.

Kenneth   Together in the eyes of God.

Sid   What about your lot?

Kenneth   'Til death us do part.

Sid   Every last one of you . . .

Kenneth   Love, honour and obey.

Sid   Disgustingly promiscuous.

Kenneth   That's rich from a man who thinks Errol Flynn missed a lot of opportunities.

Sid   And he was bent, and all.

Kenneth   And almost as well-hung as me, apparently.

Sid   Only place you'd be well-hung is the Isle of Man.

Barbara   Sidney.

Sally   Done it.

Barbara   All right, unclip the dooh-dah, give it a good yank. Sid, turn your back.

Sid   Are you gonna tell the cameraman to turn his back?

Barbara   Turn round.

Sid   Point his arri in the opposite direction? (*He laughs.*)

Barbara   I want to practice getting me hands up.

Sid   I could help you there.

Barbara   Sidney.

Sid   Strewth.

Kenneth   Libidinous cretin.

Sid   You can talk. The moral climate's gone right down the pan since they legalised you lot.

Kenneth   Go on, that's right; assuage your own sordid guilt by casting slurs on my entirely more refined sexual orientation.

Sid   I couldn't care less what you do to each other in private; it's your flouncing bleeding effeminacy gets up my nose.

Barbara   Sidney, turn round and face the wall.

Sid   It was bad enough, you and Charlie mincing through scene after scene; suddenly it's legal and you both turn into screaming queens.

Kenneth   I have never screamingly queened in my life.

Barbara   Ready?

Sally   Right.

Barbara   One, two . . . Sid; close the door.

Sid *closes the mirrored door.*

Barbara   One, two, three.

Sally *pulls the line.* **Barbara** *grabs her bra.* **Sid** *turns round.*

Sid   Ow!

Barbara   Serves you right. I knew you'd turn round.

Sid   I'm only flesh and blood.

Sally   You were too quick.

Barbara   You didn't pull hard enough.

Sally   I pulled really hard. Look, it's come off.

Sid   Here, let me.

Barbara   Get off. Go and find another horse to curse.

Sid   Gawd blimey, I'm missing the three o'clock.

Turns on his portable telly.

Kenneth   There's more to life than sex and horses, you know.

Sid   Shuttup, you poofta.

Barbara   Right, let's try again.

Kenneth   It's lucky you left South Africa. If the crops had failed you'd have shot your entire family.

Sid   Not before I'd shot you lot.

Barbara   Sidney! Watch your telly and no bloody peeping.

Kenneth   If you expect your average Odeon-full of punters to do the decent thing and all close their eyes in unison, I suggest you think again.

Barbara   God, I hate this.

Sid   Not to mention the crew.

Barbara   There won't be any crew; it'll be a closed set, don't you worry.

Sally   Turn round.

Sid   Blow me, they're almost home.

Sally   I'm going to use less tape.

Sid   Bloody thing.

He struggles with the aerial.

Barbara   I'm gonna keep me elbows bent so my hands are closer.

Sid   Where's Sudden Eclipse? Hold this, will you?

He gives **Sally** *the aerial.*

Sally   Yes sir, no sir, three bags full sir.

Barbara   Ready?

Sid   Hang on. They're neck and neck.

Sally   My tongue's free if anyone wants their shoes cleaning.

Sid   Come on, Sudden Eclipse.

Barbara   One . . .

Sid   Wait until they've crossed the line, will you?

Barbara   Two . . .

Sid   Hang on a minute . . .

Barbara   Three.

Sally *pulls the line.* **Barbara***'s bra flies off.* **Sid** *ricks his neck.*

Sid   Ow!

Barbara   Da da!

Kenneth   Oh, Bravo!

Barbara   What'd you see, Sid?

Sid   Nothing. And I've ricked me bleedin' neck.

Barbara   Serves you right. Give us me coat, Kenny.

Kenneth   Ooh. Dresser on set.

Sally   I've hurt me finger.

Sid   Who's winning? Will you please get out of the way!

Sally   Oh, pardon me for breathing.

Sally *falls out the caravan and disappears, tugging the aerial. The TV falls on* **Sid***'s foot.*

Sid   Ow!

Barbara   What happened?

Sid   Gawd Streuth!

Kenneth *and* **Barbara** *laugh.*

Sid   What's so bloody funny?

Barbara   Hard luck, Sid.

Sid   I think I broke my toe.

Kenneth   You're a voyeuristic disgrace and it serves you right.

Sid   Unnatural acts, mate. Look in the Bible.

Kenneth   That's right; throw your little stones. Hide behind the ruined greenhouse of your own sad lechery. By all means pronounce judgement on the divine splinter of my sexual proclivities, if you can catch sight of it through the Epping Forest of your own lustful eye.

Sid   Don't lecture me on sexual relationships, mate. Not from your perspective.

Barbara   I wish you two'd pack it in.

Sid *returns the telly, that's still got some life in it.*

Sid   Who won the bloody race?

Barbara   You're really getting on my nerves.

Sid   Lift up the aerial. Where's the bleedin' aerial? Sally, will you please . . . Where's she gone?

Barbara   Sally?

Sally *enters covered head to foot in mud, with a bent aerial.*

Sally   Look at me! Look at the state of me!

Barbara   Oh, Sally.

Sid   Oh well, that's knackered, isn't it?

Barbara   Lets get your clothes off.

Sid   Good idea.

Barbara   Leave her alone!

Kenneth   It's incessant, isn't it? At least my lot are unfettered by the dual agendas of heterosexual desire.

Sid   Oh, give it a rest.

Kenneth   At least we're capable of frank and honest sexual relationships.

Sid   Your lot? Relationships? What sort of relationship is it begins in a toilet and ends with a hammer in the head.

A stunned pause. **Kenneth** *goes to the door.*

Kenneth   The boy shone. You met him. He made you laugh. You liked him.

Kenneth *leaves*.

Barbara   Oh, Sidney.

Sid   Well.

Sally   I haven't got a change of clothes.

Barbara   Sidney, sort her out some clothes.

Sid   Who won the bloody race?

Sally   I don't care who won the bloody race. Whichever horse you didn't have money on won the bloody race!

Sid   If you'd held the aerial still it might have just nipped by on the inside.

Barbara   And the horrifying thing is: he believes that.

Sally   I bloody hate location.

Barbara   Calm down. Go take a shower.

Sid   No.

Barbara   Why not? Look at her.

Sid   All right then, but do it quietly.

Barbara   Why quietly?

Sid   I've got a splitting headache.

Sally   Good.

Sally *disappears*.

Sid   Do you fancy a drink?

Barbara   Vodka, please.

Sid   I meant let's go to a pub.

Barbara   I don't want us to be seen in a pub. I want to talk to you.

Sid   Let's go for a walk then.

Barbara   In this weather?

Sid   Bit of fresh air.

Barbara   Sidney, I want to talk.

Sid   We can talk in the dining bus.

Barbara   I want to talk about us.

Sid   Us?

Barbara   You snogged me, Sidney.

Sid   Yes, well, I'm sorry about that.

Barbara   It was my fault.

Sid   I forgive you. Let's go and get a cup of tea.

Barbara   I'll tell you what I think, Sidney. I think we're in danger here. I think we're in danger of having a horrible messy affair.

Sid   No no no . . .

Barbara   No, let me finish. I've been thinking about it all day and I've come to a decision. And I warn you, Sid, my decisions are final.

Sid   Don't say that.

Barbara   No, I've decided.

Sid   No, please, girl . . .

Barbara   I think we should get it over with.

Sid   You what?

Barbara   Nothing permanent. Nothing public. One night of bliss and that's your lot. Take it or leave it.

Sid   I'll take it.

Barbara   Thought you might.

Sid   You mean it?

Barbara   I've been to bed with enough men I didn't like. I suddenly seemed ridiculous to keep turning you down.

Because I do like you, Sidney. I like you very much. I warn you though, if Ronnie finds out, we're both for the high jump.

Sid　Come here.

They move towards each other. We hear **Kenneth** *off.*

Kenneth　Mind your step, it's like the swamplands of the Matagasi round here . . .

Sid *glances through the window.*

Enter **Kenneth** *leading a huge, dangerous-looking man called* **Eddie**.

Eddie　I'm supposed to be keeping an eye on Mrs Knight, not nobbing it up with you lot. Ronnie reckons you lot get up to allsorts.

Kenneth　Yes, well that's a commonly held myth, you see. In actual fact we're all very familial.

Sid *glances through the window.*

Sid　Gawd, strewth. He's bringing him over!

Barbara　Who?

Sid　Eddie.

Barbara　Eddie? Oh, bloody hell; I don't want Eddie to find me here.

Eddie　There's nothing dodgy goes on then, like in Hollywood?

Kenneth　Good heavens no. We all keep ourselves to ourselves. That's why you must say hello to Sidney; he gets very lonely in his little van.

Barbara　Sod this for a game of soldiers.

Sid　What you doing?

Barbara　Hiding.

Sid　No!

Barbara   Ronnie's told him to look out for any hankypanky.

Sid   Tell him we're working. Doing our lines. What's he going to think, we're sitting here, talking, fully dressed.

Sally *pops her head out, soap in her eyes.*

Sally   Is there a towel?

Sid   Oh Gawd, strewth.

Barbara   Oh, bloody hell; it's an orgy.

Sid   It's all perfectly innocent.

Barbara   That's not how it looks, Sid. And besides, it isn't, is it?

Sally   Towel, please!

Eddie   Hold on, Kenny, I've lost my shoe.

Kenneth   Where?

Eddie   It's behind me.

Kenneth   Hang on.

Sally   What's going on?

Barbara   Sally, do us a favour and keep quiet for five minutes, will you?

Sally   Why?

Sid   Because you haven't got your clothes on. And get your clothes on.

Sally   Which?

Sid   Which what?

Sally   I can't do both in here.

Sid   Keep quiet then.

Barbara   Please, Sally; or Ronnie'll do his nut.

Sally   This is ridiculous.

Barbara   Sally, please.

Sally   All right. Jesus.

Eddie   That's ruined that is. Ronnie got me these in Bond Street.

Kenneth   Nearly there now.

Barbara   I'll be in the bedroom.

Sid   No!

Barbara   Sidney!

Sid   That'll be the first place he looks. Hide in here.

He offers her the toilet.

Barbara   In there?!

Sid   Think of your health.

Barbara   I'm claustrophobic.

Sid   Think of mine then.

She hides. **Imogen** *appears from the bedroom.*

Imogen   I'm feeling a bit sick, actually . . .

Sid *closes the door on her.* **Eddie** *and* **Kenneth** *arrive.*

Kenneth   Anybody home?

Sid   I was just on my way out.

Kenneth   Oh, well then, lucky we caught you. May we *entré*? Oh, *quel surprise*. All on your ownsome. In you come, Eddie.

Sid   It's a bit inconvenient at the moment.

Kenneth   Don't be so inhospitable; he's got a soggy sock. Eddie's a big fan of yours, well, enormous in fact, as you can see.

Eddie   I'm pleased to meet you.

Sid   Mutual, I'm sure. Thing is I'm a bit um . . .

Kenneth   Overwhelmed he is; he's always overwhelmed by public adoration, even in small dollops.

Sid   Do you think we could . . .

Kenneth   Can I have a lie-down?

Sid   No.

Kenneth   Why not?

Sid   Well, it's a bit . . . inconvenient at the moment.

Kenneth   Yes. Too inconvenient to sign his poor mother's book. That's all he wants you know; he wants you to sign your moniker in his poor old mother's book.

Eddie   If you wouldn't mind.

Sid   Sure. No problem. Who to?

Eddie   My mother.

Sid   What's her name?

Eddie   Mum.

Sid   Right. There.

Eddie   Thanks.

Sid   Pleasure.

Kenneth   Have you seen Miss Windsor?

Sid   Hardly ever.

Kenneth   She's wanted on the set.

Eddie   There is another thing.

Sid   What's that?

Eddie   Well . . . would you mind if I spoke to Mr James in private?

Kenneth   Not at all. In fact, why don't you two sit down and have a nice long tête-à-tête?

Eddie   No thanks; I've eaten.

Kenneth   I'll leave you to it. If you do see Miss Windsor, they're ready for her close-up and they're losing the light.

Sid   Why don't we all go to the bus?

Kenneth   No, it's much cosier in here. Nice and private. Take your time.

Sid   Kenny . . .

Kenneth   Best of British.

Kenneth *leaves, but hangs about the end of the van, listening.*

Eddie   I'm a bit embarrassed, tell you the truth, but Ronnie asked me to have a word in your ear.

Sid   A word?

Eddie   He asked me to ask you nicely if you'd got designs on his wife.

Sid   Designs? That's . . .

Eddie   Have you?

Sid   Have I what?

Eddie   Are you shaggin' his missus?

Sid   No. Absolutely not. Absolutely not at all.

Eddie   Thing is, you've got a bit of a reputation and Ronnie thought . . .

Sid   Well, you can tell Ronnie there is absolutely nothing to worry about.

Eddie   Thing is you hear all sorts of things about you lot.

Sid   Eddie. I can completely reassure you about this. All those stories about showbiz antics are a complete myth. Me and Mrs Knight are just fellow artistes, in fact we're barely friends, in actual fact I haven't set eyes on her in days.

Kenneth *has discovered the caravan is supported at one end with a dodgy pile of bricks. He gives the bricks a malicious kick. The caravan tips up to a wild angle, spilling* **Sid** *on to the divan.*

Barbara *falls out of the toilet and lands on top of him.* **Sally** *tumbles out of the shower, loses her towel, bounces off* **Eddie** *and lands on* **Sid** *and* **Barbara**. **Imogen** *flies in and lands on top of them all.* **Eddie** *manages to stay upright.*

Sid   And I'll tell you something else. This is the last time I share a dressing-room.

Blackout.

Act Three

Dick. 1974.

The van stands in a pub car park. The curtains are drawn against a crisp spring day. **Sid** *is lying like a corpse in a seventeenth-century shift. He looks much older.* **Sally** *enters, draped with various bits of seventeenth-century costume. She sees* **Sid** *and looks at him curiously. It occurs to her he might be dead. Then* **Sid** *snores loudly and she relaxes. Her little fright galvanises a decision she's been trying to make. She rummages in her bag for a letter, and in her purse for a small rather crumpled photograph. She puts the photo in the envelope, seals it, and places it prominently where* **Sid** *usually sits. He wakes.*

Sid   Whassat?

Sally   It's me. Heath's resigned.

Sid   Has he?

Sally   Harold Wilson's gone to see the Queen.

Sid   She will be pleased.

Sally   It's a new era. A new beginning. There's some post for you.

Sid   Bin it.

Sally   No. I'm not going to bin it any more.

Sid *picks up the letter.*

Sid   It'll be from that mad nun in Shrewsbury.

Sally   You don't know who it's from, so read it.

Sid *discards the letter.* **Sally** *begins dressing a female blonde wig.*

Sally   I've been offered a job.

Sid   That's nice.

Sally   I've been offered a job on James Bond.

Enter **Kenneth**.

Kenneth   There's been something of a discussion at lunch and it has fallen to me on behalf of your fellow cast and the entire crew to make you cogniscent of the fact that you're behaving like a lovesick teenage imbecile.

Sally   Leave him alone, Kenny.

Kenneth   We're of a single mind that the sooner you two put an end to this ludicrous affair, the better.

Sally   Kenneth, please. He's not well.

Sid   I'm perfectly all right.

Sally   Oh, please yourself!

Sally *leaves*.

Kenneth   This thing is affecting the morale of the entire unit.

Sid   What morale?

Kenneth   You were never good for morale. When Phil Silvers stood in for you there was better morale.

Sid   You all hated Phil Silvers.

Kenneth   Exactly; and it was great for morale! Whereas your partial return to health has had entirely the opposite effect. Behind the crapulent scenery as well as in front.

Sid   Have you heard something?

Kenneth   What about?

Sid   Don't mess me about, Kenneth. Have you heard any rumours?

Kenneth   I don't know what you mean, I'm sure.

Sid   Are they gonna drop me?

Kenneth   Well, it's about time.

Sid   That's very supportive of you.

Kenneth   Yes, well, I wouldn't worry. Peter won't.

Sid   Gerald wants to.

Kenneth   Ignore 'em. It's just the usual bollocks. Put the fear of God into us and keep the money down.

Sid   When they got rid of Charlie . . .

Kenneth   They didn't get rid of Charlie. Charlie got rid of himself. Charlie was so full of lemonade he couldn't perambulate let alone articulate.

Sid   But what have you heard?

Kenneth   Only the patently obvious. That your battered old mug running around leering up skirts and God help me snogging girls half your age is no longer the side-splitting sight it used to be.

Sid   I know.

Kenneth   There comes a time in every man's life he can no longer lech without appearing something of a dirty old sod. A benchmark you passed in the late nineteen fifties.

Sid   I know.

Kenneth   The sight of your face near a heaving bosom is positively excruciating.

Sid   I know.

Kenneth   You've got a very grubby image.

Sid   All right, all right; don't rub it in. That's why I took the sitcom. Family man.

Kenneth   Tip of the week; when you're playing her dad, don't think about Sally Geeson's bum.

Sid   I never look at her bum. I never look anywhere near her bum.

Kenneth   Yes, that's how I knew you were thinking about it. The boy's nice.

Sid   Robin? He's a good lad. I've got him a part in this.

Kenneth   You want to watch your back. He reminds me of you when you were younger.

Sid   Oh, fuck 'em.

Kenneth   This is my last, anyway. Positively my last. I said I'd only do it if they cut the stocks scene; I'm not being pelted with rubbish at my age.

Sid   Stocks scene's still in.

Kenneth   It is not.

Sid   It's on the call sheet.

Kenneth   Oh no it isn't.

Sid   Stoke Poges. Tuesday. Scene 97. Captain Fancy. Villagers and Yokels. Construction erect stocks.

Kenneth   What day is it?

Sid   Tuesday.

Kenneth   Give me the phone. I've had enough of this duplicity. They think they can get away with blue murder. I can't look at a tomato without breaking out. It'll play havoc with me skin and I've got the Cabaret on Sunday. (*Phone.*) This is Kenneth Williams. Is Peter there? Yes, he's always out to lunch, isn't he. Well, you can tell him from me, he'd better get his obese old backside down to the set because I categorically refuse to be humiliated any further.

Sid   You'll do it, mate.

Kenneth   I will not.

Sid   If you don't, they won't use you next time.

Kenneth   Well, that'll be a blessing.

Sid   Are they going to drop me?

Kenneth   Way things are going they won't have to. Let's face it; the whole things running out of steam. Rothwell's had it. I'm getting gags the third time round. Windsor's doing another flash. I sometimes think we should all just grow up.

Barbara *enters. She's not happy.*

Barbara   I thought you'd be in here. I saw you all, gossiping in the bus.

Kenneth   We were not gossiping, we were having a compassionate discussion . . .

Barbara   My arse. I can fight my own battles thank you very much.

Sid   I hope you've calmed down.

Barbara   Yes, I've calmed down. This is me calmed down, all right? Is this calm enough for you?

Sid   Kenny; sling your hook.

Barbara   No, Kenny; stay where you are.

Sid   You want to talk in front of him?

Barbara   I don't want you jumping me.

Sid   When have I ever done that?

Kenneth   I could stand by with a bucket of water.

Sid   You'll stand by with a thick ear in a minute.

Kenneth   Sexaholic.

Sid   Shirt-lifter.

Kenneth   Dick.

Sid   Bum bandit.

Kenneth   South African.

Sid   How dare you.

Barbara   Will you stop it! You're as pathetic as each other.

Kenneth   That is a slur. I do not feel the necessity to wield my penis in the pursuit of dominance. My ego is not hostage to my gonads. Women exist for me to bitch with or bitch about or bitch about with, not to satisfy an addled libido.

Sid   And how's your mother?

Kenneth   Irrelevant.

Sid   Domineering mother plus weak or absent father equals poofta, mate. It's common knowledge.

Barbara   Sid; we have to talk.

Kenneth   Well, if it's psychology you want, what about six-year-old boy gets dumped by mother who buggers off to Australia as one half of a comedy dance duo, and grows up a misogynist comedian who only fancies younger women and argues incessantly with Joan Sims?

Sid   Very perceptive. Who was it had to beg the Best Boy not to tell his mother what he'd been up to behind the honey wagon?

Barbara   Look, will you both stop it!

Sid   It's unnatural for a man to fancy other men!

Barbara   Kenny doesn't fancy other men. He fancies himself. Other men are just the next best thing.

Sally *enters.*

Sally   Kenny; you're wanted on set. Scene 97.

Kenneth   Right. It's about time they learned they can't muck me about. The final showdown. *Finito. La fin.* And you watch your steaming great gob or I'll do you for slander.

Sid   Slander, you couldn't do the Marquis de Sade for slander, mate!

Exit **Kenneth**.

Sally   Sid, they're gonna want you in your frock.

Sid   Oh, bollocks.

Sally   It's a lovely colour.

Sid   I hate drag.

Sally   Be a brave soldier.

Sid   It's all right; I'll do it.

Sally   Do you know how to get into it?

Barbara   Yes, he does.

Sally   Hurry up then.

Sally *leaves.* **Sid** *changes costume.*

Barbara   And when you're dressed, the first thing you're gonna do is apologise to Bernie.

Sid   All I said to Bernie was . . .

Barbara   All he was doing was helping me off a horse.

Sid   He was taking liberties.

Barbara   Hairy bloody great thing.

Sid   He is an' all.

Barbara   Not Bernie; the horse! He was helping me down.

Sid   He was touching you up.

Barbara   I hate horses.

Sid   Lecherous sod.

Barbara   I'd told him I hated horses.

Sid   You never told me you hated horses.

Barbara   You never bleeding asked.

Sid   Well, if you don't like horses you shouldn't be on a horse. You shouldn't have let them put you on a horse.

Barbara   Sidney.

Sid   He had his hand on your bottom. You don't need to put your hand on someone's bottom to help them off a horse.

Barbara   You don't need to put your tongue in someone's ear to wish them Merry Christmas, but it's never stopped you. Scenes with a horse are a doddle compared to scenes with you. I've seen you do ten lines of dialogue juggling half a dozen props and hit your mark for the sight gag with no rehearsal in one bloody take. But give you the feed and me on your knee freezing my tits off in underwear and no; we're there for two and a half hours. Talk to me about groping and it's not Bernie springs to mind. Talk about gentlemanly conduct and you're talking Bernie. Talk to me about trying to act with another actor taking personal liberties and it's you. It's you I think of. It's you who's happy to humiliate me in front of the entire crew.

Sid   I don't like that sort of scene any more than you.

Barbara   It was ghastly. I felt sick and degraded.

Sid   I have never treated you with disrespect.

Barbara   I know a real kiss when I get one.

Sid   It was scripted.

Barbara   It was meant. It was embarrassing.

Sid   It was a kiss. A kiss is a kiss.

Barbara   And work is work.

Sid   What about Brighton?

Barbara   What about it?

Sid   I don't recall a camera.

Barbara   Brighton was Brighton.

Sid   Was it that much of a disaster?

Barbara   It wasn't a disaster, it was . . .

Sid   Well, what was it?

Barbara   I just wanted to get it over with. I wanted you to get it out of your system. I thought you just wanted to give me one; wallop.

Sid   Well, that's a terrible thing to think.

Barbara   Sidney, I'm thirty years younger than you, we're both married, we're both unfaithful; it doesn't exactly augur well, does it?

Sid   You're gonna have to leave him now, you know.

Barbara   I'm not leaving him.

Sid   You said you were going to.

Barbara   No I didn't.

Sid   You did. You said you'd had enough.

Barbara   That was about him and me, not you and me.

Sid   I'm leaving mine.

Barbara   Sidney . . .

Sid   No, enough's enough.

Barbara   You can't leave Val.

Sid   Why not?

Barbara   Because you love her. And you love your kids. I've seen you with them.

Sid   It's not about Val.

Barbara   How do you think I'd feel, imagining Val? Sitting on her own in Iver? If it wasn't for her you'd be skint, drunk and unemployed. Whatever happened to whatsisname.

Sid   I know. I'm not denying it.

Barbara   Well then.

Sid   I reckon I've got a good ten years left in me. And I want to spend them with you.

Barbara   Oh great. I get your last ten years, then a few more mopping up after you, and then what? I'm high and dry at forty.

Sid   In Brighton you said . . .

Barbara   Will you leave off about bloody Brighton?

Sid   Didn't you enjoy it?

Barbara   The foreplay especially. Forty-five minutes drinking warm champagne and waiting for Val to phone.

Sid   I know the earth didn't exactly move.

Barbara   I'm not going to massage your ego, Sid. Look where it's got me so far. You don't want me; it's the idea of me you want.

He hands her a chit.

Barbara   What's this?

Sid   It's a doctor's certificate.

Barbara   What for?

Sid   Fit as a fiddle.

Barbara   I don't want to see your doctor's certificate.

Sid   You said you were worried about me ticker. Me ticker's fine.

Barbara   Sidney.

Sid   There it is in black and white.

Barbara   Oh my God.

Sid   What's in Stanmore anyway? You said yourself you never see him. A Merc in the drive . . .

Barbara   A Daimler.

Sid   A Daimler in the drive . . .

Barbara   The Merc's in the garage . . .

Sid   A Merc in the garage . . .

Barbara   Next to the Jag.

Sid   But apart from the motors, what is there in Stanmore?

Barbara   About two hundred thousand in used notes. And a marriage, Sidney.

Sally *enters.*

Sally   Barbara, they're ready for you.

Barbara   My marriage.

Barbara *leaves.*

Sally   Kenny's being difficult; you may as well relax.

Sid *pours a drink.*

Sally   Read your letter.

Sid   I can't. I've got that double vision thing again.

Sally   I wish you'd stop drinking.

Sid   Read it to me.

Sally   No. It's addressed to you.

Sid   Chuck it then.

Sally   All right; I'll read it. I'm opening it. Oh there's a photo.

Sid   Is it a nun?

Sally   No.

Sid   Bin it.

Sally   No.

Sid   Oh . . . read it then.

Sally   'Dear Sidney James.'

Sid   Read it quietly.

Sally   'Dear Sidney James. It's been hard to decide if I should contact you or not, but as you can see I have decided to write. The photo enclosed is of someone you will recognise. It is a picture of my mother. Her name was Jenny, her maiden name was Barlow. You'll remember her as one half of Heaven on Wheels, the speciality act with which you toured the Midlands in 1944.'

Sid   That's enough.

Sally   There's more.

Sid   I wouldn't be surprised.

Sally   'You were performing as Max Miller at the time, and suggested she join with you to rehearse a short tap routine. Sadly, the routine never saw the light of day, but rehearsals went on throughout the tour. My mother always believed I was conceived in Wolverhampton, but not that you had any knowledge of my subsequent arrival. Shortly after the tour ended she was suprised to learn of your sudden marriage. Rather than cause any trouble, she chose to marry an old admirer, a solicitor from Berkshire. My stepfather's generosity towards her did not, sadly, extend to myself, and as I grew so did a degree of bitterness between them. They divorced when I was six years old, and my mother brought me up alone. She died ten years ago of a miserable cancer. Sorting through her things I came apon her diaries and some photographs. It was not hard to deduce my true parentage. It's only after a great deal of thought that I'm writing to you. I want you to understand I want nothing from you, but I do want to meet you. I want you to know me. I want to talk to you about my mother.

Sid   That's enough.

Sally   To hear that you remember her with affection would mean a great deal to me . . .'

Sid   I said that's enough.

Sally   There's a picture.

Sid   Bin it.

Sally   A picture of her mother.

Sid   Sally. If it happened in the mid-nineteen forties, I don't remember it. It's water under the bridge. She's got her life, I've got mine.

Sally What if she hasn't?

Sid What?

Sally Got a life?

Sid Well, she should get one. I think I'll just take another little nap.

He lies back, closes his eyes.

Sally Do you remember her?

Sid God, I'm tired.

Sally She's wearing her skates. Do you?

Sid What?

Sally Remember her?

Sid Of course I do. She used to whizz round. Hopeless bloody hoofer, though.

Sally Look.

Sid No.

Sally Look at her.

Sid No.

Sally But . . .

Sid Sally, I'm knackered. Please. I need a kip.

Sally, *subdued, carefully puts the photo in her cardigan pocket. The corners of her mouth start to dip down in reflex misery. She is trying hard not to cry when the door opens and* **Eddie** *enters.* **Sally** *turns her back to hide her state and* **Eddie** *takes out a gun.* **Sally** *turns to see it, and is silenced by a single finger to the lips. She crumples backwards in surprise. He cocks the gun and points it at Sid's knee.* **Sally** *gurgles incoherently.*

Eddie Wake up, Sidney.

Sid *opens his eyes and is suddenly very awake.*

Eddie   I've got a message from Ron.

Sid   Have you? That's nice.

Eddie   He told me to tell you it's not so much the money, and it's not so much you shagging his wife, it's more you shagging his wife when you owe him so much money. He feels that's taking the piss somewhat.

Sid   I hadn't thought about it quite like that, but on reflection he's absolutely right.

Eddie   I told him you've got a dodgy ticker, so he told me be sure not to frighten you too much.

Sid   How much is too much?

Eddie   Bit more than not enough, I suppose.

Sid   Well, I'd say you've done a bit more than not enough, hovering on the much more, which is dangerously close to too much, wouldn't you say?

Sally   Please; leave him alone.

Eddie   It's all right love, I'm not going to hurt him. Ronnie was very particular about that. Don't want you to have a heart attack, do we?

Sid   That's very kind. I'll try not to.

Eddie   Ron said I shouldn't bring a shooter or nothing 'cos if I did you might.

Sid   I might, yes. It's a distinct possibility.

Eddie   That's what I thought. So I said I wouldn't fire it.

Sid   Good idea.

Eddie   He's very fond of you.

Sid   Is he?

Eddie   Compared to the other arty farties she hangs out with, he loves you.

Sid   Me too; it's mutual.

Eddie   I can never get over how much bigger you look on the telly.

Sid   I'm . . . usually standing up.

Eddie   I think I'll pull the trigger after all.

Sid   No, no. Don't.

Sally   No please, don't.

Sid   I wouldn't if I were you.

Eddie   Just don't have a heart attack, all right?

Sid   Well, I'm not sure I can guarantee that.

Sally   *Please* don't.

Sid   In fact I think it just missed a beat.

Eddie   You little fibber.

Sid   No, definitely.

Eddie *releases the safety catch.*

Sally   Ahh!

Sid   Ooh; there it goes again.

Eddie   Now, watch. Watch!

Sid   No.

Eddie   No, don't close your eyes; watch.

Sid   I should cocoa.

Eddie   I'm not going to do it if you don't open your eyes.

Sid   I'm not bloody gonna then.

Eddie   Open your eyes.

Sally   Don't make him open his eyes!

Eddie   Open your eyes or the girl gets it.

Sally   Open your eyes! Sid, open your eyes.

Sid   All right! My eyes are open. Look. Open eyes. My eyes are wide open, only please; let's talk about this.

Eddie   Just watch. And don't tell Ron.

Sally   No!

Sid *whimpers. A little flag with BANG on it pops out of the gun.*

Sid   Ahhh! Euhhh. Ohh. Mm.

Eddie *laughs.*

Sally   You bastard.

Eddie   That's good, innit? I got that from Alan Alan.

Sally   You complete bastard!

Sid   Agh.

Eddie   You all right?

Sid   Fine . . . .

Sid *gets pains down his arm and gesticulates.*

Sally   Oh, Jesus.

Eddie   What does he want?

Sally   He wants his tablets.

Eddie   His what?

Sally   His nitroglycerine.

Eddie   What? Oh, no. Now listen. Listen to me. You are NOT having a heart attack, all right!

Sid *can't breath.*

Eddie   Did you hear me! Give him his fucking tablets! Listen, you ponce; if you have a bleeding heart attack I will fucking shoot you. You listening to me? Sid? Please don't have a heart attack. Please? Please don't. It's not a real gun, Sid. Look. It's for kids. I was thinking; they shouldn't sell them to kids really. Could have someone's eye out with that. Listen, Sid, don't die, mate. Please? Ron'll fucking kill me.

Sid Go away.

Eddie You all right?

Sid Never better.

Sally I'll get a doctor.

Sid No! Stop fussing.

Sally That was your last one.

Sid There's another bottle in the car, in the glove compartment.

Sally *leaps up.*

Sally You could have killed him.

Eddie No, be fair.

Sally You stupid bloody animal.

Eddie It would have been strictly unintentional.

Sally You should be locked up.

Exit **Sally**.

Eddie She's not entirely alone in that opinion. It breeds prejudice, this profession. People tend to forget we're all individuals. Ronnie didn't want to hurt you. Dampen his ardour; that's what he said. Is your ardour dampened?

Sid Sopping.

Eddie Right then. Anyway; he sends his love.

Sid That's nice of him.

Eddie He's a nice bloke.

Sid He's a diamond.

Enter **Kenneth**, *covered in tomatoes and assorted rotten grocery,* **Barbara** *bringing up the rear.*

Kenneth   Don't look at me. Don't speak to me. I have never been so humiliated in my life.

Barbara   Don't bang on about it, Kenny; it's only fruit and veg.

Kenneth   Oh, the filth. The disease!

Barbara   I've never seen walk-ons so enthusiastic.

Kenneth   Poxy Middlesex wankers.

Barbara   There was a fight for the fruit between them and the props boys. Hello, Eddie. What are you doing here?

Kenneth   Get me to the shower. Cleanse me immediately.

Barbara   Oh, get in there and cleanse yourself. What do you want, Eddie?

Eddie   Ronnie asked me to come and have a little chat with Sid.

Barbara   Oh, he did, did he.

Kenneth   This has made me mind up. There's going to be no more of this. This is absolutely the last one. I'd rather do *Call My Bluff*.

Exit **Kenneth** *to the shower. Enter* **Sally** *with tablets.* **Sid** *takes a couple more.*

Sally   Here.

Barbara   Are you all right?

Sid   I'm fine, for Christ's sake.

Barbara   Eddie, he's not well!

Eddie   No, he's fine. Aren't you, Sid?

Sally   Could you get the hell out of here please!

Eddie   Manners.

Sally   There's some other gorilla over in the car park come looking for you.

Eddie   Yeh?

Barbara   Sounds like Charlie.

Eddie   Looking for me?

Barbara   Ronnie must want you for some other little errand. Go on then.

Eddie   Right. Keep it damp, Sid.

Eddie *leaves.*

Sally   Twenty-seven's next. Shall I get Peter to reschedule?

Sid   No.

Barbara   How are you feeling?

Sid   Stop fussing, will you.

Sally   I'm going to call a doctor.

Sid   No.

Barbara   I think she should Sid.

Sid   I'm fine.

Sally   I'll phone from the pub.

Sally *leaves.*

Sid   I'm going to be needed soon.

Barbara   Let's be on the safe side, shall we?

Sid   Just leave it alone. I'm fine.

Barbara   Oh, Sidney. What am I going to do with you?

Sid   Take me home.

Barbara   Oh, right. Yours or mine?

Sid   I just want to go home of an evening and find you there.

Barbara   Sid, you have to stop this.

Sid   Tell me I'm wrong.

Barbara   This is making you ill. You look lovely.

Sid   Don't start.

Barbara   Where's your sense of humour?

Sid   In my trouser pocket. Let's get a place of our own.

Barbara   People would laugh, Sid. People would laugh at us.

Sid   No they wouldn't.

Barbara   I think they would.

Sid   Well, it's a living.

Barbara   Behind our backs.

Sid   Let 'em. I don't care.

Barbara   Well I do. I've been a joke too much of my life. I don't want my private life public; I don't want to be laughed at, I don't want to be pitied, I want to lock my door at night and leave Her outside.

Sid   Leave her in Stanmore. We'll get our own place.

Barbara   Sid, when you look at me you don't see me you see Her. So when I look at you I see Her in your eyes. I try to be me when I'm with you but I'm not. She's there between us. And He's between us too; good old Sid. Yuck yuck yuck. When I'm with you, Sid, I don't know who the fuck I am.

Sid   You are the finest woman I ever set eyes on. The noblest, the brightest, the kindest. You could make my entire life worth living.

They gaze into each other's eyes.

I mean it.

Barbara   I know you do.

She leans forward to kiss him, and **Eddie** *enters.*

Eddie   Mrs K. Ronnie's got a little problem.

Barbara   What sort of little problem?

Eddie   He's been arrested.

Barbara   He's been what?

Eddie   Banged up.

Barbara   What for?

Sid   Nothing trivial, I hope?

Eddie   Suspicion of murder.

Barbara   What?

Sid   You're joking.

Barbara   That's ridiculous.

Eddie   I know.

Barbara   He's not that sort of bloke.

Eddie   He *knows* that sort of bloke.

Barbara   But he's not one of 'em.

Eddie   I know.

Sid   Who got murdered?

Eddie   Some Italian geezer.

Barbara   Zamperelli?

Eddie   Yep.

Barbara   Oh, Jesus.

Sid   Why would Ronnie murder an Italian?

Barbara   He didn't.

Eddie   He wouldn't.

Sid   I know; he never would. So why'd they arrest him?

Eddie   The Italian murdered Ronnie's brother.

Sid   I see.

Eddie   Lucky for him Ronnie's not like that.

Sid   Absolutely. He's dead though?

Eddie   He is. And Ronnie's a bit pissed off, I can tell you.

Barbara   I bloody knew it. I knew they'd pick up Ronnie.

Sid   You sure he didn't do it?

Barbara   I know he didn't.

Sid   Were you with him?

Barbara   No, as a matter of fact I was with you.

Eddie   He says you're to get to Hendon nick straight away.

Barbara   Tell the stupid bastard I'm working.

Eddie   He was very insistent.

Barbara   Tell him he can go to hell. I told him not to threaten Zamperelli. Tell him I bloody warned him.

Eddie   He won't like it.

Barbara   Go on, Eddie; get gone.

Eddie   Couldn't I tell him you love him and you'll stick by him no matter what?

Barbara   No, Eddie, you stick by him. You tell him you love him.

Eddie   Well, I'll give it a try.

Barbara   Goodbye, Eddie.

Eddie   Bye then.

She's ushered him out.

Barbara   Oh, sod him.

Sid   It's a sign, this is.

Barbara   Sod him, sod him, sod him.

Sid   It's fate, that's what it is.

Barbara   What am I going to do?

Sid   Well, you can stop worrying for a start. He's made his bed and he can lie in it. You can get on with your life. You know what I fancy?

He gets out a bottle of champagne.

Barbara   I don't know what to do.

Sid   It'll all turn out for the best. You'll see. It's all gonna be hunky-dory. End of the shoot, you and me, Capri. Or a Cortina down to Camber Sands. Come on, we'll have the time of our lives.

She suddenly runs out of the caravan.

Barbara   Eddie!

Eddie (*off*)   Yeh?

Barbara   Tell him I love him.

Eddie (*off*) That's more like it.

Barbara   Tell him I'll be there as soon as I can. Eddie! And for as long as it takes.

Eddie (*off*)   Right. I will.

She returns to the van.

Sid   How long's that then?

Barbara   How long's what?

Sid   As long as it takes?

Barbara   Depends what they think they've got on him. Days. God help him, months.

Sid   What if he goes down?

Barbara   He won't go down.

Sid   What if he does?

Barbara   He won't.

Sid   He might. What if he does?

Barbara   We'll appeal.

Sid   That could take years.

Barbara   Well, that's what I mean, that's what it means. As long as it takes.

Sid   I'm fifty-nine.

Barbara   You're sixty-one.

Sid   You see?

A terrible pause. She sees the champagne bottle he still holds.

Barbara   You selfish sod.

Sid   Yeah but . . .

Barbara   You fuck.

Sid   No listen . . .

Barbara   Don't say it, Sidney. Whatever it is don't even think it.

Sid   He's a villain! He's a useless waste of ruddy space.

Barbara   He's my husband.

Sid   Yeah but why him? Why choose him? Why has it always been, why does it have to be *him*?

Barbara   Because there's a bit of me Ronnie holds in trust, in perpetuity. The me he looks after is the me that's me. The me I recognise. I can come home to him and there I am.

Sid   You can't if he's in bloody Wandsworth.

Barbara   That's not the point. The point is, whether you like it or not you belong with Val. You belong to her.

Sid   No, no no.

Barbara   Yes. Like a coat on a hook. If it's cold out, you want your coat; you know where it is. You want reminding who you are; you know who to go to. That's love, isn't it?

Sid *is suddenly near to tears. He bites his hand.*

Barbara   Isn't it?

Sid (*hardly audible*)   But I don't like him.

Barbara   What?

Sid   I don't like him.

Barbara   Ronnie?

Sid   No. The bloke I am when I'm with Val. I don't like him any more.

Barbara   Well, that's very sad. There are times I could strangle Ronnie, but the me that's there with him is always the me I love.

Sid   Well, this is the me I love. The me you're looking at.

Barbara   What about when you're alone, Sid; do you love him then? Well that's very sad Sidney, because it's not going to work. All this desire; it's just self-pity.

Sid   Please, girl . . .

Barbara   This is the thing, Sid. This is what it is. This is the problem. You used to make me laugh. That was a long time ago. You don't make me laugh any more. You make me unhappy. Being with you makes me unhappy. Your wanting me makes me unhappy. I'm unhappy because you're unhappy and you're unhappy because of me. That's a whole lifetime of unhappiness piling up around us unless one of us has the strength to give it up.

Sid   I can't live without you. I'm not sure I can. I'm getting old. I'm worn out. I'm wearing out. My back aches. This eye's all blurred every morning. I've had a cough since 1969. Nothing heals any more. I don't want to get old.

Barbara I can't stop you getting old, Sid. If we were together I wouldn't be new any more. And all you ever want is someone new. If you feel old Sid, it's because all you dream of is new.

Barbara *kisses his knuckles and leaves.*
Kenneth *returns silently, towelling his hair.*

Kenneth Yes, well. That's better. No good sitting there covered in muck; you want to give yourself a good hose down. I came to see you last month, at the Victoria Palace. I didn't come round. Sitting in the circle being force-fed that puerile tat was bad enough. I don't blame you; it's the same swill we've all been slopping about in for years. You were dreadful. And you know it. So was everyone else. Except her. She was doing her Marie Lloyd and suddenly I heard heavy breathing over my shoulder. I thought I know that wheeze. It was you, breathless, leaning on the back of the circle. It's a big place, Victoria Palace. I thought, if he's up and down those stairs twice nightly just for a gawp at madam he's not long for this world. [Mind you,] the saddest thing was the audience. They weren't even in with a chance of a fumble. All they could do was watch. Then at the curtain call you came forward and said 'Did you like it?' And they all shouted 'Yes!' and you said 'Good, 'cos we're going to do the whole ruddy thing over again' and I thought God help us, that's all we've ever done.

Sid *drinks.*

Kenneth You know why you love her, Sid? She's vivid. From the Greek. Vivace. She's vivacious; and she vivifies. She pertains to life. She's somehow got the hang of it, unlike us.

Sid *bows his head.* **Kenneth**, *in an unthinking moment of compassion, touches the back of* **Sid**'*s head.* **Sid**, *surprised, flinches. Stares at him aggressively.* **Kenneth** *backs off.* **Sally** *enters.*

Sally Your GP's on a housecall and the Slough ambulance is on strike and do we want one from Hammersmith and have you actually collapsed and I said no and they said well find out if you had and phone them back.

Kenneth   He's all right. Back to his old self.

Kenneth *leaves.*

Sally   Are you all right?

Sid *nods.*

Sally   Do you need another pill?

Sid *shakes his head.*

Sally   What's the matter?

Sid   She's gone.

Sally   Have another pill.

He brushes her off.

I don't want you to die!

Sid   I don't intend to.

Sally   takes out the photo.

Sally   Look at her?

Sid   Why?

Sally   Please.

Sid   What for?

Sally   For me.

He takes the photo. Looks at it. Puts it down.

Sally   Well?

Sid   Well what?

Sally   Is it her?

Sid   Yes it's her. Jane.

Sally   Jenny.

Sid You're right. Jenny with the two left feet. Don't look at me like that. It's just there's so many of you. Bin it.

Sally She'll turn up one day. One of your misdemeanours'll walk right through that door.

Sid God help me.

Sally What would you do then?

Sid I'd give her a cup of tea and her train fare home. Let me get some kip, will you?

Sally What if she wanted to be part of your life?

Sid No room.

Sally You've room enough for all your women.

Sid There's only one woman in my life. And she's not in my life.

He drinks a large shot.

Sally They're going all over the world.

Sid Would you do me a favour?

Sally All over the world, I'd get to go.

Sid Sally.

Sally What?

Sid Would you give me a kiss?

Sally No.

Sid Please.

Sally I gave you a kiss.

Sid That was years ago. Give us another.

Sally You said one'd be enough.

Sid One's never enough.

Sally Singapore they're going. And Australia.

Sid If you won't give us a kiss, undress for me.

Sally   No.

Sid   I won't touch you. Let me just . . . look.

Sally   No.

Sid   Please.

Sally   No.

Sid *begins to cry. It's a deep and rending sorrow.* **Sally** *is frozen, torn between surprise and compassion.*

Sally   It's alright.

She touches him. He takes her face between his hands and kisses her. She pushes him away. Her mind is suddenly made up. She swiftly goes around the caravan collecting her things. She puts on her coat, grabs her bag, and goes to the door.

Sally   I'll send you a card.

The lights fade.

Act Four

Emmanuelle. 1978.

The caravan sits disused in a scrappy corner of Pinewood Studios, leaning at a permanent slant. The tatty curtains are pulled shut, the room dank and cold. It's raining outside. **Barbara** *stands just inside the door, just looking.* **Kenneth** *enters with a raincoat round his head and two plastic cups of tea.*

Kenneth   I thought I'd find you here.

Barbara   Oh, Kenny, don't get wet.

Kenneth   A little late, alas.

Barbara   Mind your step, it's all skew-wif.

Kenneth   Brought you a cuppa.

Barbara   Oh, ta.

Kenneth *enters the van.*

Kenneth   Oh dear.

Barbara   The rain's got in.

Kenneth   Well, it's had it, hasn't it?

Barbara   They shouldn't have let it rot.

Kenneth   They should have given it to me.

Barbara   They should have towed it away.

Kenneth   I think they took your point. Peter summoned the site manager as soon as we finished the read-through.

Barbara   How was it?

Kenneth   We struggled through without you.

Barbara   I couldn't face it.

Kenneth   I'm not surprised.

Barbara   I knew it was only a cameo, I knew it wouldn't be much . . .

Kenneth   I know.

Barbara   I didn't want to do much . . .

Kenneth   Me neither.

Barbara   Then I flicked through to my scene, took one look at it, and I thought, oh no.

Kenneth   They think you've flounced off home.

Barbara   I went to the bar. Thought I'd come for one last look.

Kenneth   Nice to see you anyway, however briefly. How's Stanmore?

Barbara   Ronnie's gone.

Kenneth   Well, good riddance.

Barbara   Don't be flippant, Kenny, nothing's that simple. Years ago, when he was on remand he used to say to me; 'I can't do life. Life's a bleeding long time.' It is 'n all.

Kenneth   And just when you've had enough of it you've got your sixties to get through and your seventies to look forward too.

Barbara   Except Sid.

Kenneth   No. No seventies for Sid. Lucky swine.

Barbara   Oh, poor Sid. I miss him.

Kenneth   And poor Imogen.

Barbara   Oh, and Imogen. Why would anyone do that to themselves? Anyone as beautiful as that.

Sid's *playing cards are on the table.* **Barbara** *toys with them.*

Kenneth   She was thirty-eight and she didn't like herself. You're the only person I know who likes themselves. The rest of us grieve. We grieve for the person we dreamed of being but never grew into.

Barbara   Oh, cheer up. What's the rest of the script like?

Kenneth   Positively vile. It wasn't a read-through, it was a wade-through. One long relentless stream of badly written jokes cobbled together with disdain for the actors and complete contempt for the audience. One of the most morally and aesthetically offensive pieces of work I've ever read. I think I'll just camp it up.

Barbara   That's what I admire about you, Kenny; always searching for an original approach.

Kenneth   You've quit then?

Barbara   I don't want to get my tits out again, not for a naff cameo, not at my age.

Kenneth   They all had 'em out in *England.* Jack said he couldn't look anyone in the eye. I blame Robin Askwith's bottom.

Barbara   They're desperate.

Kenneth   I've got to get mine out in this.

Barbara   Really desperate. How is your bum?

Kenneth   Ask the Spanish inquisition; they seem to have taken up permanent residence. Desperate's not the word.

Barbara   You all got your botties out in *Constable.*

Kenneth   That was in context. And I was younger then. Do us a favour.

Barbara   What?

Kenneth   Will you have a butcher's?

Barbara   At what?

Kenneth   From a medical perspective?

Barbara   Kenneth!

Kenneth   I tried in the mirror, but I couldn't see a thing. Then I pulled a muscle. I can't just walk into make-up. I fear I may have cultivated a small vineyard down there.

Barbara   Oh, please.

Kenneth   Have a look.

Barbara   No.

Kenneth   Fifteen years we've known each other and you won't even take a quick peek at me anus.

Barbara   If that's your definition of friendship, I'm not surprised you haven't got any. It's all right for you anyway; people don't have any expectations of a bottom.

Kenneth   Oh, well, yes, I'm well aware that your twin contributions to world culture stand at an altogether higher echelon.

Barbara   Slightly lower lately.

Kenneth   You've never disappointed.

Barbara   How would you know? I've watched you in rushes; you always look away.

Kenneth   I do no such thing.

Barbara   The slightest threat of a bare boob and you put sugar in your tea even though you've finished your tea and you don't take sugar.

Kenneth   Don't talk such utter drivel.

Barbara   You're all mouth and no trousers.

Kenneth   I've haunted the fleshpots of Morocco and the wings of the Talk of the Town. I've encountered more bosoms than you could shake a stick at . . .

She lifts up her sweater. He stirs his tea.

Kenneth   Well, I'm the wrong man to ask anyway. Isn't there some sort of test you can do with a pencil?

Barbara   I've tried it. I got as far as six pencils, a ruler and a fountain pen, then I gave up.

Kenneth   Well, if you ever get tired of acting, you'd do well at W.H. Smith's.

Barbara   I don't want to be humiliated any more.

Kenneth   I've been clenching my buttocks all week, which is above and beyond the call of duty for a man with my afflictions.

Barbara   I've been doing press-ups.

Kenneth   Bet you never got your chin off the floor.

Barbara   I never got my chin on it.

They laugh.

Kenneth   Here we go then; Venus unveiled.

Barbara   Oh, Kenny, no.

Kenneth   No, fair do's. I want to walk on to that soundstage exuding confidence from every orifice.

Barbara   Oh, go on then; get it over with.

He bares his bum.

Kenneth   Well?

Barbara   Oh, it's . . .

Kenneth   What?

Barbara   It's fine.

Kenneth   Fine?

Barbara   As bottoms go.

Kenneth   I know how bottoms go; that's what I'm worried about.

Barbara   Put it away.

Kenneth   Would you say it was perky?

Barbara   Not exactly.

Kenneth   Amusing?

Barbara   Well . . .

Kenneth   It's gruesome, isn't it?

Sally   Toupee tape.

Barbara   Ahh!

Kenneth   God in heaven!

Sally *appears from the shadows.*

Sally   Sorry.

Barbara   Oh. You frightened the life out of me.

Sally   Sorry.

Barbara   Where'd you come from?

Sally   I heard you coming so I sort of hid. Sorry. I thought you'd just pop in and go out again. You could use toupee tape. To lift the buttocks?

Kenneth   Yes. This was a private consultation. Thank you.

Barbara   What are you doing here?

Sally   Nothing. Same as you.

Barbara   What's that?

Sally   Remembering.

Barbara   You were close to Sid, weren't you? I always thought that.

Sally *gathers up the playing cards, places them tidily.*

Barbara   You didn't come to funeral. I remember being surprised you weren't there.

Sally   I was in Sunderland.

Barbara   Sunderland?

Sally   I wanted to see where he died. It's a huge theatre. I expected it to be closed but it wasn't. So I bought a ticket. It

was a different show of course. It had that bloke from On
The Buses in it. And a big fish-tank with some naked girls
swimming in it. Sid would have liked that.

Barbara   You should have come to the funeral.

Sally   I went to Sunderland.

Kenneth   How was the show?

Barbara   Kenneth.

Sally   Dreadful.

Kenneth   Well, miss him if you must, but don't mourn for
the manner of his passing. He died laughing at his own
jokes, which was perfectly apt.

Barbara   Have some compassion, Kenny. He worked
himself to death.

Kenneth   A number one tour of the provinces is too long
and lingering a suicide, even for Sid to contemplate.

Barbara   It was the drink then.

Kenneth   I shouldn't think so. He could have entered his
liver in the Olympics.

Barbara   Well then what?!

Kenneth   He had a heart attack, dearie. He was probably
humping the ASM.

Barbara   I should have called him back. He called me
half a dozen times and I never called him back.

Kenneth   Everything ends in silence. It has to be
someone's. No love affair lasts for ever.

Sally   Sid managed it.

Barbara   What do you mean?

Sally   It was for ever for Sid.

Barbara   Don't.

Sally   I'm glad for him.

Barbara   Do you believe in heaven?

Kenneth   You're no doubt expecting a cynical retort, but yes I do, as a matter of fact.

Barbara   What's it like, do you think?

Kenneth   It's whatever you most fancy.

Barbara   It's not lounging about on a cloud with angels in togas, then?

Kenneth   Well, in my case that's just about spot on. They'd have to be lewd little angels, though. I imagine a banqueting table piled high with whatever you never got enough of. One long eternal Roman orgy.

Barbara   You're so deep. I think heaven's being left alone with a Steenbeck in the edit suite. You sit in front of your life and you're allowed to re-edit it. Cut the rotten bits, loop the good sex, montage the highlights . . . watch it over and over. Live it again and again, a bit better every time. And eventually . . . make it perfect. What about you, Sally?

Sally   I don't believe in heaven.

Kenneth *feels the familiar nagging pain in his gut.*

Barbara   You all right?

He nods, in pain.

Barbara   Oh, Kenny.

Kenneth   Oh, I'm sick of this. I wish I could just retire, jack it all in.

Barbara   Why don't you?

Kenneth   Because I'm a narcissistic nitwit, and the little pond of my celebrity is the only source of water in this desert of a life. I couldn't survive my flat night after night if I wasn't on the telly. I just wish they'd leave my bottom out of it.

Barbara   Toupee tape. Have you got some?

Sally *tries to find some in her bag.*

Kenneth   They don't even like me any more. The public loathe me.

Barbara   Don't be ridiculous. There are millions out there who just adore you.

Kenneth   Yes, most of whom I seem to run into between my flat and the bus stop, all carrying two large carrier bags and a can of Special Brew.

Barbara   It's brilliant for boobs. We got through six rolls on Dick. Drop 'em, Kenny.

Kenneth   Do what?

Barbara   Trousers down.

Kenneth   Oh, this is ridiculous.

Barbara   Little trick of the trade, that's all.

She tapes his buttocks up.

Kenneth   It's hard to describe the abject horror of being recognised in the street by terminally ugly unwashed ignoramuses who think etiquette's an expensive catfood.

Barbara   They love you.

Kenneth   I don't want the love of the nation, it's unhygienic.

Barbara   There.

Kenneth   How is it?

Barbara   Pretty as a picture.

Kenneth   Oh yes.

Barbara   Well, it's not quite a Michelangelo.

Kenneth   As long as it's less of a Stanley Spencer.

Barbara   It belongs in the British Museum, Kenny.

Kenneth   Oooh yes, I should be a permanent feature.

Facing the door as you come in with an inscription on me buttocks; The End is Nigh.

They laugh. **Kenneth** *suffers sudden stabbing pains. He stops laughing.* **Barbara** *holds his hand. He grips her tight until the pain subsides.*

Barbara   All right?

Kenneth   Oh . . . what's the bloody point?

The pain subsides.

You know when I knew it was all over? I got home one night last year and turned on the Cabaret. It had been a wet Sunday; it hadn't gone well but it hadn't been disastrous. And I turned it on and I heard canned laughter. They'd smothered me in canned laughter. And I recognised it. It was the same tape they use for all the sitcoms. They use it on *Bless This House.* You can actually recognise individual morons in the audience cackling away like the living dead. I didn't know who to feel sorrier for, them or me. Them mindlessly guffawing through eternity or me slogging me guts out for laughs that weren't even mine. I realised with some horror they could well have been laughing at Sid. Then they started putting out the films diced up like stewing steak and I swear I felt like they'd done it to me. Chopped me up and laid me out on six different trays in the butcher's window to be gawped at by millions of idiot plebeians who think talent's a substance that oozes out of game-show hosts and can't even laugh for themselves. Then me kidneys appeared on the *Parkinson* show and I knew we'd had it. We're dead already, we just lack the good taste to lie down.

Kenneth *leaves.*

Barbara   Come on; I'll buy you a gin.

Sally   No thanks.

Barbara   You can't sit here. You'll get mildew.

Sally   I'll be fine.

Barbara   You don't look fine.

Sally   They're going to tow it away! It's all there is left and you told them to tow it away.

Barbara   I'm sorry. Oh, sweetheart, I'm sorry.

Sally   I couldn't get him out of my head. I tried for months I went to Sunderland I stood outside the house I went to the grave at Kilburn and I couldn't get him out until I came back here and I came in here and this is where I left him.

Barbara   Shhh.

Sally   And you told them to tow it away.

Barbara   I'm sorry. Sally, I'm sorry.

Sally   I miss him.

Barbara   You loved him, I know.

Sally   I'm lonely.

Barbara   It'll pass, Sally. It passes.

Sally   I've been alone my whole bloody life.

Barbara   Me too. And never a sodding moment to myself. Love's not a safe haven, it's a choppy bleedin' ocean. And 'I love you' 's not a lightship, it's a distress signal. Come on.

Sally *shakes her head.*

Barbara   You can't stay here.

Sally   I want to stay here.

Barbara   He's gone, Sally. I was lying in bed the other night and I was cuddling my pillow. Silly sod, but I do. And I heard myself whisper: 'You'll never leave me. You'll always be here.' And I realised I wasn't talking to my pillow, I was talking to myself. And I realised something really obvious, something I've always known but never quite acknowledged. There are two of me. There's the me that needs looking after and there's the me that looks after me. And they've both been there since the very beginning. And the one who looks after me is always going to be there. So whatever happens I'll always have myself, and I'm bleeding good company.

Sally *laughs.*

Barbara   We were laughing.

Sally   What?

Barbara   Kenny asked what the point was. Just before he felt the pain. Well, we were laughing. Come on. Come on. There's a small steakhouse in Stanmore where the owner, if she's in the mood, will ply the clientele with so much free booze you can get way beyond depressed; you can get to fuck it all and the horse it rode in on.

Sally   I can't really drink, I feel really bad next day.

Barbara   That's because you haven't discovered the cure.

Sally   What's the cure?

Barbara   Brent Cross. Come on.

Sally   What if the owner's not in the mood?

Barbara   Don't worry sweetheart; she is.

Barbara *leaves.* **Sally** *turns to follow her and* **Sid** *appears. A tune begins; 'For All We Know'.* **Sally** *hesitates, taking in his shambling posture, his familiar grin. Then she leaves, abruptly. Sid goes to the table, gathers the pack and shuffles. Out of the shadows comes* **Imogen**. *He smiles, she smiles, and she joins him. He deals the cards and they pick up their hands. Imogen stakes her watch.* **Sid** *stakes his watch. They look at their cards.* **Imogen** *smiles, takes off her top and puts it on the table. The lights fade.*

End.

The Graduate

based on the novel by Charles Webb *and the screenplay by* Calder Willingham *and* Buck Henry

The Graduate was first presented by John Reid and Sacha Brooks at the Gielgud Theatre, London, on 24 March 2000, with the following cast (in order of appearance):

Benjamin Braddock	Matthew Rhys
Mr Braddock	Paul Jesson
Mr Robinson	Colin Stinton
Mrs Braddock	Amanda Boxer
Mrs Robinson	Kathleen Turner
Elaine Robinson	Kelly Reilly
Desk Clerk, Waiter, Psychiatrist	Alan Barnes
Belligerent Man, Priest	Geoffrey Towers
Stripper	Sally Chattaway
Wedding Guests	Sara Bienvenu
	Josh Cohen

Director Terry Johnson
Set & Costume Designer Rob Howell
Lighting Designer Hugh Vanstone
Sound Designer Mike Walker
Music Barrington Pheloung & Original Artists
Assistant Director Caroline Hadley
Company Stage Manager Alan Hatton
Deputy Stage Manager Natalie Wood
Assistant Stage Managers Marcus Watson
                             Rosemary McIntosh

Produced by special arrangement with Canal+ Image
Executive for Canal+ Image Ron Halpern

The original production continued at the Gielgud Theatre from 31 July 2000 with the following cast:

Benjamin Braddock	Josh Cohen
Mr Braddock	Alex Giannini
Mr Robinson	Colin Stinton
Mrs Braddock	Amanda Boxer
Mrs Robinson	Jerry Hall
Elaine Robinson	Lucy Punch
Desk Clerk, Waiter, Psychiatrist	Alan Barnes
Belligerent Man, Priest	Geoffrey Towers
Stripper	Julie McKenna
Wedding Guests	Coral Beed
	Christine St. John
	Andres Williams

Director Terry Johnson
Set & Costume Designer Rob Howell
Lighting Designer Hugh Vanstone
Sound Designer Mike Walker
Music Barrington Pheloung & Original Artists
Assistant Director Caroline Hadley
Company Stage Manager Alan Hatton
Deputy Stage Manager Lorna Cobbold
Assistant Stage Managers Brad Fitt
Rosemary McIntosh
Ian Slater

Characters

Benjamin
Mrs Robinson
Mr Robinson
Elaine
Dad, Mr Braddock
Mom, Mrs Braddock
Stripper
Desk Clerk
Two Men
Psychiatrist
Wedding Guests
Priest

The Desk Clerk doubles the Priest and the Psychiatrist. The Two Men and the Wedding Guests are doubled by the company.

Setting

California, 1960s.

A flexible, minimalist setting with one door USR and another DSL. Simple furnishings transform the space into: Benjamin's bedroom; the lobby of the Taft Hotel; Room 515, the Taft Hotel; a downtown bar; the Robinsons' living room; the Braddocks' poolside; a rooming house bedroom, Berkeley; a vestry; a motel room.

The light beyond the windows of these rooms is bright and Californian, slamming through curtains or blinds, lending sharp contrast to the interiors. Similarly, the night scenes share the illusion of illumination from source, with rich amber light spilling from lamps or through doors, sculpting well-defined playing areas from deep shadow.

The effect should be slightly claustrophobic.

Act One

Scene One

In the darkness, the sound of amplified breathing as if through an oxygen mask.

Lights come up on **Benjamin**'s *room. Door to en suite bathroom, door to hallway. A bed, a chair. Airfix aeroplanes. A fish-tank.*

It's night. **Benjamin** *sits in semi-darkness amidst the remnants of his pre-pubescence. He is perfectly still, and wears a diving suit. The sounds of a party filtering up from downstairs. The door opens to throw a shaft of bright light across the room.* **Benjamin**'s *father silhouetted.*

Dad   Ben? Ben?

Benjamin *removes the mask.*

Dad   What are you doing?

Benjamin   You said I should put the suit on.

Dad   I said you should put the suit on and come downstairs.

Benjamin   I put the suit on.

Dad   Then come on downstairs.

Benjamin   I lost the inclination.

Dad   It's a hell of a suit, isn't it?

Benjamin   Yes, it is.

Dad   Happy graduation.

Benjamin   Thank you.

Dad   So, come on down.

Benjamin   I'll be down.

Dad   The guests are all here.

Benjamin   I'll be down soon.

Dad   What is it, Ben?

Benjamin   Nothing.

Dad   Then why don't you come down and see your guests?

Benjamin   I have some things on my mind right now.

Dad   What things?

Benjamin   Just some things.

Dad   Ben, these are our friends down there. You owe them a little courtesy.

Benjamin   I'd rather be alone right now.

Dad   Hal Robinson and I have been doing business together in this town for seventeen years. He's the best friend I have. He has a client in Chicago that he's put off seeing so he could be here tonight . . .

Benjamin   I don't want to see the Robinsons.

Dad   The Terhunes have come all the way from . . .

Benjamin   I don't want to see the Terhunes. I don't want to see the Robinsons, the Terhunes, the Pearsons or anyone else.

Dad   I don't know what's got into you but whatever it is I want you to snap out of it and march right on down there!

Benjamin   I just need to be alone right now.

The door opens and **Mr Robinson** *strides in with* **Benjamin**'s *mother.*

Mr Robinson   All hail the conquering hero!

Mom   Ben, where are you?

Benjamin   I'm here.

Mr Robinson   Ben!

Benjamin   Mr Robinson.

Dad   He's wearing the suit.

Mom   You're wearing the suit!

Dad   He loves it.

Mom   Do you like it Ben?

Dad   He'd better, or I'm out a coupla hundred bucks!

Mr Robinson   It's a hell of a suit.

Dad   Isn't it?

Mom   Ben, the guests are all downstairs.

Dad   Come on Ben, let's go down.

Mr Robinson   Ben, I want to shake your hand. Goddammit I'm proud of you.

Mom   We're all so proud of you, Ben.

Dad   Everyone's lining up down there to shake your hand.

Mr Robinson   I took a look at your yearbook, Ben. Head of the debating club. Captain of cross-country. Editor of the school newspaper.

Dad   No one appears in that yearbook more than Ben.

Mr Robinson   Social secretary of his house. I'm running out of fingers . . . First in your class . . .

Benjamin   I wasn't first.

Mr Robinson   Oh?

Benjamin   I *tied* for first. I tied with Abe Frankel.

Mr Robinson   Well, the luck of the Jews. Now give me the low-down on that prize of yours.

Benjamin   Well, I'm not . . .

Dad   Tell him about it, Ben.

Mom   It's called the Frank Halpingham Education Award and it puts Ben through two years of graduate school when he goes into teaching.

Mr Robinson   And they chose Ben.

Dad   He's into Harvard and he's into Yale. And what's that other one?

Mom   Columbia.

Dad   Columbia.

Mr Robinson   Well . . . good God Frank, you bred a genius.

Dad   I guess we did.

Mom   I don't know how.

Dad   We don't know where he got it from, but well yes, Ben has quite an intellect.

Mr Robinson   I've got one thing to say to you Ben. May I say one thing to your son?

Dad   Go right ahead.

Mr Robinson   I've just got one thing to say, Ben.

Benjamin   What's that, sir?

Mr Robinson   One word, Ben.

Benjamin   One word?

Mr Robinson   Plastics, Ben. Plastics. Will you think about that?

Benjamin   Yes I will.

Mom   Benjamin is going to teach; aren't you Ben?

Benjamin   Well . . .

Dad   Don't hound the boy, now.

Mom   Well . . .

Dad   Whatever this boy does . . .

Mr Robinson   Whatever he chooses to do . . .

Dad   This boy is gonna shine.

Mr Robinson   I couldn't be prouder of you Ben, if you were my own son.

Dad (*touched*)   Thank you, Hal. Say thank you, Ben.

Benjamin   Thank you.

Mr Robinson   I have to get to the airport.

Dad   You need a cab?

Mr Robinson   I'm gonna drive. My wife will need a cab.

Dad   We'll put her in a cab.

Mr Robinson   Just wait until you can't stand her a moment longer, then put her in a cab. Call a cab and just pour her in.

Mom   Oh scoot.

Dad   She knows how to enjoy herself.

Mr Robinson   She certainly does.

Mom   She just needed a little lie down, that's all she needed.

Mr Robinson   Ben, don't be a stranger.

Mr Robinson *leaves.*

Dad (*turning*)   Ben, you come on down now. Are you coming down, Ben?

Benjamin   No I'm not.

Dad   Those people down there . . .

Benjamin   Those people down there are grotesque!

Dad Grotesque?

Benjamin And you're grotesque.

Dad You're calling me grotesque?

Benjamin You are grotesque, and *I'm* grotesque, we're all grotesque. Not actually grotesque, you're not grotesque, but I have this feeling of grotesqueness when I even think about leaving this room, all right?

Dad Ben, you're all tied up in knots. You've just had the four most strenuous years of your life back there . . .

Benjamin They were nothing.

Dad Four golden years . . .

Benjamin Which add up to nothing.

Dad I'm going to have words with you later. I'm going downstairs to tell these people you are suddenly sick, and I am going to entertain these people on your behalf. And I do not wish to see your face.

Benjamin's *father leaves.*

Mom Are you sick, Ben?

Benjamin Oh, yes.

Mom Well then I guess you'd better get out of that suit.

Benjamin's *mother leaves.* **Benjamin** *struggles to get out of the suit. The door opens to silhouette* **Mrs Robinson**. *She watches* **Benjamin** *as he struggles, half undressed.*

Mrs Robinson I guess this isn't the spare room, is it?

Benjamin Oh good God . . . evening, Mrs Robinson.

Mrs Robinson Good evening, Benjamin.

Benjamin It's down the hall.

Mrs Robinson That's a hell of a thing.

Benjamin Yes, it is. Would you excuse me?

He struggles to make himself decent. **Mrs Robinson** *watches.*

Mrs Robinson   Is this what they're wearing back east?

Benjamin   It's a graduation gift.

Mrs Robinson   You sleep in it?

Benjamin   My father wanted me to show it off. He wanted a demonstration in the pool.

Mrs Robinson   It looks like a prophylactic.

Benjamin   A what?

Mrs Robinson   For the severely anxious.

Benjamin   It's at the end of the hall.

Mrs Robinson   What is?

Benjamin   The spare room.

Mrs Robinson   Ah.

Mrs Robinson *enters the room, a little unsteady.*

Benjamin   Mrs Robinson, I'm kind of distraught at the moment. I'm sorry to be rude but I have some things on my mind. It's good to see you.

Mrs Robinson   How are you?

Benjamin   I'm sorry not to be more congenial, but I'm trying to think.

Mrs Robinson   Is there an ashtray in here?

Benjamin   No.

He meant she should leave. She lights a cigarette. He takes her the waste bin. She puts her match in it.

Mrs Robinson   What are you upset about?

Benjamin   Some personal things.

Mrs Robinson   Girl trouble?

Benjamin   What?

Mrs Robinson   Do you have girl trouble?

Benjamin   Look, I'm sorry to be this way but I'm just, well right now I'm sort of . . .

Mrs Robinson   I was feeling a little unsteady myself. Your mother said I should lie down for a while.

Benjamin   The spare room's at the end of the hall.

Mrs Robinson   Are you drinking?

Benjamin   I don't drink.

Mrs Robinson   You don't drink?

Benjamin   As a rule. Of course I drink, but not as a rule.

Mrs Robinson   What do you drink? Bourbon?

Benjamin   Mrs Robinson, I have some things on my mind. And I have guests downstairs I should . . .

Mrs Robinson   May I ask you a question?

Benjamin   Uh-huh.

Mrs Robinson   What do you think of me?

Benjamin   What?

Mrs Robinson   What do you think of me?

Benjamin   Um . . .

Mrs Robinson   You've known me nearly all your life, you must think something . . .

Benjamin   Look, this is a rather strange conversation and I really ought to get downstairs . . .

Mrs Robinson   Don't you have any opinions at all?

Benjamin   No. Look, my father may be up again any minute, and . . .

Mrs Robinson   Benjamin.

Benjamin   What?

Mrs Robinson   Did you know I was an alcoholic?

Benjamin   Mrs Robinson, I don't want to talk about this.

Mrs Robinson   Did you know that?

Benjamin   No.

Mrs Robinson   You never suspected?

Benjamin   No.

Mrs Robinson   My God Benjamin, I fall out of cars. I insult senators at fondue parties. Surely you must have formed some sort of . . .

Benjamin   Mrs Robinson, this is none of my business . . .

Mrs Robinson   You never even suspected?

Benjamin   Would you excuse me?

Mrs Robinson   Sit down.

Benjamin   I'm going downstairs now.

Mrs Robinson   Why?

Benjamin   Because I want to be alone.

Mrs Robinson   There are three dozen people down there.

Benjamin   Then I'll go for a walk. I need to get out of here.

Benjamin *puts on a raincoat. It's older than he is.*

Mrs Robinson   Would you drive me home?

Benjamin   I'm sorry?

Mrs Robinson   I want you to drive me home. My husband's flying to Chicago. I don't like to be alone.

Benjamin   My God.

Mrs Robinson   What?

Benjamin   No. No, Mrs Robinson. Oh no.

Mrs Robinson   What's wrong?

Benjamin   Mrs Robinson, you didn't – I mean you didn't expect . . .

Mrs Robinson   What?

Benjamin   I mean you didn't really think I would do something like that.

Mrs Robinson   Like what?

Benjamin   What do you think!

Mrs Robinson   Well, I don't know.

Benjamin   For God's sake Mrs Robinson, you come to my room, you sit on the bed, you . . . smoke a cigarette, then you start opening up your personal life to me and now you're asking me to take you home because your husband's flying to Chicago.

Mrs Robinson   So?

Benjamin   Mrs Robinson, you are trying to seduce me. (*Certain.*) Aren't you. (*Uncertain.*) Aren't you?

Mrs Robinson   Why no. I hadn't thought of it. I feel rather flattered that you . . .

Benjamin (*mortified*)   Mrs Robinson, would you forgive me?

Mrs Robinson   What?

Benjamin   Will you forgive me for what I just said?

Mrs Robinson   It's all right.

Benjamin   It's not all right. That's the worst thing I've ever said to anyone!

Mrs Robinson   I've heard worse.

Benjamin   Please forgive me. Because I don't think of you that way. It's just I'm all mixed up.

Mrs Robinson   All right, calm down.

Benjamin   It makes me sick that I said that to you.

Mrs Robinson   I forgive you.

Benjamin   Can you? Can you ever forget I said that?

Mrs Robinson   We'll forget it right now.

Benjamin   I don't know what's wrong with me.

Mrs Robinson   It's forgotten.

Benjamin   Good.

Mrs Robinson   Benjamin?

Benjamin   Yes?

She stands and turns her back to him.

Mrs Robinson   Would you unzip my dress?

Benjamin   Un your what?

Mrs Robinson   Your mother said I should lie down. The spare bed is piled high with coats. Do you mind if I lie down, Benjamin?

Benjamin   No. Be my guest. Good night.

Mrs Robinson   Benjamin, would you please unzip the dress?

Benjamin   I'd rather not.

Mrs Robinson   Do you still think I'm trying to seduce you?

Benjamin   No I don't.

Mrs Robinson   With your parents just downstairs?

Benjamin   I ought to go down . . .

Mrs Robinson   You've known me all your life.

Benjamin   I know that.

Mrs Robinson   Would you please? It's hard for me to reach.

After a moment, **Benjamin** *unzips her dress.*

Thank you.

Benjamin   You're welcome.

Mrs Robinson   What are you scared of?

Benjamin   I'm not scared of anything.

Mrs Robinson   Then why do you keep moving away?

Benjamin   Because this is my room and if you're going to lie down I don't think I should be here.

She lets her dress fall.

Mrs Robinson   Haven't you ever seen anyone in a slip before?

Benjamin   Not in my parents' house, no.

Mrs Robinson   You still think I'm trying to seduce you, don't you?

Benjamin   No. But what if they walked in?

Mrs Robinson   Well, what if they did?

Benjamin   Well it would look pretty funny, wouldn't it?

Mrs Robinson   Do you think they'd be horrified that you saw me in my slip?

Benjamin   Well, they might get the wrong idea.

Mrs Robinson   I don't see why. I'm twice your age.

Benjamin   That's not the point.

Mrs Robinson   Benjamin, I am not trying to seduce you!

Benjamin   I know that.

Mrs Robinson   Would you like me to seduce you?

Benjamin   What?

Mrs Robinson   Is that what you're trying to tell me?

Benjamin   I'm going downstairs now. I apologise for what I said. I hope you can forget about it. I'm going downstairs.

He steps out the door.

Mrs Robinson   Benjamin.

Benjamin   What?

Mrs Robinson   Could you bring me my purse before you go?

Benjamin   No.

Mrs Robinson   Please?

Benjamin   I have to go downstairs.

Mrs Robinson   I really don't want to put this on again; won't you bring it to me?

Benjamin   Where is it?

Mrs Robinson   In the spare room. Beside the bed.

Benjamin   I'll get your purse. Then I have to go downstairs.

He leaves. **Mrs Robinson** *finishes her drink and goes into the bathroom, leaving the door ajar.* **Benjamin** *returns.*

Mrs Robinson?

Mrs Robinson (*off*)   I'm in the bathroom.

Benjamin   Well, here's your purse.

Mrs Robinson (*off*)   Could you bring it in?

Benjamin   I'll hand it to you.

Mrs Robinson (*off*)   Benjamin, I'm getting pretty tired of this.

Benjamin   What?

Mrs Robinson (*off*)   I'm getting pretty tired of all this suspicion. Now if you won't do me a simple favour, then I don't know what.

Benjamin   I'll put it on the bed.

Mrs Robinson (*off*)   For God's sake Benjamin, will you hand me the goddam purse.

Benjamin   I'd rather not.

Mrs Robinson (*off*)   All right then, put it on the bed.

Benjamin   OK. It's on the bed.

He crosses the room to the bed. **Mrs Robinson** *crosses the room behind him, closes the door and turns the key. She is naked.*

Benjamin   Oh, God.

She looks at him.

Oh, my God.

Mrs Robinson   Don't be nervous.

Benjamin   Let me out.

Mrs Robinson   Benjamin?

Benjamin   Get away from that door.

Mrs Robinson   I want to say something first.

Benjamin   Jesus Christ.

Mrs Robinson   Benjamin, I want you to know that I'm available to you . . .

Benjamin   Oh, my God . . .

Mrs Robinson   I want you to know you can call me up any time you want and we'll make some kind of arrangement.

Benjamin   Let me out.

Mrs Robinson   Do you understand what I said?

Benjamin   Yes! Yes! Let me out!

Mrs Robinson   Because I find you very attractive, and any time . . .

Mr Robinson (*off*)   Judith!

A moment, then **Mrs Robinson** *strides into the bathroom, grabbing her dress.* **Benjamin** *stares at the door as footsteps approach up the stairs.*

Mr Robinson (*off*)   Judith?

At the last moment, **Benjamin** *unlocks the door.*

Mr Robinson (*off*)   Benjamin?

And opens it.

Mr Robinson   Ah hah!

Benjamin   Ha hah!

Mr Robinson   Man of the moment.

Benjamin   Mr Robinson.

Mr Robinson   Have you seen my squiffy little wife?

Benjamin   I thought you were going to the airport.

Mr Robinson   I turned on the radio and lucky I did. The pilots came out in support of the cabin crews and nothing's flying out until morning. You know how much a stewardess thinks she's worth?

Benjamin   No I don't.

Mr Robinson   I never saw one didn't think she was God's gift. Wait a minute; that's not stewardesses, that's women, period. Know what I mean?

Benjamin   Yes.

Mr Robinson   Where is she?

Benjamin   Er . . . she's in the bathroom. She felt unwell.

Mr Robinson   She puke?

Benjamin   Well, she . . . I don't know.

Mr Robinson   She drinks so little, you understand. So when she drinks . . . Judith? Are you throwing up?

Mrs Robinson   I wasn't, but I might.

Mr Robinson   I've come to take you home.

Mrs Robinson   Give me a few minutes.

Mr Robinson   Is anything wrong? You look a little shaken up.

Benjamin   No, I'm just – I'm just – I'm just a little worried about my immediate future.

Mr Robinson   Ben, how old are you now?

Benjamin   I'll be twenty-one next week.

Mr Robinson   That's a hell of a good age to be.

Benjamin   Thank you.

Mr Robinson   I wish I was that age again. Because Ben?

Benjamin   What?

Mr Robinson   You'll never be young again.

Benjamin   I know.

Mr Robinson   Ben, can I say something to you?

Benjamin   Plastics?

Mr Robinson   No, Ben. I want to give you a bit of friendly advice.

Benjamin   I'd like to hear it.

Mr Robinson   I think you should take it a little easier than you seem to be. Have a good time with the girls and so forth. Sow a few wild oats. Because Ben, you're going to spend most of your life worrying. But right now you're young. Don't start worrying yet, for God's sake.

Benjamin   No.

Mr Robinson   Before you know it you'll find a nice little girl and settle down and have a damn fine life but until then try to make up a little for all the mistakes you're gonna make down the line. And while you're at it, make up for a few of mine.

Benjamin   I will, sir.

Mrs Robinson *comes out of the bathroom.*

Mr Robinson   I was just telling Ben here to sow a few wild oats. You think that's sound advice?

Mrs Robinson   Yes, I think that's sound advice.

Mr Robinson   You look like the kind of guy that has to fight them off.

Mrs Robinson   Are we going?

Mr Robinson   Say, when does Elaine get down from Berkeley?

Mrs Robinson   Saturday.

Mr Robinson   Ben, I want you to give her a call. Not that she's *any* girl, if you know what I'm saying?

Benjamin   I think I do.

Mr Robinson   Elaine's a wonderful girl. She's the sort of girl you'd only ever want to treat just right, you understand.

Benjamin   Yes I do.

Mr Robinson   I just know you two would hit it off really well. Wouldn't they?

Mrs Robinson   What?

Mr Robinson   Ben and Elaine. They'd like each other.

Mrs Robinson   I'm sure.

Benjamin*'s mother comes in.*

Mom   Oh, you found each other.

Mr Robinson   We certainly did.

Mom   A shame about your trip, but nice you get to drive home.

Mrs Robinson   Good night, Olive.

Mom   Oh.

Mrs Robinson   Good night Benjamin.

Benjamin   Good night.

Mrs Robinson *leaves.*

Mr Robinson   Be seeing you, Ben. Olive.

Mom   Good night, Hal.

Mr Robinson *leaves.* **Benjamin** *puts on some sneakers.*

Mom   What are you putting on, Ben? Ben, it's a party; you can't wear those old things.

Benjamin   I'm not coming to the party, Mom.

Mom   Then what are you doing?

Benjamin   I'm leaving home.

Mom   What?

Benjamin   I'm leaving home. I'm clearing out.

Mom   You're going away?

Benjamin That's right.

Mom You're taking a trip?

Benjamin That is right.

Mom Well, where are you going?

Benjamin I'm going on the road.

Mom On the road?

Benjamin I believe that's the conventional terminology.

Mom You mean you're just going to pack your bag and go?

Benjamin I'm not taking any bags.

Mom What?

Benjamin I'm taking what I have on.

Mom Are you serious?

Benjamin Yes.

Mom Well, how much money are you taking?

Benjamin Ten dollars.

Mom Well, how long will you be gone?

Benjamin Maybe five years. Maybe ten. I don't know.

Benjamin's *father comes in.*

Dad Ben, you get your sorry ass down those stairs right now. (*To his wife.*) What's the matter with you?

Mom Ben, you tell your father, because he's not going to let you do this.

Dad Do what?

Benjamin I'm going on a trip.

Mom He's not taking any clothes. It's nine o'clock at night and he has ten dollars in his pocket and he's . . .

Dad   He's what?

Mom   He's going to do the road.

Dad   He's what?

Benjamin   I'm leaving.

Dad   You're what?

Mom   Ask him where he's going.

Benjamin   I don't know where I'm going.

Mom   He's going God knows where and he's leaving tonight.

Dad   He's what?

Mom   Tell him he's doing no such thing.

Dad   You're doing what?

Benjamin   I'm heading out. Across the country. Around the world. If I can get the papers, the passport, the whatever you need. I'll go right around the world.

Dad   You're gonna bum around the world?

Benjamin   I'm gonna work. I'm gonna meet a lot of interesting people. I'm through with all this.

Dad   All what?

Benjamin   All this. I don't know what it is but I'm sick of it. I want something else.

Dad   Well what the hell else do you want?

Benjamin   You know what I want?

Dad   No, son, I do not.

Benjamin   I want simple people. I want simple honest people that can't even read or write their own name. I want to spend my life with those sort of people.

Dad   Ben . . .

Benjamin   Farmers. Truck drivers. Ordinary people who don't have big houses. Who don't have swimming pools.

Dad   Don't get carried away now, son.

Benjamin   Real people, Dad.

Mom   Aren't we real?

Dad   You have a romantic notion here, Ben.

Benjamin   Real people like Gramps. You remember his hands?

Dad   Your grandfather built half of Toledo.

Benjamin   If you want the cliché Dad, I am going out to spend some time with the real people of this country.

Benjamin's father thinks, then takes out his pocketbook and gives Benjamin the contents.

Dad   I want you to take this.

Benjamin   I don't want it.

Dad   Here.

Benjamin   No.

Dad   Take it.

Benjamin   I won't.

*His father puts it in **Benjamin**'s pocket.*

Thank you.

Mom   So do we approve of this?

Dad   Do we *approve*? Son, lets you and I walk down those stairs. Let's show that bunch of . . . *grotesques* down there just what Benjamin Braddock is made of.

Benjamin   OK.

Dad   OK?

Benjamin   OK.

Dad   Call collect if you get into trouble.

Benjamin   I will.

They make for the door.

Mom   You have your father's approval, Ben.

Benjamin   I know.

Mom   Do you think you might be back by Saturday?

Dad   By Saturday? Heck no, he won't be back by Saturday.

He and **Benjamin** *laugh together.*

Benjamin   Why would I be back by Saturday?

Mom   Well, I invited the Robinsons over for dinner.

Benjamin   Well, I won't be back by Saturday.

Lights fade.

Scene Two

The same. Early morning. **Benjamin** *on the bed, grimy and exhausted. His father in a bathrobe.*

Dad   So, you're back.

Benjamin   I'm back.

Dad   Looks like you got a little beard started there.

Benjamin   It comes off tomorrow.

Dad   Well, how are you?

Benjamin   Tired.

Dad   You're all tired out.

Benjamin   That's right.

Dad   Well, two weeks.

Benjamin   No. Nine days.

Dad   That's a fair amount of time. How far did you get?

Benjamin   I don't know. Caluha. One of those towns.

Dad   Well, that's where the big fire is. You must have seen it.

Benjamin   Dad, I'm so tired I can't think.

Dad   How much did you spend?

Benjamin   Some.

Dad   Did you get some work?

Benjamin   Yes.

Dad   What kind of work?

Benjamin   Dad . . .

Dad   Come on Ben, I'm interested in this.

Benjamin   I fought the fire.

Dad   That big fire up there? You fought it?

Benjamin   That's right.

Dad   Well that's right up there by Shasta. You must have been right up there by Shasta country. That's beautiful country.

Benjamin   Yes it is.

Dad   How much they pay you on a deal like that?

Benjamin   Five an hour.

Dad   Five dollars an hour?

Benjamin   That's right.

Dad   They give you the equipment and you go in and you try to put out the flames?

Benjamin   That's right.

Dad   Well what about the Indians? I was reading they transported some Indians up there from Arizona. Professional fire-fighters. Did you see some of them?

Benjamin   I saw some Indians, yes.

Dad   This is exciting. What else happened?

Benjamin   Nothing.

Dad   Where did you stay?

Benjamin   Hotels.

Dad   Expensive hotels?

Benjamin   Cheap hotels.

Dad   Talk to a lot of interesting people?

Benjamin   No.

Dad   You didn't?

Benjamin   I talked to a lot of people. None of them were particularly interesting.

Dad   Did you talk to some Indians?

Benjamin   Yes.

Dad   They speak English?

Benjamin   Yes.

Dad   Well, what else did you . . .

Benjamin   Dad, the trip was a complete waste of time and I'd rather not talk about it. It was a bore.

Dad   Well it doesn't sound too boring if you were up there throwing water on that fire.

Benjamin   It was a boring fire.

Dad   Well, tell me about it Ben. What kind of people did you bump into? What kind of people gave you rides?

Benjamin   Queers.

Dad What?

Benjamin Queers usually stopped. I averaged about five queers a day. One queer I had to hit in the face and jump out his car.

Dad Homosexuals?

Benjamin Ever met a queer Indian?

Dad A what?

Benjamin Ever had a queer Indian try to jump you while you're trying to keep your clothes from burning up?

Dad Did this happen?

Benjamin Mainly I talked. I talked to farmers.

Dad What about?

Benjamin Crops.

Dad Crops?

Benjamin That's all they know to talk about.

Dad And that's who you talked to?

Benjamin I talked to tramps. I talked to drunks. I talked to whores.

Dad Whores?

Benjamin Yes. I talked to whores. One of them swiped my watch.

Dad A whore stole your wristwatch?

Benjamin Yes.

Dad While you were . . . talking to her?

Benjamin No.

Dad Then you – then you spent the night with a whore?

Benjamin There were a few whores included in the tour, yes.

Dad   More than one?

Benjamin   It gets to be a habit.

Dad   How many?

Benjamin   I don't remember. There was one in a hotel. There was one at her house. There was one in the back of a bar.

Dad   Is this true, Ben?

Benjamin   One in a field.

Dad   A field?

Benjamin   A cow pasture. It was about three in the morning and there was ice in the grass and cows walking around us.

Dad   Ben, this doesn't sound too good.

Benjamin   It wasn't.

Dad   I guess you did quite a bit of drinking on this trip.

Benjamin   Well, it's not too likely I'd spend the night with a stinking whore in a field full of frozen manure if I was stone-cold sober, now is it?

Benjamin's *mother enters.*

Mom   Here's coffee. Now, let's hear all about this trip.

Dad   I think Ben needs some sleep.

Mom   Where did you go? What did you do?

Dad   Let's go down and leave him be.

Benjamin   I have to take a shower.

Benjamin *leaves the room.*

Mom   Welcome home, Ben . . . Is something wrong?

Dad   Leave the boy alone. He's fine.

Mom   Did something happen?

Dad   Nothing happened.

Mom   He seems a little disillusioned.

Dad   Disillusioned?

Mom   Increasingly disillusioned. Today's young people . . .

Dad   What the hell would you know about *disillusioned*?

He leaves. She follows.

Mom   I read in the digest that today's young people . . .

Dad   Don't talk to *me* about disillusioned.

Benjamin *appears in a phone booth.*

Benjamin   Mrs Robinson? This is Ben Braddock. Hi. I was wondering if we could . . . no! No. If we could meet for a *drink* or . . . Or something. Well . . . Where would you suggest?

Scene Three

Lobby of the Taft Hotel. Well appointed. Door USR becomes entrance from street, door DSL becomes a reception desk. **Benjamin**, *hair slicked, rigid with false nonchalance, walks in. As he looks around him, the* **Desk Clerk** *looks up.*

Desk Clerk   Good evening, sir.

Benjamin   Good evening.

Desk Clerk   Can I help you?

Benjamin   No thank you.

Desk Clerk   Will you be wanting a room, sir?

Benjamin   No. No, thank you.

A phone rings just off-stage. The **Desk Clerk** *disappears to answer it.* **Mrs Robinson** *walks in.*

Mrs Robinson   Hello, Benjamin.

Benjamin   Oh. Hello.

Mrs Robinson   How are you?

Benjamin   Very well. Thank you.

Mrs Robinson   Did you get us a room?

Benjamin   What?

Mrs Robinson   Have you gotten us a room yet?

Benjamin   I haven't, no.

Mrs Robinson   Do you want to?

Benjamin   Well, I . . . I mean I could. Or we could just talk. We could have a drink and just talk if you'd rather I'd be perfectly happy to . . .

Mrs Robinson   Do you want me to get it?

Benjamin   You? No. No, I'll – now?

Mrs Robinson   Yes. Why don't you get it now?

Benjamin   Right now?

Mrs Robinson   Why don't you?

Benjamin   I will then.

Benjamin *crosses to the desk. Taps the bell, which rings uncomfortably loud. He muffles it. The* **Desk Clerk** *returns.*

Desk Clerk   Yes sir?

Benjamin   I changed my mind. I'd like a room, please.

Desk Clerk   A single room or a double room?

Benjamin   A single. Just for myself, please.

Desk Clerk   Will you sign your name, please.

Benjamin *signs a card, crumples it, puts it in his pocket and signs a second card.*

Desk Clerk   Is something wrong, sir?

Benjamin   No. Nothing.

Desk Clerk   Very good sir. We have a single room on the fifth floor. Twelve dollars. Would that be suitable?

Benjamin   Yes, that would be suitable.

Benjamin *gets his wallet out.*

Desk Clerk   You can pay when you check out, sir.

Benjamin   Oh, right. Excuse me.

Desk Clerk   Do you have any luggage?

Benjamin   Yes I do.

Desk Clerk   Where is it?

Benjamin   What?

Desk Clerk   Your luggage.

Benjamin   Well, it's in the car. It's out there in the car.

Desk Clerk   I'll have the porter bring it in.

He rings for the porter.

Benjamin   Oh no . . .

Benjamin *puts his hand over the bell. The* **Desk Clerk** *accidentally thumps* **Benjamin**'s *hand.*

Desk Clerk   Sir?

Benjamin   I mean I'd rather not go to the trouble of bringing it all in. I just have a toothbrush. I can get it myself. If that's all right.

Desk Clerk   Of course. I'll have a porter show you the room.

Benjamin   No, that's all right. I just have the toothbrush to carry up and I think I can handle it myself.

Desk Clerk   Whatever you say, sir.

He hands **Benjamin** *the key.* **Mrs Robinson** *comes over.*

Mrs Robinson   Is everything all right?

Benjamin   Oh, yes. Thank you. This is er . . . This is my, er . . . Did you get it?

Mrs Robinson   Did I get what?

Benjamin   My toothbrush? I left it in the car.

The phone rings again.

Desk Clerk   Excuse me.

The **Desk Clerk** *leaves.*

Mrs Robinson   Shall we go up?

Benjamin   Well, yes. But um – well, there might be a problem.

Mrs Robinson   What's that?

Benjamin   I got a single room and he um . . . the man . . .

Mrs Robinson   The clerk.

Benjamin   The desk clerk. I think he'll be suspicious now.

Mrs Robinson   Well, do you want to go up alone first?

Benjamin   May I? I mean yes. I would. I mean, I don't know what their policy is here.

Mrs Robinson   I'll be up in ten minutes.

Benjamin   Ten minutes. Right. OK.

Benjamin *walks away.*

Mrs Robinson   Benjamin.

Benjamin   Yes?

Mrs Robinson   Aren't you forgetting something?

Benjamin   Mm? Oh. Mrs Robinson, I really am very grateful for— (this opportunity).

Mrs Robinson   The room number, Benjamin.

Benjamin   Oh, it's um . . . five-eleven.

The **Desk Clerk** *returns.*

Desk Clerk   I beg your pardon.

Benjamin   That's fine. We're . . . I'm just . . .

Desk Clerk   Would a double room be more suitable?

Benjamin   Um . . .

Mrs Robinson   Thank you.

Desk Clerk   I think you'll find it altogether more spacious.

He and **Benjamin** *switch keys.*

Benjamin   Thank you.

Mrs Robinson   And some champagne?

Desk Clerk   No problem at all madam. The elevator's just there.

Benjamin   Thank you.

Desk Clerk   Thank *you*. Goodnight, Mr Gladstone.

The lights change suddenly, isolating **Mrs Robinson** *and* **Benjamin** *in an illuminated square representing the rising elevator. The scene changes in the surrounding darkness.*

Benjamin   You seem very . . .

Mrs Robinson   What?

Benjamin   Er . . .

Mrs Robinson   Do you think I've done this before?

Benjamin   Have you?

Mrs Robinson   What do you think?

Benjamin   I don't know.

Mrs Robinson   There's only one right answer Benjamin, and that wasn't it.

Ben   I'm nervous.

Mrs Robinson   Try small talk.

The lights fade swiftly.

Scene Four

Room 515, the Taft Hotel. Doors to corridor, bathroom and closet. **Benjamin** *standing with his hands in his pockets.* **Mrs Robinson** *sitting on the bed. She has champagne.*

Benjamin   About that high. Which may not seem very high, but that's quite high. For actual flames. If you're actually in them . . .

Mrs Robinson   So did you put it out?

Benjamin   Personally?

Mrs Robinson   You and the Indians.

Benjamin   Yes, we did. And the firemen. We eventually – put it out.

Mrs Robinson   I'm impressed. I'll get undressed now. Is that all right?

Benjamin   Sure. Fine.

She stands up, takes a last pull on her cigarette and turns to put it out. **Benjamin** *moves closer and kisses her. When their lips part she exhales her cigarette smoke. Then she unbuttons her blouse.*

Benjamin   Do you—

Mrs Robinson   What?

Benjamin   I mean, do you want me to just stand here? I don't know what you want me to do.

Mrs Robinson   Why don't you watch.

Benjamin   Oh. Sure. Thank you.

She takes off her blouse. He puts his hand on her breast. She notices a smudge on her blouse, and rubs it off. He takes his hand away.

Mrs Robinson   Would you get me a hanger?

Benjamin   Certainly.

He goes to the closet.

A wood one?

Mrs Robinson   What?

Benjamin   They have wire ones or wooden ones.

Mrs Robinson   A wooden one is fine.

He struggles to get a wooden hanger out, but they're fixed in. She takes off her skirt. He returns with a wire hanger.

Benjamin   The wood ones are fixed to the rail.

Mrs Robinson   Would this be easier for you in the dark?

Benjamin   No.

Mrs Robinson   Are you sure?

Benjamin   Yes.

She gives him the hanger with her skirt on it, which he takes to the closet. She's reaching to undo her bra when he begins to bang his head against the closet door.

Mrs Robinson   Benjamin?

Benjamin   I can't do this. Mrs Robinson, I cannot do this!

Mrs Robinson   You don't want to do this?

Benjamin   You have no idea how much. I do. And don't. I do, but I can't. Now I'm just, I'm sorry I called you up but I—

Mrs Robinson   Benjamin—

Benjamin   I mean don't you see? Don't you see how this is the worst thing I could possibly do?

Mrs Robinson   Is that why you're doing it?

Benjamin   No. I just – Mrs Robinson, could I take you to a movie?

Mrs Robinson   Are you trying to be funny?

Benjamin   No! But I don't know what to say, because I've got you up here and now I—

Mrs Robinson   You don't know what to do with me.

Benjamin   Well, I know I can't do this!

Mrs Robinson   Benjamin, do you find me desirable?

Benjamin   Mrs Robinson, you are the most attractive of all my parents' friends. And that includes Mrs Terhune. I find you more than adequately desirable, but for God's sake; can you imagine my parents? Can you imagine what my parents would say if they saw us in here right now?

Mrs Robinson   What *would* they say?

Benjamin   I have no idea Mrs Robinson, but for God's sake. They've brought me up. They've made a good life for me. I think they deserve something a little better than this.

Mrs Robinson *nods.*

Benjamin   I mean, this has nothing to do with you. But I respect my parents, and I appreciate what they've . . .

Mrs Robinson   Benjamin?

Benjamin   Yes?

Mrs Robinson   Can I asked you a personal question?

Benjamin   Ask me anything you want.

Mrs Robinson   Is this your first time?

Benjamin   Is this what?

Mrs Robinson   It is, isn't it? This is your first time.

Benjamin   Well, that's a laugh, Mrs Robinson. That really is a laugh.

He laughs weakly.

Mrs Robinson   Well, it's nothing to be ashamed of—

Benjamin   Are you kidding?

Mrs Robinson   It's perfectly natural to be nervous if it's your first time—

Benjamin   Now wait a minute.

Mrs Robinson   Just because you're a little inadequate in one area it doesn't mean—

Benjamin   Inadequate!

Mrs Robinson   Well I guess I'd better be— (going)

Benjamin   Stay on the bed! Sit on the bed. Stay there.

Benjamin *tears off his clothes, loses his balance, falls over.*

Blackout.

Scene Five

The same. Music. The light through the blinds plays a fugue of passing time as **Benjamin** *and* **Mrs Robinson** *make love, unseen beneath the sheets. Summer days come and go. Dawn breaks and the love-making forms a tableau as the closet door (which was also* **Benjamin**'s *bedroom door) opens and we see* **Benjamin**'s *mother beyond it. The lighting indicates we are in two places and two times at once.*

Mom   Ben? It's nearly eleven o'clock. It's a beautiful day, Ben. Are you going to spend all summer in bed?

She closes the door. **Benjamin** *climaxes and the lovers change positions. More time passes until the door opens again and we see* **Benjamin**'s *father beyond it.*

Dad   Ben, will you please get up off that bed and clean the pool or trim the lawn, or do *something* for Heaven's sake. You come in at all hours and your scholarship, Ben. When are you going to take up your scholarship?!

Dad *disappears and* **Benjamin** *climaxes again. The lovers change positions once more,* **Mrs Robinson** *firmly guiding* **Benjamin**'s *head beneath the covers. Finally the lights settle to early evening and* **Benjamin** *emerges.*

Mrs Robinson   Don't stop. Benjamin? What's wrong?

Benjamin   Mrs Robinson, do you think we could have a conversation?

Mrs Robinson   A conversation?

Benjamin   Yes.

Mrs Robinson   Why?

Benjamin   Well we've been coming here and doing this for a couple of months now and we never seem to talk about anything. I just wondered if you'd mind very much if we had a conversation. I mean we're not stupid people are we?

Mrs Robinson   I don't know.

Benjamin   Well we're not, but all we ever do is come up here and throw off our clothes and leap into bed together.

Mrs Robinson   Are you tired of it?

Benjamin   I'm not, no. But do you think we could liven it up with a few words now and then?

Mrs Robinson   What do you want to talk about, darling?

Benjamin   Anything. Anything at all.

Mrs Robinson   Do you want to tell me about your childhood?

Benjamin   No I don't.

Mrs Robinson   Kiss me then.

Benjamin   No. Now we are going to do this thing. We are going to have a conversation. Think of a topic.

Mrs Robinson   How about art?

Benjamin   Art. That's a good subject. You start it off.

Mrs Robinson   I don't know anything about it.

Benjamin   You what?

Mrs Robinson   Do you?

Benjamin   Well, yes I do. I know quite a bit about it.

Mrs Robinson   Go ahead then.

Benjamin   Are you interested in modern art or classical art?

Mrs Robinson   Neither.

Benjamin   You're not interested in art?

Mrs Robinson   No.

Benjamin   Then why do you want to talk about it?

Mrs Robinson   I don't. Could we go back to what we were doing?

Benjamin   No. Think of another topic.

Mrs Robinson   Why don't you tell me what you did today?

Benjamin   This is pathetic.

Mrs Robinson   What did you do?

Benjamin   I got up around twelve. I ate breakfast. I had some beers. I went out to the pool. I blew air in my raft, I put the raft in the water, I floated on the raft. I ate dinner, I watched two quiz shows, then I came here. What did you do?

Mrs Robinson   I got up.

Benjamin   Is that all?

Mrs Robinson   I came here.

Benjamin   What did you do in between?

Mrs Robinson   I read a novel.

Benjamin   An entire novel?

Mrs Robinson   Five or six pages.

Benjamin   What was the novel?

Mrs Robinson   I can't remember.

Benjamin   Is that all you did?

Mrs Robinson   I fixed dinner for my husband.

Benjamin   There! That's something we can have a conversation about! Your husband. I mean I don't know anything about how you work this, how you get out of the house at night, what are the risks involved.

Mrs Robinson   There's no risk.

Benjamin   How do you get out of the house?

Mrs Robinson   I walk out.

Benjamin   You walk right out the door?

Mrs Robinson   That's right

Benjamin   What do you tell him?

Mrs Robinson   Benjamin, this isn't a very interesting topic.

Benjamin   Please, tell me.

Mrs Robinson   He's out all day. He comes home, he takes two Seconal, then it's tomorrow.

Benjamin   So I guess you don't sleep together or anything?

Mrs Robinson   No, we don't.

Benjamin   How long has this been going on?

Mrs Robinson   Four or five years.

Benjamin   Are you kidding me?

Mrs Robinson   No.

Benjamin   You have not slept with your husband for four or five years? Man, this is interesting.

Mrs Robinson   Calm down, Benjamin.

Benjamin   We're talking, Mrs Robinson. We are talking.

Mrs Robinson   We certainly are.

Benjamin   So you don't love him. You wouldn't say you—

Mrs Robinson   I think we've talked enough.

Benjamin   But you loved him once, I assume. When you first knew him.

Mrs Robinson   Well, no.

Benjamin   Never?

Mrs Robinson   I never did. Now would you please—

Benjamin   Well, wait a minute. You married him.

Mrs Robinson   Yes I did.

Benjamin   Well why did you do that?

Mrs Robinson   Let's see if you can guess.

Benjamin   His money?

Mrs Robinson   Think really hard, Benjamin.

Benjamin   You had to? I mean you *had* to? Did you have to?

Mrs Robinson   Don't tell Elaine.

Benjamin   You really had to.

Mrs Robinson   Are you shocked?

Benjamin   Well, I never thought of you and Mr Robinson as the sort of people who, I mean . . . how did it happen? Do you feel like telling me the circumstances?

Mrs Robinson   Not particularly.

Benjamin   Was he a law student at the time?

Mrs Robinson   Yes.

Benjamin   And you were a student also?

Mrs Robinson   Yes.

Benjamin   What was your major?

Mrs Robinson   Benjamin . . .

Benjamin   I'm interested. What was your major subject?

Mrs Robinson   Art.

Benjamin   Art?

Mrs Robinson   Art.

Benjamin   How did you get pregnant?

Mrs Robinson   Pardon me?

Benjamin   Did he take you to a hotel?

Mrs Robinson   Benjamin . . .

Benjamin   I'm curious.

Mrs Robinson   We did it in his car.

Benjamin *is delighted.*

Benjamin   In his car!? Oh boy. In a car?! What kind of car?

Mrs Robinson   What?

Benjamin   Do you remember the make of car?

Mrs Robinson   My God.

Benjamin   Really. I want to know.

Mrs Robinson   It was a Ford, Benjamin.

Benjamin   A Ford? A Ford! Goddammit, a Ford! That's great.

Mrs Robinson   Benjamin, I'm beginning to think sleeping with younger men may have its disadvantages.

Benjamin   So old Elaine Robinson got started in a Ford.

Mrs Robinson   Don't talk about Elaine.

Benjamin   Don't talk about Elaine?

Mrs Robinson   No.

Benjamin   That reminds me.

Mrs Robinson   What?

Benjamin   I have to talk about her.

Mrs Robinson   I don't want you to.

Benjamin   I have to. I've been meaning to all night. I have to talk about Elaine.

Mrs Robinson   What about her?

Benjamin   I have to see her. I have to go out with Elaine. I have to go on a date with Elaine.

Mrs Robinson   You have to what?

Benjamin   You see Mr Robinson called my dad and my dad said I was still hanging around the house and they arranged that I should take out Elaine.

Mrs Robinson   Benjamin, don't you dare.

Benjamin   I have no choice. It turned into a whole big thing about my wasting my life and watching TV all the time and he, my dad, said if I didn't take out Elaine he'd cut off my allowance and throw me out the house. He became irrational, so I said OK. I'll just take her to a movie. Why are you getting so upset?

Mrs Robinson   I'm not getting upset, Benjamin, I am telling you you are not to see Elaine.

Benjamin   Are you jealous of her? Are you afraid I might like her?

Mrs Robinson   No.

Benjamin   Well then what?

Mrs Robinson   Drop it, Benjamin.

Benjamin   I want to know why you feel so strongly about this.

Mrs Robinson   I have my reasons!

Benjamin   Then let's hear your reasons, Mrs Robinson. Because I think I know what they are.

She ducks beneath the covers.

Your daughter shouldn't associate with the likes of me, should she? I'm not good enough for her to associate with, am I? That's the reason, isn't it? I'm a dirty degenerate, aren't I? I'm good enough for you but I'm too slimy to associate with your daughter. That's it, isn't it? Isn't it?

Mrs Robinson   YES!

Benjamin   You go to hell.

He gets dressed.

You go straight to hell, Mrs Robinson.

Mrs Robinson   Benjamin.

Benjamin   Do you think I'm proud of myself? Do you think I'm proud of this?

Mrs Robinson   I wouldn't know.

Benjamin   Well, I'm not. No sir. I am not proud of spending my time in hotel rooms with a lascivious alcoholic.

Mrs Robinson   I see.

Benjamin   And if you think I come here for any reason beside pure boredom, then you're all wrong.

She nods.

Because . . . Mrs Robinson?

Mrs Robinson   What?

Benjamin   You make me sick! I make myself sick. This is the sickest, most perverted thing that ever happened to me and you do what you want but I'm getting the hell out.

A pause as he dresses.

Mrs Robinson   Do you mean those things?

Benjamin   Damn right I do.

Mrs Robinson   Well, I'm sorry.

Benjamin   Well, I'm sorry too, but that's the way it is.

Mrs Robinson   That's how you feel about me?

He nods.

That I'm a sick and disgusting person.

Benjamin   Now, don't start acting hurt, Mrs Robinson. You told me yourself you were an alcoholic. You lie there and call me trash, what do you expect me to say?

Mrs Robinson   Did I call you that?

Benjamin   You did. You lay there and told me I was not good enough for your daughter.

Mrs Robinson   If that's the impression you got
Benjamin, I would like to apologise. You're as good a
person as she is. It's just that under the circumstances I
don't think you'd be right for each other.

Benjamin   I'm as good as she is?

Mrs Robinson   You're as good as she is. Brighter,
certainly. In many ways her equal.

She gets up and dresses.

Benjamin   What are you doing?

Mrs Robinson   Well, it's obvious you don't want me
around any more.

Benjamin   Well, I was kind of upset.

Mrs Robinson   I can understand why I might disgust
you.

Benjamin   No, no. I like you.

Mrs Robinson   I should have realised how sickening this
might be for you . . .

Benjamin   It's not! I like it. I like it very much. I look
forward to it. It's the one thing I have to look forward to.

Mrs Robinson   You don't have to say that.

Benjamin   I wouldn't say it if it wasn't true.

Mrs Robinson   But you think we should stop seeing each
other?

Benjamin   No.

Mrs Robinson   Shall we go back to bed then?

Benjamin   Yes. OK.

Mrs Robinson   I'd like that.

Benjamin   I just need the bathroom.

He goes into the bathroom.

Mrs Robinson   And you won't go out with Elaine.

Benjamin   I'm going to lose my allowance.

Mrs Robinson   Benjamin!

Benjamin   I have no intention of going out with Elaine.

Mrs Robinson   Give me your word.

Benjamin   This is absurd.

Mrs Robinson   Promise me.

Benjamin   I promise! I will not go out with Elaine!

Mrs Robinson   Well, good. Immature son of a bitch.

Blackout.

Elaine *appears downstage, waiting on a downtown street corner.*
Shadows and neon.

Elaine   Oh, thank you no. I'm waiting for someone. Well,
thank you. No. No, I'm fine. I'm waiting for someone.
Pardon me? No!

Benjamin *enters.*

Benjamin   Hi.

Elaine   Oh, hi.

Benjamin   Am I late?

Elaine   Oh, no.

Benjamin   Good.

Elaine   Where are we going?

Benjamin   Inside.

Elaine   Oh. Well . . . that's nice.

Scene Six

The Club Renaissance. A tacky Hollywood bar. A jukebox USR. Two men sit with a pitcher of beer and one of their heads on the table. **Benjamin** *sits with* **Elaine**. *She looks childlike and out of place. The* **Waiter** *passes.*

Elaine   What is this place?

Benjamin   It's a very lively place. It livens up eventually. You like beer?

Elaine   Um, well . . .

Benjamin   Could we have two beers, please?

Elaine   . . . yes.

Benjamin   Would you like some dinner?

Elaine   I'd love some.

Benjamin   Could we have a menu?

Waiter   Dinner for two, sir?

Benjamin   No, just for her.

Elaine   Aren't you eating?

Benjamin   I'm not hungry, if it's all the same to you.

Elaine   Oh. Oh well.

A difficult pause.

Elaine   I heard you got a scholarship.

Benjamin   I don't want to teach.

Elaine   Oh, but a good teacher is a rare and wonderful thing.

Benjamin   That's what my parents think.

Elaine   Well, it's true.

Benjamin   That's not what the world thinks. The world thinks you failed before you began.

The **Waiter** *brings beer.*

Elaine   So do you have a job lined up?

Benjamin   No.

Elaine   Do you have anything in mind?

Benjamin   No.

Elaine   Would you like to guess what I saw last month?

Benjamin   What did you see?

Elaine   You'll never guess.

Benjamin   Then I won't try. What was it?

Elaine   I saw the *Mona Lisa*.

Benjamin   Did you?

Elaine   The *Mona Lisa*. It's on loan to the Washington Museum and my room-mate Diane and I went on the civil rights march? There were two hundred thousand people. We were lucky to get a hotel room and the day after we went to see the *Mona Lisa*.

Benjamin   Was she smiling?

Elaine   Well of course she was. Aren't you interested in beautiful things?

A **Stripper** *enters and puts a dime in the jukebox. Music begins. She flicks a switch to dim the room and another to light some tacky coloured spots.*

Elaine   Oh.

Elaine *turns. The* **Stripper** *drops her robe and starts her act. One of the men slaps the other on the shoulder. He lifts his head.* **Elaine** *realises what she's watching and turns around again, bowing her head.*

Elaine   Could we get a table somewhere else?

Benjamin   I didn't make a reservation.

Elaine *takes a sip of a drink, then pushes it to* **Benjamin**.

Elaine   Would you drink this for me, please.

Benjamin   Why don't you watch the show?

Elaine   Benjamin, do you dislike me?

Benjamin   What?

Elaine   Do you dislike me for some reason?

Benjamin   No, why should I?

Elaine   I don't know.

The **Stripper** *swings her tassels to desultory applause.*

Benjamin   You're missing a great effect here.

Elaine *looks.*

Benjamin   How about that?

Elaine *turns back.*

Benjamin   Could you do that?

The **Stripper** *comes up behind* **Elaine** *and tousles her hair with her tassels. The men laugh. One applauds.* **Elaine** *starts to cry.* **Benjamin**'s *discomfort grows until he suddenly leaps up and pulls the plug on the jukebox.*

Man   Hey!

Benjamin   I'm sorry.

Stripper   What do you think you're doing?

Benjamin   I'm sorry. My friend's not feeling well.

He offers her a dime. She just looks at him.

Sorry.

He offers her some crumpled dollars, which she takes.

Stripper   Excuse me if I earn a living.

Glances at **Elaine**, *then strides away.*

Man Hey, babe!

Stripper Back room, kiddo.

She leaves. One man's head sinks back down on the table. The other looks at **Benjamin**.

Man What's the matter with ya?

Benjamin I'm sorry.

He follows the **Stripper**. **Benjamin** *returns to* **Elaine**, *who is clinging to her chair.*

Elaine Would you take me home now, please?

Benjamin I'm sorry.

Elaine Could you get the cheque, please?

Benjamin Elaine, listen . . .

Elaine Please, just take me home.

Benjamin I have to tell you something. This whole idea of the date and everything. It was my parents' idea. They forced me into it.

Elaine Oh. That's nice of you to tell me.

Benjamin I'm not like this.

Elaine Will you drive me home now, please?

Benjamin Well, can't we have dinner or something?

Elaine NO!

Music filters through from the back room.

Benjamin Can we just sit somewhere and talk?

Elaine I want to go home!

Benjamin I want to talk to you first.

Elaine Please, Benjamin.

Benjamin   Could you stop crying, please?

Elaine   No I couldn't.

Benjamin   But could you try?

Elaine   No.

Benjamin   This is embarrassing. You want to leave?

Elaine   No.

Benjamin   You said you wanted to.

Elaine   I changed my mind.

Benjamin   Let's go outside.

Elaine   This is where you took me, Benjamin. If it's all the same to you, this is where I'll cry.

Benjamin   I want you to know I hate myself.

Elaine   Thank you for saving me the trouble.

Benjamin   I've been going through a difficult time lately.

Elaine   I'm sorry to hear it.

Benjamin   My life is bullshit.

Elaine   Your life is what?

Benjamin   Well, bullshit.

Elaine   How can you say that?

Benjamin   It's what I think.

Elaine   Life is bullshit?

Benjamin   My whole life.

Elaine   Then I feel sorry for you.

Benjamin   I feel sorry for myself.

Elaine   I don't believe I'm sitting here with a nihilist. I'm always being attached on to by nihilists. I hate nihilists. I try to avoid them.

Benjamin   Feel free to avoid me from now on.

Elaine   Have you ever read *The Fountainhead*?

Benjamin   No.

Elaine   Have you ever seen the *Mona Lisa*?

Benjamin   No.

Elaine   Well, I have.

Benjamin   I know you have.

Elaine   The world is full of wonderful things. How can you sit there and say life is bullshit?

Benjamin   I've had a very good education.

Elaine   Then be grateful. There are people fighting for an education in Alabama. Fighting state troopers for a good education. Do you think they think life is bullshit?

Benjamin   Very possibly.

Elaine   A monk just set fire to himself in Saigon . . .

Benjamin   Well, hey.

Elaine   Life is precious, Benjamin. How dare you. How dare you sit there and say life is bullshit. When you have so much. When whatever you want you could probably have.

Benjamin   You like your life?

Elaine   I *love* my life. Don't you?

Benjamin   Once, I guess. When I was a kid.

Elaine   What happeed?

Benjamin   It was unrequited.

Elaine   Well, nothing's perfect Benjamin. I'd have liked a nicer nose. I wish my mother didn't drink so much. I wish I'd never fallen out of that tree and broken my thumb because it so affects my fingering I'll probably never play the violin as well as I'd love to but that's about it for the bullshit,

Benjamin. It's only bullshit if you let it pile up. Heaven's in the details. Someone said that. I think Robert Frost said that.

The **Stripper** *returns having finished her act. Picks up her robe from somewhere near* **Elaine**.

Elaine   You have beautiful breasts.

The **Stripper** *looks at* **Elaine** *and* **Elaine** *looks right back.*

Stripper   Thank you.

Elaine   I'm sorry I cried.

Stripper   I'm sorry I made you.

She eyes **Benjamin**, *turns back to* **Elaine**.

Stripper   So, what, are you screwing him for practice?

Elaine *laughs, surprisingly loudly. The* **Stripper** *smiles.*

Stripper   OK, babe.

The **Stripper** *leaves.* **Elaine** *continues talking to* **Benjamin**.

Elaine   She's nice.

Ben   Nice?

Elaine   Nice people. I was in this diner with my room-mate Diane? And this guy came in with a goat on a rope and it turns out the reason he's got a little goat on a rope is he was thrown out the day before for bringing in his dog? But the point is Diane had stood up to leave when she saw the man walk in and she sat straight down again and said, Well if there's a goat I think I'll have dessert. And that's why I love Diane, because if you think like that you not only notice more little goats, you get more dessert. Will she dance again?

Benjamin   I don't think so.

Elaine   Then let's go!

She leaps up. **Benjamin** *follows her.*

Do you have a car?

Benjamin   No.

Elaine   Good. I love cabs. Don't you? And cab drivers? I think cab drivers are mostly fallen angels.

Benjamin *kisses her.*

Elaine   Why did you do that?

Benjamin   Your mouth. It's very beautiful.

Elaine   No it isn't.

Benjamin   Very *Mona Lisa.*

Elaine   No bullshit.

Benjamin *laughs.*

Benjamin   No bullshit?

Elaine   Well, don't do it again.

Benjamin   Don't you like me?

Elaine   You're cute Benjamin, but you're kind of morose.

Benjamin   I'm cute?

Elaine   Way too serious.

Benjamin   But cute?

Elaine   Yes.

Benjamin   How?

Elaine   I really have no idea.

Benjamin   Like a goat?

Elaine   Maybe.

Benjamin   So would you like to go somewhere and get some dessert?

Elaine   Way to go, Benjamin.

She smiles. Lights fade.

Scene Seven

The Robinsons' living room. Front door and stairs. **Benjamin** *waits anxious yet brash, spinning car keys on his finger.* **Mrs Robinson** *enters more quickly than she intended. A stony silence.*

Benjamin   Mrs Robinson, I hope you won't be offended if I say I think you're being a little melodramatic about this. Elaine and I are just going for a drive. I don't think there's any great crisis that necessitates any degree of acrimony here.

Mrs Robinson   Turn around and leave the house, Benjamin. Get back in your car and drive away.

Benjamin   What exactly are you trying to say, Mrs Robinson?

Mrs Robinson   I'm telling you never to see her again. Do I make myself clear?

Benjamin   Yes you do.

Mrs Robinson   Then the matter's closed.

Benjamin   No it's not, because I have no intention of following your orders, Mrs Robinson.

Mrs Robinson   Benjamin, if you think . . .

Benjamin   Why don't you tell me exactly what your objections are instead of . . .

Mrs Robinson   Elaine is a very simple girl. She is sweet, uncomplicated and thoroughly honest. And she is thoroughly sincere. And Benjamin, you are none of these things. You are a lot of things, but you add up to nothing.

Benjamin   What time does she usually get up?

Mrs Robinson   I don't think you need to worry about that.

Benjamin   I think we do. I think we have a date and I think she's expecting me.

Mrs Robinson   I could make things most unpleasant.

Benjamin   In what way would that be?

Mrs Robinson   To keep her away from you I would tell Elaine anything I had to.

A pause.

Benjamin   I don't believe you.

Mrs Robinson   Well, you'd better.

Benjamin   I don't think you would do that.

Mrs Robinson   You want to watch?

Benjamin   Would you do that? Mrs Robinson, I'm asking you not to do that. Please don't do that.

Mrs Robinson   Go home now.

Benjamin   Please, don't wreck it. I'm asking you please not to wreck it.

Mrs Robinson   Wreck it?

Benjamin   Please.

Mrs Robinson   Wreck what?

Benjamin *hangs his head.*

Mrs Robinson   Are you in love Benjamin? Do you have the audacity? The indecency?

Enter **Elaine** *in her dressing gown.*

Elaine   Benjamin?

Mrs Robinson   Elaine, go back upstairs.

Elaine   Why are you so early?

Benjamin   It's a beautiful day; would you like to get in the car?

Elaine   I'm not dressed.

Mrs Robinson   Go back upstairs, Elaine.

Benjamin   Get dressed, I'll wait down here.

Mrs Robinson   Benjamin was just leaving.

Benjamin   No he wasn't. No I'm not.

Elaine   Is something wrong?

Benjamin   I'll be right here.

Mrs Robinson   Benjamin's not feeling well.

Benjamin   I'm perfectly all right.

Elaine   I don't understand.

Benjamin   Get dressed, Elaine.

Mrs Robinson   Goodbye, Benjamin.

Elaine   Would someone please tell me what's going on? Mother?

She looks at her mother. So does **Benjamin**. **Mrs Robinson** *looks at* **Benjamin**, *then back at her daughter. Before she can speak,* **Benjamin** *does.*

Benjamin   Elaine, I have something to tell you.

Mrs Robinson   Benjamin.

Benjamin   I have been having an affair. I have been having an affair with an older woman.

Elaine   What are you talking about?

Mrs Robinson   Get dressed Elaine.

Benjamin   With a married woman.

Mrs Robinson   Benjamin's waiting to take you for a ride.

Benjamin   I just wanted you to know.

Elaine   Well, thank you. I'll get dressed.

She makes to leave, then stops dead. She slowly turns to her mother and
Benjamin.

Oh my God.

Mrs Robinson   Elaine . . .

Elaine   Oh my God.

Benjamin   Listen, Elaine.

Elaine   Oh my God. Get out of here.

Benjamin   Elaine . . .

Elaine   Would you please? Oh my God. Oh my God.
Would you please get out of here? My God.

Benjamin   Should I come back later?

Elaine *looks at him. He leaves. She looks at her mother.* **Mrs
Robinson***'s knees slowly buckle and she sits on the floor. Using ice
and a shaker,* **Elaine** *fixes a vodka cocktail and gives it to her mother.*
Elaine *returns to the shaker and pours the rest for herself. The glass
is half empty, so she tops it up with vodka. Sits opposite her mother.*
Mrs Robinson *has never seen her drink before. She never* has
drunk before. **Elaine** *drinks her cocktail in two long drafts. Lights
transform to evening.*

Scene Eight

Later. **Elaine** *and* **Mrs Robinson** *have been drinking.*

Mrs Robinson   'Laine.

Elaine   Don't want to.

Mrs Robinson   Go to bed.

Elaine   . . . no.

A pause.

Mom?

Mrs Robinson   Mm?

Elaine   'ove you.

Mrs Robinson   'ove you too.

Elaine   Huh!

Mrs Robinson   Oh yes.

Elaine   Don' believe you.

Mrs Robinson   In my *way*, OK? 'Laine . . .

Elaine   I don't be sick on my blouse.

Mrs Robinson   *Don't* be.

Elaine   No.

Mrs Robinson   Are you?

Elaine   No.

Mrs Robinson   Don't.

Elaine   No, I won't.

Mrs Robinson   I'm not apologise.

Elaine   Disgusting.

Mrs Robinson   I told you.

Elaine   Mmmng.

Mrs Robinson   . . . believe me?

Elaine   Mm.

Mrs Robinson   Gu.

Elaine *lurches over on to her hands and knees.*

Mrs Robinson   Not on the rug.

Elaine   Not going to.

Mrs Robinson   Get off the rug. Turn your head round.

Elaine *rolls on to her back. Begins to cry.*

Elaine   He sorrible. Everybody sorrible. Why so everybody horrible?

Mrs Robinson   My horrible?

Elaine   Yes.

Mrs Robinson   Mnot.

Elaine   Nnn. Nwhat are you then?

Mrs Robinson   Mbored. Sbored. N I din't anyway I tol' you. Was him.

Elaine   Hmph. Hm.

She sits up.

Be sick.

Mrs Robinson   Not my rug! . . . in your skirt!

Elaine   'S my favourite.

Mrs Robinson   'S horrible. Doesn't suit you.

Elaine   It's all right. It's all right. I don't want to.

Mrs Robinson   No fashion sense of dress. Never had.

Elaine   Rooms going over and over and over.

Mrs Robinson   It's . . . no, it's the little muscles. In your eyes. You got to relax a little muscles.

Elaine   Mmm?

Mrs Robinson   In the corner of your eyes. And let your eyes go up.

Elaine   Eragh . . . !

Mrs Robinson   Asright; they just want to drift up so just let 'em and they stay up there.

Elaine   Mmmhah.

Mrs Robinson   Relax and up they go an get stuck up there. Mmm?

Elaine   Oh yeh.

Mrs Robinson   And the room stops going over.

Elaine   Yeh.

Mrs Robinson   Mm?

Elaine   Mm.

Mrs Robinson   Little tip.

Elaine   'Kyou.

Mrs Robinson   Now just be still.

Elaine   Where's love go?

Mrs Robinson   Love?

Elaine Where's it all go?

Mrs Robinson   When you was little, I love you all the time.

Elaine   When I was little, yes, when I couldn't remember if you say so.

Mrs Robinson   I did.

Elaine   Well I don't remember and what about when I'm big? You love me? Look I'm big and you love me I don't think so.

Mrs Robinson   I do.

Elaine   You don't. Love gets littler and littler and goes away until it isn't there. It's all gone away.

Mrs Robinson   You love me?

Elaine   No. S'gone. You love daddy?

Mrs Robinson   No.

Elaine   See.

Mrs Robinson   That's long gone away somewhere I don't know.

Elaine   So where's it go?

Mrs Robinson   I met your father, he used t'sing t'me.
We'd be go someplace in the car and he used sing. He could
sing. He could. Same thing as Sinatra. Key. But not the
range. Not the high notes. I used to love him. Singing. In
the wee small hours. Just some songs he couldn't get to the
end. Couldn't get through those high notes to the end. You
know those notes. So. So. At school I'd had this teacher.
Who taught the choir. And the piano and oboe and things,
but the choir. So I know if you singing and you think you
breathing *in* as you go up . . . You understand? You imagine
you singing *in*, not up, not out, but *in*, then those high notes
can happen. La la la la . . .

Elaine   La la la la la la . . .

Mrs Robinson   La la . . . la la.

Elaine   La la!

Mrs Robinson   A's right. See? So. One night. In the car.
I taught him. I taught him how to do that. And right away,
he got it. How to do it. All the way. Half a thing. Octave.
(*She sings a snatch of Sinatra.*) And all the songs he used to sing
. . . to *want* to sing . . . suddenly he could. He could sing
them. And you know what? He never sang to me again.

Elaine   I never heard him sing.

Mrs Robinson   He'll never sing.

Elaine   I'm going to have a forever love.

Mrs Robinson   Ha.

Elaine   No ha, never mind ha.

Mrs Robinson   You never find it, sweetie.

Elaine   I will.

Mrs Robinson   You look hard as you like.

Elaine   You don't look. That's the thing. Everyone there's something.

Mrs Robinson   Something what?

Elaine   Worth loving.

Mrs Robinson   Hah.

Elaine   No, that's the point. You see? Don't *look*, that's not the point. The point . . . The *point* . . . You *choose*. You unnerstand?

Mrs Robinson   So young.

Elaine   The love's in *you*, and you just choose.

Mrs Robinson   Anyone 'cept Benjamin.

Elaine *laughs loudly.* **Mrs Robinson** *joins in. They laugh together.*

Mrs Robinson   'Xcept Benjamin.

Elaine   'Xcept Benjamin. *Anyone* except Benjamin.

Lights fade.

Scene Nine

The Braddocks' front lawn. **Mr Braddock** *is outside.* **Benjamin** *comes out the front door with a suitcase.*

Benjamin   Dad.

Dad   Mm?

Benjamin   Sir?

Dad   What?

Benjamin   I'm going to marry Elaine Robinson.

Dad   Are you serious?

Benjamin   Yes.

Dad I'll go get your mother. You wait right here.

He leaves. **Benjamin** *puts on his jacket. His father comes back with his mother.*

Mom What's all the excitement?

Dad Ben.

Benjamin I'm going to marry Elaine Robinson.

Mom Oh, Ben!

Dad Ha hah!!!

Mom Ah, Ben!

Dad Ben and Elaine are getting married.

Mom Oh Ben, I'm crying.

Mom *hugs him.*

Dad Now let him go, let him go.

Mom *holds his hand.*

Dad Let's get the whole story here. Have you set the date yet?

Benjamin No.

Dad Have you told the Robinsons yet?

Benjamin No.

Dad Let's call them right now.

Benjamin No.

Mom Oh, Ben.

Dad Ben, we are . . . just delighted.

Benjamin I think I should tell you that Elaine doesn't know about this yet.

Dad She doesn't know about what yet?

Benjamin That we're getting married.

Dad   What?

Benjamin   I just decided an hour ago.

Dad   And you talked it over with her?

Benjamin   No.

Dad   But you've written her about it?

Benjamin   No.

Dad   You called her?

Benjamin   No.

Dad   Well good God Ben, you get us all excited here and you haven't even proposed?

Benjamin   I'm driving up to Berkeley today.

Dad   To propose to her?

Benjamin   Yes.

Dad   Well that sounds kind of half-baked.

Benjamin   I'm moving up there.

Dad   To live?

Benjamin   Yes.

Mom   To *live*?

Dad   Now just a damn minute; she's up there finishing school and you're just going to move up there?

Benjamin   Yes.

Dad   Move up there and pester the girl because you have nothing better to do?

Benjamin   I love her.

Dad   You hardly know the girl, Ben; how do you know she wants to marry you?

Benjamin   Oh, she doesn't.

Dad   She what?

Benjamin   I'm pretty sure she won't want to initially.

Mom   Ben, does she like you?

Benjamin   No.

Dad/Mom   No?

Benjamin   She hates me.

Mom   Oh, Ben.

Blackout.

Act Two

Scene One

Attic room, Berkeley boarding house. Evening. **Benjamin** *stands holding the door open for* **Elaine**.

Elaine Benjamin, why are you here?

Benjamin Would you like to come in?

Elaine I want to know what you're doing here in Berkeley.

Benjamin Would you like some tea? I have tea.

Elaine I want to know why you're stalking me.

Benjamin I'm not.

Elaine I see you on campus. You duck into doorways. On the bus you hid behind a magazine.

Benjamin I've been meaning to speak to you.

Elaine You've been following me around for days.

Benjamin Would you like to come in?

Elaine No.

Benjamin Why not?

Elaine I don't want to be in a room with you. Now why are you up here?

Benjamin I'm just living here temporarily. I thought I might be bumping into you. I thought I remembered you were going to school up here.

Elaine Did you move up here because of me?

Benjamin No.

Elaine Did you?

Benjamin   I don't know.

Elaine   Well, did you?

Benjamin   Well, what do you think?

Elaine   I think you did.

Benjamin   I'm just living in Berkeley. Having grown somewhat weary of family life. I've been meaning to stop by and pay my respects but have not been entirely certain how you felt about me after the incident with your mother which was certainly a serious mistake on my part but not serious enough I hope to permanently alter your feelings about me.

Elaine *comes in, slamming the door.*

Elaine   Benjamin, you are the one person in the world I never want to see again. I want you nowhere near me. I want you to leave here and never come back.

He holds his hands in front of his face.

Promise me you'll go.

Benjamin   Elaine . . .

Elaine   Promise me.

Benjamin (*stares at her a moment*)   All right.

Elaine   Pack you bags and go tonight.

Benjamin   All right!

Elaine   So promise me.

Benjamin   All right!

He flops down, his head in his arms.

Elaine   Goodbye, Benjamin.

Benjamin (*into his arms*)   I love you!!!!

Elaine   You what?

Benjamin   I love you! I love you and I can't help myself
and I'm begging you to forgive me for what I did. I love you
so much I'm terrified of seeing you every time I step outside
the door I feel helpless and hopeless and lost and miserable,
please forget what I did please Elaine oh God Elaine I love
you please forget what I did Elaine I love you. I love you.
Forget what I did. Please forget what I did Elaine, I love
you.

Elaine   I don't think so.

Benjamin   I do.

Elaine   How can you love me Benjamin when you're so
full of hate?

Benjamin   Of hate?

Elaine   How else could you have done that?

Benjamin   Done what?

Elaine   How could you have raped my mother?

Benjamin   What?

Elaine   You must have so much hate inside you.

Benjamin   Raped her?

Elaine *starts to cry.*

Benjamin   Did you say raped her?

Elaine   Virtually raped her.

Benjamin   Did she say that?

Elaine   I want you out of here by the morning.

Benjamin   No!

He runs between her and the door.

Elaine   Don't you touch me.

Benjamin   I'm not.

Elaine   Then get away from the door.

Benjamin   What did she say? Tell me what she said.

Elaine   Why?

Benjamin   Because it isn't true.

Elaine   She said you virtually raped her.

Benjamin   Which isn't true.

Elaine   Is it true you slept with her?

Benjamin   Yes.

Elaine   All right then, get away from the door.

Benjamin   What did she say?

Elaine   She said you dragged her up to the hotel room . . .

Benjamin   I dragged her!?

Elaine   . . . and you made her pass out and you raped her.

Benjamin   I what I drugged her?   I dragged her up five floors and I drugged her? I *raped* her?

Elaine   You *virtually*, yes.

Benjamin   I *what?*

Elaine   Could I leave now please?

Benjamin   That is not what happened.

Elaine   I have to leave.

Benjamin   My parents gave me a party when I got home from college. Your mother came up to my room.

Elaine   I don't want to hear this.

Benjamin   She asked me to unzip her dress.

Elaine   May I go now?

Benjamin   She took off all her clothes. She stood there entirely naked and she said . . .

Elaine *screams, long and hysterical.* **Benjamin** *frozen. She calms down. He brings her a chair. He brings her a glass of water. She drinks it.*

Elaine   What did you think would happen?

Benjamin   What?

Elaine   When you came up here?

Benjamin   I don't know.

He begins to pack.

Elaine   You just came up here?

Benjamin   I drove up. I made reservations at a restaurant.

Elaine   You were going to invite me to dinner?

Benjamin   Yes.

Elaine   Then what did you do?

Benjamin   I didn't invite you.

Elaine   I know.

Benjamin   I just came up here. I got this room. I kind of wallowed around. I wrote you some letters.

Elaine   Love letters?

Benjamin   I don't remember.

Elaine   So what are you going to do now?

Benjamin   I don't know.

Elaine   Where are you going?

Benjamin   I don't know.

Elaine   Well, what are you going to do?

Benjamin Are you deaf?

Elaine What?

Benjamin I don't know what I'm going to do.

Elaine Well, will you get on a bus or what?

Benjamin Are you concerned about me or something?

Elaine You came up here because of me. You messed up your life because of me, and now you're leaving because of me. You made me responsible! I don't want you drunk in some gutter because of me.

Benjamin You want me to stick around?

Elaine I want you to have a definite plan before you leave, then I want you to leave.

Benjamin I have no plans.

Elaine Then just make up your mind.

Benjamin What?

Elaine Don't you have a mind?

Benjamin Of course.

Elaine Then make it up.

Benjamin I could go to Canada.

Elaine You want to go to Canada?

Benjamin No.

Elaine You think I can study? You think I can think with you here?

Benjamin Just tell me to leave and I'll leave.

Elaine I have so much work this semester.

Benjamin Would you just tell me to leave, please?

Elaine Are you simple?

Benjamin   What?

Elaine   I mean what do I have to say to you?

Benjamin   I don't know.

Elaine   Can't you see the way I feel?

Benjamin   Shall I go then?

Elaine   Why don't you?

Benjamin   Why don't I go?

Elaine   Yes.

Benjamin   All right. That's all you had to say.

Elaine *goes to the door.*

Elaine   You know what she gave me for my eleventh birthday? She gave me a bartender's guide. I made her cocktails all day.

Benjamin   She's a strange woman.

Elaine   Is she attractive?

Benjamin   Yes. Not really.

Elaine   Well is she or not?

Benjamin   I don't know.

Elaine   You don't know which she is or you don't know which I'd like to hear?

Benjamin   Either.

Elaine   And am I?

Benjamin   I'm sorry?

Elaine   Am I as attractive as her?

Benjamin   Oh, yes.

Elaine   I have to go now.

Benjamin   Would you marry me?

Elaine   Would I what?

Benjamin   Marry me. Would you?

Elaine   Marry you?

Benjamin   Yes.

Elaine Marry you?

Benjamin   Would you?

Elaine   Why would I?

Benjamin   I think we have a lot in common.

Elaine   Well, that's true.

Benjamin   So will you?

Elaine   Marry you?

Benjamin   Yes.

Elaine   Hah. Ha ha ha. Oh Benjamin, you are something.

Benjamin   Am I?

Elaine   Yes you are, but I don't know what. Why do you want to marry me?

Benjamin   It's the way I feel. I feel we should.

Elaine   What about the way I feel?

Benjamin   How do you feel?

Elaine   Confused.

Benjamin   Are you fond of me?

She sniffs.

Are you?

Elaine   Yes, fond.

Benjamin   Then let's get married.

Elaine   And can you imagine my parents?

Benjamin   You mean your mother?

Elaine   I mean my father.

Benjamin   I think he'd be very happy for us.

Elaine   And what if he found out what happened?

Benjamin   He won't.

Elaine   But what if he did?

Benjamin   I'd apologise. I'd say it was a stupid foolish thing and he'd say he was a little disappointed in me but if it's all in the past then that's that.

Elaine   You're so naïve.

Benjamin   Forget about your parents. This isn't about our parents. This is about us. Have you any other objections?

Elaine   Yes I do.

Benjamin   What are they?

Elaine   We're too young to be married. You should do other things first.

Benjamin   What other things?

Elaine   Well, *go* somewhere. Asia. Africa. See different places, different people.

Benjamin   Elaine, I have no desire to hop around the world ogling peasants. So do you have any other objections?

Elaine   Have you thought about finding a place to live and buying the groceries every day?

Benjamin   Sure.

Elaine   No you haven't.

Benjamin   You mean which brand of cereal we should buy?

Elaine   Yes.

Benjamin   No I haven't.

Elaine   Well why not? I mean that's the kind of thing you'll have to be thinking about, Benjamin, and I think you'd get sick of it after two days.

Benjamin   But I wouldn't get sick of you, would I?

Elaine   Well yes, I think you probably would.

Benjamin   Well no, I wouldn't.

Elaine   I'm not what you think I am, Benjamin. I'm just a plain ordinary person. I'm not smart or glamorous or anything like that.

Benjamin   So what?

Elaine   So why me?

Benjamin   Well. You're reasonably intelligent. You're striking-looking.

Elaine   Striking?

Benjamin   Sure.

Elaine   My ears are too prominent to be striking-looking.

Benjamin   No, they're very striking.

Elaine   I wouldn't be enough for you, Benjamin.

Benjamin   That isn't true.

Elaine   You're an intellectual, and I'm not.

Benjamin   Now listen . . .

Elaine   You should marry someone who can discuss politics and history and art . . .

Benjamin   Ah, shut up. Would you just . . . thank you. Now have you ever heard me talking about any of that crap?

Elaine   You majored in that crap.

Benjamin   Have you ever heard me talk about it?

Elaine   That crap?

Benjamin   Yes.

Elaine   No I haven't.

Benjamin   All right then. Goddammit, I hate all that. So will you marry me?

Elaine   No!

Benjamin   Why not?

Elaine   Well for a start I'm studying and you haven't got any money!

Benjamin   I'll move up here. I'll get a job teaching.

Elaine   I thought you didn't want to be a teacher.

Benjamin   Yes, but I could teach.

Elaine   You don't have the right attitude. Teachers are meant to be inspired.

Benjamin   That's a myth.

Elaine   Is it?

Benjamin   Oh yeh.

Elaine   It is not.

Benjamin   Any other objections?

Elaine   Plenty.

Benjamin   Take your best shot.

Elaine   Well, what about babies?

Benjamin   Babies?

Elaine   Do you want babies? Because that's what I want.

Benjamin   Well, I do too.

Elaine   Oh, come on.

Benjamin   I do.

Elaine   You do not.

Benjamin   Goddammit Elaine I want babies! Your babies. Triplets! I want to smother in a huge pile of diapers!

She laughs.

I'm serious here. Let's get married.

Elaine   Benjamin.

Benjamin   What?

Elaine   I can't see why I'm so attractive to you.

Benjamin   You just are.

Elaine   But . . . I don't understand.

Benjamin   What don't you understand?

Elaine   I mean you're a really brilliant person.

Benjamin   Elaine, don't start that. I mean it.

She nods. He takes her hand.

So, shall we get married?

Elaine   If you want to marry me so much why don't you just . . . drag me off.

Benjamin   All right, I will. We'll get a blood test in the morning and I'll just drag you off.

Elaine   But you can't. I mean I couldn't. I'd have to see Carl.

Benjamin   Carl?

Elaine   I'd have to talk to Carl first.

Benjamin   Who's Carl?

Elaine   The boy I met last semester. Carl Smith.

Benjamin   Well, what does he have to do with it?

Elaine   I said I might marry him.

Benjamin   What?

Elaine   He asked me to marry him and I said I might.

Benjamin   Well, Elaine . . .

Elaine   What?

Benjamin   Why in the hell didn't you tell me about this?

Elaine   I'm telling you.

Benjamin   Now? You're telling me now?

Elaine   Well there wasn't a before. It was none of your business before.

Benjamin   My God Elaine, how many people have done this?

Elaine   Proposed to me?

Benjamin   Yes.

Elaine   I don't know.

Benjamin   You mean more than him have?

Elaine   Well, yes.

Benjamin   How many?

Elaine   I don't know.

Benjamin   Well, could you try and remember? Six? Seven?

Elaine   About that, yes.

Benjamin   Are you kidding me?

Elaine   No.

Benjamin   You mean you have actually had six or seven people ask you to marry them?

Elaine   Is this any of your business?

Benjamin   Well yes, I think it is. When did he ask you?
Was it him on the bus?

Elaine   What bus?

Benjamin   On the bus to the zoo?

Elaine   You followed me to the zoo?

Benjamin   No, I missed the bus! When did he ask you?
Did he ask you that day? My God, he asked you that day,
didn't he? Where did he ask you, did he ask you at the zoo?

Elaine   Benjamin, why are you getting so excited?

Benjamin   He asked you at the zoo. I missed the bus and
he asked you in the monkey house or somewhere. Did he
get down on his knees? I hope he didn't get down on his
knees. He did, didn't he? What did he say?

Elaine   Benjamin . . .

Benjamin   What did he say?

Elaine   He said he thought we'd make a pretty good
team.

Benjamin   Hah!

Elaine   What?

Benjamin   He said that?

Elaine   Benjamin, what is wrong with you?

Benjamin   So what is he, a student?

Elaine   A medical student. Final year.

Benjamin   And he got down on his knees at the zoo and
he said . . .

Elaine   It wasn't at the zoo, it was at his apartment.

Benjamin   His apartment?

Elaine   Yes.

Benjamin   You went to his apartment?

Elaine   Yes.

Benjamin   But you . . . I mean you didn't . . . ?

Elaine   No, I did not spend the night.

Benjamin *grins.*

Benjamin   So good old Carl, the final-year medic, took you up to his apartment and popped the big one, did he . . . ?

Elaine   Goodbye Benjamin.

Benjamin   Did he put music on?

Elaine   I have to study.

Benjamin   No wait. Wait. Are we getting a blood test tomorrow?

Elaine   No.

Benjamin   The day after?

Elaine   I don't know.

Benjamin   Are we getting married?

Elaine   Maybe we are and maybe we aren't.

She leaves, closing the door behind her. **Benjamin** *sits. Suddenly the door opens,* **Elaine** *walks in, kisses him hard, and waltzes out again.* **Benjamin** *grins.*

Scene Two

The same. Morning. A knock on the door. **Benjamin** *opens it eagerly.* **Mr Robinson** *stands there. He's been travelling all night. He's dishevelled.*

Mr Robinson   Do you want . . . Do you want to try and tell me why you did it?

Benjamin   I don't . . . I don't . . .

Mr Robinson *comes in and sits down.*

Mr Robinson   Do you have any special grudge against me you'd like to tell me about? Do you feel a particularly strong resentment for me for some reason?

Benjamin   No. It's not . . .

Mr Robinson   Is there something I've said that's caused this contempt? Or is it just the things I stand for that you despise?

Benjamin   It was nothing to do with you, sir.

Mr Robinson   Well Ben, it was quite a bit to do with me. And I'd like to hear your feelings about me if you have any. I'd like to know why you've done this to me.

Benjamin   There was no personal . . . It was nothing personal.

Mr Robinson   Nothing personal?

Benjamin   No, sir.

Mr Robinson   Well that's an interesting way of looking at it, Ben. You sleep with another man's wife . . .

Benjamin   Mr Robinson, there was no reason for it . . .

Mr Robinson   Ben, you're a little old to abdicate responsibility . . .

Benjamin   I'm entirely responsible. It was altogether my own fault, Mr Robinson, but I would like you to know that . . .

Mr Robinson   I think we're two civilised human beings; do you think it's necessary to threaten each other?

Benjamin   No I don't.

Mr Robinson   Then do you want to unclench your fists please? Thank you.

Benjamin   I'm trying to tell you that I have no personal feelings about you, Mr Robinson. I'm trying to tell you I do not resent you.

Mr Robinson   You don't respect me terribly much either, do you?

Benjamin   No, I don't.

Mr Robinson *nods.*

Mr Robinson   Well, I don't think we have a whole lot to say to each other, Ben. I do think you should know the consequences of what you've done. I do think you should know my wife and I are getting a divorce.

Benjamin   A divorce? Why?

Mr Robinson   Why?

Benjamin   Well, it shouldn't make *that* much difference, surely? I mean we . . . we . . . got into bed with each other but it was nothing compared to . . . It was nothing at all. We could have been shaking hands.

Mr Robinson   I always thought when you took your clothes off and got into bed with a woman and had sexual intercourse with her that was just a little more than shaking hands.

Benjamin   Not in this case.

Mr Robinson   Well, that's not saying much for my wife, is it?

Benjamin   You miss the point.

Mr Robinson   Not at all Ben. I'm sure my wife's bedroom technique could do with a little brushing up.

Benjamin   You are distorting everything I say!

Mr Robinson   Don't shout at me, Ben.

Benjamin   The point is I don't love your wife; I love your daughter.

Mr Robinson   Well, I'm sure you think you do Ben, but after a few times shaking hands with Elaine I'm sure you'll find her just as disappointing.

Benjamin   I'm sorry?

Mr Robinson   A boy called us up and he asked for her hand. Carl is to be a doctor, and he asked for her hand in marriage. There are some fine young men in this world.

Benjamin   Mr Robinson . . .

Mr Robinson   I don't know if I can prosecute or not, but I think maybe I can. In light of what's happened I think maybe I can get you behind bars if you even so much as look at my daughter again. I don't want to mince words with you. I think you're totally despicable. I think you're scum. I think you're filth.

He leaves. Enter **Dad**.

Benjamin   Dad?

Dad   I have just driven a grown man four hundred miles, Ben. A grown man crying like a child because of what you did to him. He was sobbing, Ben, beating his hand on the armrest like a little baby. Now pack your case.

Benjamin   I can't leave here.

Dad   You're driving back with me tonight.

Benjamin   I appreciate your concern but I can't leave here.

Dad   Hal's going to spend a couple of days with his daughter. And you have an appointment in the morning with a psychiatrist.

Benjamin   I beg your pardon?

Dad   Get to it, Ben.

Benjamin   Well, I don't know if you brought a straitjacket up here with you, but if you didn't . . .

Dad *hits his son very hard with the back of his hand.* **Benjamin** *goes flying.*

Dad   Forgive me for that, Ben. I'm very badly shaken. I want you to forgive me for that.

Blackout.

Scene Three

A psychiatrist's study.

The **Psychiatrist** *with his back to us.* **Benjamin**, **Dad** *and* **Mom** *in chairs facing us.* **Mom** *is nearly hysterical.*

Mom   Well, I just don't understand what I'm supposed to have done! Why is it all my fault?

Dad   Now, that's not what he said.

Mom   He said it was my fault.

Dad   He didn't say that.

Benjamin   It certainly sounded like that.

Dad   You keep your goddam opinions to yourself!

Mom   Why is everything *my* fault?

Dad   Would you . . . Would you please . . . Could you just, for the love of Mike . . . *say* something?

A pause.

Psychiatrist   Nothing is anyone's fault.

Benjamin   Well, that's encouraging.

Mom   I don't understand if you do your very best and you're a perfectly decent person how you can be blamed for things you didn't do even if the person who did them you once, you what, you didn't take him to the zoo or something or he didn't like green beans? I cooked three vegetables half my whole life, I stood in line for a plastic man with the right

sort of gun in a *blizzard* for Heaven's sake, all Christmas
Eve . . .

Dad   Would you just shut up for thirty seconds!

Mom   I just want to know . . .

Dad   Well then, *listen* for once in your life!

A pause.

Doctor . . .

Psychiatrist   I'm not a doctor.

Dad   You're not?

Psychiatrist   But that's OK.

Dad   Well whatever you are, I don't know what we're all
doing here but the situation's very simple. Our son – I still
like to call him our son – has behaved so reprehensibly
towards the wife and daughter of my oldest and dearest
friend there is obviously something not entirely normal . . .

Benjamin   Define normal.

Dad   I'm speaking, Benjamin.

Benjamin   You try and put your own son in a hospital
with old women muttering obscenities and and murderers
peeing in the corridor. Is that normal?

Mom   It's for your own good, Benjamin.

Benjamin   And they've hidden her. Did you know that?
The Robinsons kidnapped their own daughter and took her
to New England. Is that normal?

Dad   That's just until the wedding.

Benjamin   The what?

Dad   The whatever.

Benjamin   What wedding?

A pause.

What wedding?

Mom   I'm not saying I'm entirely blameless . . .

Benjamin   Am I insane?

Dad   It's all for the best, Ben.

Benjamin   Excuse me, I asked you a question, am I insane?

Psychiatrist   I don't believe so.

Benjamin   Thank you.

Benjamin *jumps out the window.*

Dad   Benjamin!

Mom   Benjamin!

Dad   You come back here!

Mom (*losing control*)   Oh God, it's all my fault!

Scene Four

The vestry, First Presbyterian church. Door to the body of the church, door a large cupboard.

Solemn organ music, then the sound of a row rapidly rising until **Benjamin** *bursts in pulling* **Elaine** *by the wrist.* **Elaine** *is in full white wedding gown. He slams the door behind them and runs to the other door.*

Elaine   Benjamin!

Benjamin   It's OK Elaine, everything's going to be OK now.

Elaine   What are you doing? Benjamin!

He flings open the other door and an old pew falls out on him.

Benjamin   Oh God.

Elaine   What are we doing?

Benjamin   We went the wrong way.

Mr Robinson (*off*)   YOU SON OF A BITCH!

Mrs Robinson *runs in just before* **Benjamin** *slams the door and uses the old pew to barricade it. Immediately,* **Mr Robinson**'s *weight hits the door from the other side.*

Mrs Robinson   Elaine!

Mr Robinson (*off*)   Let me in there you filthy degenerate!

Others shout and holler on the other side of the door. **Mrs Robinson** *stands getting her breath back, staring at* **Benjamin**. **Benjamin** *gets his breath back staring at* **Mrs Robinson**.

Mrs Robinson   Elaine, get back in the church.

Elaine   Benjamin, what is happening?

Benjamin   We're getting married.

Elaine   I'm getting married to Carl.

Benjamin   You're going to marry me.

Elaine   I'm marrying Carl. I was just marrying him.

Mr Robinson (*off*)   Open this door, you filthy, degenerate son of bitch!

Elaine   You hit my fiancé!

Benjamin   He fainted.

Elaine   Well, you bloodied his nose.

Mr Robinson (*off*)   Judith, open the door!

Mrs Robinson   Open the door, Benjamin.

Benjamin   No.

Mrs Robinson   Open the door.

Benjamin   You think I'm mad?

Mrs Robinson   Like a dog. You should be shot.

Benjamin   I love Elaine. Elaine, I love you.

Mr Robinson (*off*)   I'm calling the police, you pervert.

Mrs Robinson   So this is, what is this, Benjamin? A big romantic gesture?

Benjamin   I just want to get married.

Mrs Robinson   So does Elaine.

Benjamin   Not to him.

Mrs Robinson   She wants to get married to Carl.

Benjamin   No she doesn't.

Mrs Robinson   Yes she does.

Benjamin   Elaine, do you want to marry Carl?

Elaine   Yes, I do.

Benjamin   No she doesn't.

Mrs Robinson   Do you want to marry Carl, Elaine?

Elaine   Yes I do.

Benjamin   No you don't.

Mrs Robinson   I think she does Benjamin.

Benjamin   You don't have to do this Elaine. You don't have to do everything your mother says.

Mr Robinson (*off*)   You're a dead man, Braddock.

Benjamin   Do you love me?

Mrs Robinson   Love?

Benjamin   Elaine, do you love me?

Elaine   No.

Benjamin   Well, I think you do.

Mrs Robinson   She doesn't love you, Benjamin.

Benjamin   Yes she does.

Elaine   I don't.

Benjamin   You see?

Mr Robinson (*off*)   This is kidnap, Braddock. You could do life for this! You could go to the chair for this!

Mrs Robinson   I don't know what you think you're going to achieve here.

Benjamin   Well that's because you have a very limited imagination.

Mrs Robinson   All that's going to happen is you're going to be seriously assaulted and Elaine is going to marry Carl.

Benjamin   I don't think so.

Mrs Robinson   Elaine, will you please put this poor boy out of his misery? Will you please tell him he's making a complete ass of himself.

Benjamin   Would you tell your mother that you love me? Would you please do that?

Elaine   Would you please both stop telling me what I think!

Benjamin   So why are you marrying Carl?

Elaine   I don't have to tell you that.

Benjamin   Because your parents told you to.

Elaine   Do you think so little of me?

Benjamin   Then why are you marrying him?

Elaine   Carl is a perfectly decent man.

Benjamin   Perfectly decent?

Elaine   I think that's a lot.

Benjamin   I think you'll make a great team.

Elaine   Well, thank you.

Benjamin   But is that enough?

Elaine   Of course that's not enough!

Benjamin   Then why are you marrying Carl?

Elaine   Because I am.

Benjamin   Is that a reason?

Elaine   Yes it is.

Benjamin   No it isn't, it's an evasion.

Elaine   Well, it's a fact, Benjamin.

Benjamin   Why is it?

Elaine   Why is it what?

Benjamin   Why are you marrying Carl?

Elaine   You know why.

Benjamin   No I don't.

Elaine   I think you do.

Benjamin   Then tell me why you're marrying him!!

Elaine   Because if I don't marry Carl you are going to ruin my life.

Benjamin   How?

Mrs Robinson   Being in it, Benjamin.

Benjamin   You're marrying Carl because you love me.

Elaine   Benjamin, that is . . .

Mrs Robinson   Absurd.

Benjamin   But it's true. Say it's not true.

Mrs Robinson   Say it's not true, Elaine.

Elaine   It's not.

Benjamin   Say it's not.

Elaine   I just said.

Benjamin   You love me. I know it.

Mrs Robinson   Keep quiet, Elaine.

Elaine   If I marry you my life is ruined.

Benjamin   No it isn't.

Mrs Robinson   Yes it is.

Benjamin   It wouldn't be.

Mrs Robinson   Believe me, both of you, it would.

Benjamin   You know something Mrs Robinson, you are a bitch. I mean I'm sorry to be rude but you are a one-hundred-carat solid gold bitch. Elaine, take off that dress.

Elaine   My dress?

Benjamin   You're not getting married. Take off the dress.

Mrs Robinson   Benjamin you are digging a very deep hole for yourself.

Benjamin   I'm sure you'd like to think so.

Mrs Robinson   Immoral behaviour, kidnapping, sexual assault . . .

Benjamin   All I want is to marry Elaine.

Mrs Robinson   He's not what you think he is Elaine. He's not the sensitive soul you think. He's got a selfish streak so wide it hides his vicious streak. What he doesn't disdain he despises. And that includes himself. He's lazy, self-loathing, and not much fun to be with. And he's terrible in bed.

Benjamin   No I'm not.

Mrs Robinson   Yes you are.

Benjamin   Oh no I'm not.

Mrs Robinson   Oh but yes you are.

Benjamin   Am I?

Mrs Robinson   Oh yes.

Benjamin   Am I?

Mrs Robinson   Yes.

Benjamin   Am I?

Mrs Robinson (*faltering*)   Yes you are. He is.

Benjamin   I love you Elaine. Take off the dress.

Elaine   Benjamin, I . . .

Benjamin   Will you TAKE OFF THAT GODDAM DRESS!

He pulls down the zip and tugs it off her shoulders.

Elaine   Ow! Benjamin!!!

Mr Robinson *starts hitting the door with a fire axe.*

Benjamin   Jesus.

Mr Robinson   You lowlife scum!

Mrs Robinson   Oh my God.

Mr Robinson   You excremental piece of garbage!

Another blow.

Benjamin   Mr Robinson . . .

Mr Robinson   You depraved son of a bitch!!!

Another blow and a panel crashes out. An arm through the hole to dislodge the bench and he's in, slamming what's left of the door behind him. **Wedding Guests** *peer in.*

Benjamin   Mr Robinson, I can understand you feeling quite upset . . .

Mr Robinson   I'm going to cut your sick head off.

Elaine   Daddy, don't.

Guests (*variously*)   Calm down, Howard./He ain't worth it, Howard./Attaboy, Howard./Frank, you shush now.

Elaine   Daddy, please.

Mr Robinson   It's all right, Peaches. I'm in control here.

Mrs Robinson   Take it easy, Howard.

Mr Robinson   Everything's under control.

The **Priest** *pushes his way to the front of the throng and examines his vestry door.*

Mrs Robinson   Put the axe down, Howard.

Priest   Mr Robinson . . .

Mr Robinson   It's all right, Reverend. I'm in control. I'm in control.

Elaine   Daddy, put it down.

Mr Robinson   You seduce my wife, you harass my daughter, you abduct her, you attempt to undress her in a holy place . . .

Mrs Robinson   Howard, put the axe down.

Mr Robinson   You said I should kill him. As we ran down the aisle you said: 'Kill him, Howard.'

Mrs Robinson   I changed my mind.

Benjamin   That's very generous of you.

Mrs Robinson   Shut up, Benjamin.

Elaine   Daddy, put the axe down. I'm marrying Carl. Nothing's going to change. Everything's OK. A door got damaged. I'm marrying Carl.

Mr Robinson *drops the axe. Slumps.*

Mr Robinson   Are you OK?

Mrs Robinson   I need a drink.

Elaine   I'm fine.

Mr Robinson *looks round at the door. Goes to the* **Priest**. *Pulls out his wallet.*

Mr Robinson   Um . . . I don't have anything on me. Reverend, would you do me the courtesy of sending me an invoice for the door?

Elaine   Everybody please go back? We'll be out with you soon.

The **Priest** *ushers the throng away.*

Priest   Could we all please move back into the body of the church? Is the groom conscious?

Elaine *tends to her father.*

Elaine   You have some varnish in your hair.

Mr Robinson   I'm fine.

Elaine   Are you OK?

Mr Robinson   Uh-huh.

Elaine   Ready to give me away?

Benjamin   Elaine . . .

Elaine   I don't want to go against the world, Benjamin. I know you hate your parents, and my parents. I know you hate everybody's parents and I know you want to go against the world but I don't want that.

Benjamin *sits, his head in his hands.*

Elaine   Daddy.

Mr Robinson   Yes.

Elaine *takes his arm and leads him out. A murmur of consent from the congregation beyond.*

Mrs Robinson   You know what? You never stood a chance. She never made a decision in her life without climbing into her father's lap for a couple of hours.

Benjamin   It's not what she wants.

Mrs Robinson   When Elaine was two years old and all the other brats were screaming, she sat and read picture books.

Unseen by **Mrs Robinson**, **Elaine** *returns for her corsage.*

When she was seven she never asked for a Tootsie Roll, let alone Disneyland. All through her teens she never came home late, drunk, her blouse unbuttoned or her ears pierced. Elaine's never *wanted* anything.

Benjamin   Is that so?

Mrs Robinson   I've waited twenty years to see if she developed any personality of her own but no, she's ten per cent me and ninety per cent him. I'm the curiosity, and the eye. He's the dreary diligence and the enduring dullness. Beyond that, Benjamin, there *is* no Elaine.

Elaine   Is that what you think?

Mrs Robinson *turns and is speechless.*

Benjamin   I don't think that, Elaine.

Elaine   That I'm what, that I'm . . .

Benjamin   I think you're a wonderful person.

Mrs Robinson   Elaine . . .

Elaine   Is that what you *think*?

Mrs Robinson   Why should you care what I think? Why should you care what anyone thinks?

Elaine   You think I'm nothing?

Mrs Robinson   I never said that.

Benjamin   That's exactly what she said.

Elaine   That I only do what I'm told?

Mrs Robinson   You're a wonderful girl.

Elaine   If I don't do what I'm told you scream at me.

Mrs Robinson   Elaine . . .

Elaine   You throw my dolls out the window, you tear my posters from the wall, you humiliate me in front of a perfectly nice boy and it's my senior prom!

Mrs Robinson   Well then scream back, Elaine. Cover your wall in weeping kittens. Go to your prom looking like a birthday cake. Ignore your mother, the unfeeling bitch, and do what you damn well want to!

Elaine   Go to the clinic and get rid of the baby?

Benjamin   I'm sorry?

Elaine   I said 'Go to the clinic and get rid of the baby.'

Mrs Robinson   Are you pregnant?

Elaine   No, I'm not. You were. So why didn't you do what you damn well wanted to?

Elaine *starts to cry.* **Mrs Robinson** *can't bring herself to step forward and comfort her.* **Benjamin** *does,* **Elaine** *clings to* **Benjamin**. **Mr Robinson** *returns.*

Mr Robinson   Elaine? What in God's name is going on?

Mrs Robinson   Leave them alone, Howard.

Mr Robinson   What?

Mrs Robinson   See to the guests.

Mr Robinson   Are you condoning this . . . this . . . what is this?

Benjamin   May I say something?

Mrs Robinson   No. Howard would you please go and announce to the guests that the wedding is cancelled.

Mr Robinson   You *are* condoning this. What the hell is this? Peaches . . .

Elaine   Leave me alone. Would you both just leave me alone. Leave us alone.

Mr Robinson   I don't understand.

Mrs Robinson   I think Peaches is rebelling, Howard.

Mr Robinson   Elaine?

Elaine   I'm sorry.

Mr Robinson   Are you going to let her *do* this? Am I the only one left in this family with a shred of decency?

Mrs Robinson   Relax Howard, give us a song.

Mr Robinson   A what?

Mrs Robinson   Sing me a song. Or speak to my attorney.

Mr Robinson (*quietly*)   Braddock, one dark night. . .

Mrs Robinson   You don't have to kill him Howard. Leave them alone and they'll *bore* one another to death.

Mr Robinson   This wedding cost five thousand dollars.

Mrs Robinson   Then for Christ's sake let's go get a *drink.*

She moves him out the door.

Elaine   Mom . . .

Mrs Robinson   It's a little late for affection Elaine. This was my sole gesture of support. Marry this conniving son of a bitch and you're on your own.

Elaine   The hell with you.

Mrs Robinson   Bless.

Elaine *swings round and kisses* **Benjamin**. *They are isolated for a few moments in their embrace before a seedy motel manager unlocks a door and they find themselves alone in . . .*

Scene Five

A motel room somewhere in Nevada. Headlights sweep through the blinds. **Benjamin** *and* **Elaine** *look around them.*

Benjamin   It's a dump.

Elaine   It's a room. It's cute. It's one o'clock in the morning.

She takes off the raincoat and stands in her wedding dress.

Well, I guess we did it. I guess we ought to get blood tests. If we want children. I mean if we want them I guess it'd be best they were normal. What are you thinking?

Benjamin   What sort of cereal.

Elaine   Huh?

Benjamin   What sort of cereal?

Elaine   Oh.

She smiles.

Cheerios.

Benjamin   Cheerios.

Elaine   OK?

Benjamin   OK.

Benjamin *puts down suitcase and is about to open it.*

Elaine   Would you undo my dress?

He does. She's shy, but continues undressing. **Benjamin** *doesn't move.*

Could I have a cigarette?

Benjamin *lights her a cigarette. She smokes like her mother. She finishes undressing and lies on the bed.* **Benjamin** *doesn't move.*

Elaine   Benjamin?

She loses confidence and covers herself.

Maybe you're right.

Benjamin *just stands there.*

Elaine   Maybe we should wait.

Benjamin *doesn't speak.*

Elaine   Maybe I should graduate.

Benjamin *can't think of a thing to say.*

Elaine   I mean, you don't have the first idea of what to do with me, do you?

Benjamin *opens his suitcase and looks at her over the lid. Then he brings out a pack of Cheerios. She laughs with delight.*

Elaine   How did you know that?

Elaine *opens the Cheerios.*

Benjamin   I'll go to the front desk. They may have some milk.

Elaine   No. Don't go. There never was any milk. I like 'em rocky.

He sits on the bed and eats a handful.

Don't just wolf them, Benjamin. You have to sort them out first. Oatmeal. Wheatmeal. Rice. OK?

Benjamin   OK.

Elaine   Improves the flavour.

Benjamin   Yes, it does.

They sit on the bed and eat Cheerios.

End.

Breinigsville, PA USA
26 August 2010
244320BV00001B/1/P